ETHNIC ISSUES
IN PAUL'S LETTER
TO THE ROMANS

ETHNIC ISSUES
IN PAUL'S LETTER
TO THE ROMANS

*Changing Self-Definitions
in Earliest Roman Christianity*

JAMES C. WALTERS

TRINITY PRESS INTERNATIONAL
Valley Forge, Pennsylvania

Trinity Press International, P.O. Box 851, Valley Forge, PA 19482-0851

Printed in the United States of America

Library of Congress Cataloging-in-Publication Data
Walters, James C.
  Ethnic issues in Paul's letter to the Romans : changing self-
definitions in earliest Roman Christianity / James C. Walters.
    p. cm.
  Includes bibliographical references and index.
  ISBN 1-56338-078-1
  1. Bible. N.T. Romans—Criticism, interpretation, etc. 2. Jews
in the New Testament. 3. Jews—Rome—History. 4. Ethnicity—
Religious aspects—Christianity—History of doctrines–Early
church, ca. 30—600. 5. Church history—Primitive and early church,
ca. 30–600. 6. Rome—Ethnic relations—History. I. Title.
BS2665.6.J44W35 1993
227'.1083058—dc20   93-32932
                                                                  CIP

Printed in the United States of America

93 94 95 96 97 98 99   10 9 8 7 6 5 4 3 2 1

To my wife, Marla,
and our daughters,
Charissa and Elizabeth

μείζονα ταύτης ἀγάπην οὐδείς ἔχει

Contents

Foreword

No document in the biblical canon has affected the history of Christian thought as dramatically as Paul's letter to the Romans. Nearly every major change of course in Christendom has been prompted by a rereading of Romans; it was the point of departure for the likes of Augustine, Luther, and Barth. However, in spite of the attention Romans has received, it has retained a remarkable ability to keep its reader at arm's length.

Scholars have become increasingly suspicious that the key to its internal coherence lies in the ethnic issues that permeate the document. The relationship between Jews and gentiles, a common motif throughout the Pauline corpus, pervades the development of the Roman letter. The motif itself is familiar; however, its treatment in Romans is nuanced. Scholars have characteristically accounted for the letter's ethnic slant by treating it as a vehicle for communicating its theological message (justification by faith) or by appealing to Paul's own experiences in the East, the impending delivery of the contribution to Jerusalem, or the westward mission. Although it would be absurd to deny that Paul's theology, ministry experiences, and plans affected the content and presentation of information in his letters, scholars have recognized for some time that the circumstances within the Christian communities Paul addressed were the central shaping factor of his letters.[1] Exegetical analyses of Paul's letters have operated on this assumption for some time; only Romans has been routinely exempted. Recently, however, attempts have been made to interpret Romans in light of Jew-gentile conflicts in Rome. Unfortunately, studies of this kind have been hindered by the paucity of ancient evidence coupled with inaccurate or simplistic portrayals of Jewish and Christian socialization in ancient Rome. It is the aim of this study carefully to interpret the available evidence for the situation of the Jews in ancient Rome and to assess the effect of early Christianity's changing relationship to the Jewish communities as a background for understanding the manner in which Jew-gentile issues are treated in Paul's letter to the Romans.

I owe a debt of gratitude to several persons whose contributions to this book are ubiquitous though not always obvious. Their criticisms would have no doubt improved the final product further were it not for the incorrigibility of the writer. I benefited from the lucid analysis of Professor J. Paul Sampley, who read the manuscript and made numerous helpful suggestions, particularly regarding the fourth chapter. Howard Clark Kee made a number of methodological suggestions and offered many helpful comments that also improved the book, especially chapter 2. The first and third chapters benefited from revisions suggested by Meyer Reinhold, especially regarding the Roman administration of non-Roman religions.

Finally, I would like to thank professor Richard Oster of the Harding Graduate School of Religion. Professor Oster was the first to open my eyes to the social world of early Christianity and to the relevance of this data for interpreting the New Testament.

Introduction

A broad reappraisal of the socio-religious context of earliest Christianity in Rome is necessary before we can test whether the ethnic issues in Romans are coherent in light of a Roman occasion for the letter. Before rushing headlong into the ancient materials, however, we must ask two interrelated questions that are often overlooked: What is it about the situation of nascent Christianity in Rome that must be clarified and how does one go about clarifying it? One critic of previous attempts has asked, "What is the specific nature of the conflict between Jewish and gentile Christians which Paul is supposed to have heard about and is trying to settle by writing Romans?" He wants to know whether the Jewish Christians were "legalists, liberals, apocalyptically-oriented or what?" and whether the gentile Christians were "legalists, antinomians, Gnostic-influenced or what?"[2] Although I appreciate the desire for specificity, I consider this line of questioning to be misguided. These questions cannot be answered decisively for any Christian community reflected in ancient literature, much less for Rome.[3] This is because the diversity of early Christianity and ancient Judaism was not simply a diversity of communities but also a diversity within communities, and no document mirrors the beliefs of every member of the community or communities that it addresses.

Instead of focusing on theological beliefs, we must look first at the boundaries that defined the Jewish and Christian communities in ancient Rome. Because the theological content of Paul's letter to the Romans centers on questions regarding the relationship of Christianity to Judaism, elucidating these boundaries should facilitate greater understanding of what Paul was saying and of the circumstances that prompted him to address these issues.

Historians who use the social sciences insist that interpreters of ancient documents must look beyond the overt profiles of persons and circumstances mirrored in a given document. Insight into the implicit

1

assumptions of a community is essential if the interpreter is to take the historical context into consideration in more than a perfunctory manner. Unfortunately, penetrating such assumptions is problematic because of their taken-for-granted character.

In order to bring these assumptions out into the open, historians must ask questions of ancient materials that are somewhat different from those routinely asked. In the introduction to his *Moral World of the First Christians,* Wayne Meeks offers a simple example that illustrates the difference of perspective this approach represents:

> It is a perfectly proper form of ethical directive to say, for example to a child, "We do not do that." Probably the response from the child, and perhaps also from the professional ethicist, will be, "Why not?" Very often that is an important question to ask, but there are other occasions when it may be more productive to ask a different question: Who are "we"? The question "Why?" calls for an explanation; "Who?" invites understanding.[4]

"Sociology of knowledge" is the common label for an approach that seeks to account phenomenologically for a community's role in constructing reality. This approach insists that what one experiences as reality is in fact a socially constructed version of reality that depends on shared experiences of community members (characteristically these result in unstated and unrecognized assumptions) that are objectified and form an interpretive framework for integrating new data.[5] Consequently, a community's self-understanding, values, beliefs, behavioral patterns, and institutional structures are dynamically affected by the social situation of that community as it stands in dialectic relation to larger society.

The implications of these phenomenological inquiries to the study at hand are obvious. The experiences of the Jewish and Christian communities in Rome, their "social world" or "life-world," must be carefully considered and sympathetically engaged before the contours of the Jew-gentile conflict can be understood. Until these contours are understood it will be impossible to assess whether the content of Romans is in fact a coherent engagement of those issues.

Data required for investigating the social world of the Christian and Jewish communities in Rome will be gathered by analyzing and interrogating ancient sources that are limited geographically and temporally. The insights of sociologists and anthropologists who interpret ancient cultures in light of models developed from the observation of contemporary peoples will be utilized in order to gain new perspectives on old materials.[6] Because the questions raised by sociologists and anthropologists are often designed to penetrate the assumptions of a society, their work can prove helpful in New Testament studies as scholars pursue the contexts of particular documents.[7] However, this author is skeptical of using such comparative models to ascertain what "must have been true" in antiquity in the absence of historical evidence.[8] Approaches of this kind assume an intrinsic commensurability between ancient and modern societies that cannot be demonstrated.[9] Esler is correct when he observes that "there are no social laws yet known which apply trans-historically to all societies."[10] Consequently, this study will rely more closely on material evidence from antiquity and use observations from the social sciences to expedite the posing of pertinent questions to the ancient sources.[11] Analogies used for hypothesizing what "must have been true" will be sought primarily in the archaeological and literary remains of groups and individuals contemporary with early Christianity and delineated further by their comparable social situation.

The first three chapters of the book investigate the socio-religious situation of emerging Christianity in Rome. The great amount of space allotted for this portion of the study results from the limited data available for the reconstruction and the consequent necessity of maximizing the yield of information while protecting the reliability of the interpretation.

Chapter 2 looks at the general social, economic, political, and religious context for the Jewish communities of ancient Rome by examining their existence among the foreign population of the city. The social situation in Rome within which various ethnic groups remained essentially foreign will be analyzed. The chapter will demonstrate the ethnic diversity of ancient Rome and highlight issues that were common to the city's foreign inhabitants. This information will help form a background for understanding Jewish socialization in the city and Christian origins in relation to the Jewish population.

Chapter 3 concentrates more narrowly on the Jewish population of ancient Rome because of the special part it played in the origin and development of nascent Christianity. First, recent advances in the study of Diaspora Judaism are reviewed because of their effect on the interpretation of data from Rome. Next, data available for reconstructing Jewish presence in the city are analyzed from the earliest records through the first century C.E. Special attention is given to the experiences of the Jews as a foreign religious cult under the supervision of Roman administrators. The chapter will demonstrate that Jewish life in Rome under certain of the Julio-Claudian emperors was turbulent and that Roman adminis-trative interventions played a determinative role in shaping the "horizon" within which Christians were interpreted by the Jewish communities to be a serious threat.

Chapter 4 will demonstrate that by the middle of the sixth decade of the first century the Romans could already distinguish administra-tively between Christians and Jews in spite of their shared history. Two events recorded by Roman authors, the edict of Claudius (ca. 49 C.E.) and the persecution of Christians under Nero (ca. 64 C.E.), offer an op-portunity to track the changing relationship between these communities during the very period in which the Roman letter was written (55–58 C.E.). The chapter not only analyzes the developing self-definition of Christianity in Rome in light of Roman administrative interventions, but also demonstrates a direct link between these events and Paul's letter to the Romans.

Chapter 5 tests whether in fact there is a correlation between the social-historical description presented in the previous chapters and the content of the letter to the Romans. The key issue is this: Does the letter address ethnic problems or concerns consonant with those one would expect under the circumstances described in the preceding sec-tions? Sections of the letter where ethnic issues are paramount receive special attention because of their utility in testing the thesis.

This author does not presume for a moment to be offering the reader a commentary on Romans or even a thorough exegesis of the texts that are treated. What I do offer, particularly in the closing chapter, are analyses of the functions of three issues addressed by Paul in Romans: The impartiality of God, the priority of Israel, and the "weak" and the "strong." Because each of these is carefully and extensively developed by Paul and because he makes ethnic applications on the basis of each one, the issues are useful for verifying the reconstruction of earliest Roman Christianity posited in the study.

An epilogue, focusing on the purpose of Romans in light of the ethnic issues that are treated in the letter, concludes this study.

CHAPTER ONE

The Socialization of Foreign Groups in Rome

In a 1922 essay, George La Piana wrote:

> Since there is no doubt that the Christians in Rome were for a long period mostly foreigners, and since it is also well known that the great majority of them belonged to the humbler social classes, the study of the life and manners of the foreign multitudes in Rome during the early centuries of the empire might throw much light on the life of the Christian community itself.[1]

This conviction no doubt provided the stimulus for La Piana's massive study of foreign groups in Rome published five years later in the *Harvard Theological Review*. The foreign groups of ancient Rome, and the Jewish community in particular, must be highlighted as the context of earliest Christianity in the capital. This chapter is concerned with the social circumstances of foreign groups, particularly the persistence of their ethnic and cultural identities, within and in the vicinity of Rome during the late republic and early empire. Locating the Jewish communities of ancient Rome and the earliest Christians within this socio-historical setting is important for reconstructing the horizon of these communities and isolating the issues that were crucial to them.

The Foreign Character of Earliest Christianity in Rome

Early Christians in Rome were concentrated within the same regions as the Jews and both groups resided primarily in areas where foreign peoples clustered.[2] The overlap of Christian and Jewish concentrations in Rome is readily explicable because earliest Christianity in Rome developed in a Jewish context. Hence, Jews who believed Jesus was the messiah not only shared a religious outlook but also a common socialization; they were part of the Jewish *ethnos* and of the foreign population of ancient Rome.

The earliest witnesses to Christian presence in Rome, the Claudian edict (49 C.E.) and Paul's letter to Rome, also suggest that nascent Christianity in the capital was primarily an intra-Jewish phenomenon.[3] In order to read the Claudian edict as an action precipitated by Christian Jews in Rome, it is necessary to assume that Suetonius's "Chrestus" is a misspelled reference to Christ. However, the independent testimony of the expulsion in Acts suggests the same conclusion; this source explicitly states that Priscilla and Aquila, a Christian Jewish couple, were evicted from Rome by the edict.[4]

The evidence from Suetonius and Acts is corroborated by the content of Paul's letter to the Romans. Modern readers of the Roman letter are struck by the sophisticated acquaintance with Jewish scriptures and practices that is assumed of the letter's original recipients. In Romans 7:1 Paul states plainly that he writes to "those who know the law." Moreover, Paul explicitly greets five Jewish Christians by name in the conclusion of the document (Rom. 16:3, 7, 11).

The advent of Christianity in Rome as an intra-Jewish phenomenon is hardly startling news in light of the large Jewish community in Rome, the facility of travel between Rome and the East, and the obvious fact that Christianity evolved from Jewish beginnings, its first missionaries (including Paul) all being Jews.[5] However, ascertaining exactly when and how Christianity made its debut in Rome is guess work. Many have suggested that residents of Rome who were present at Pentecost brought the Christian faith back to Rome (Acts 2:10). This explanation is of course possible; however, any postulation that Christianity entered Rome via Roman travelers who came in contact with Christians in the East would be equally plausible.[6] The best hypothesis is that Christianity made its way to Rome the same way other foreign religions did, as the personal baggage of individuals who journeyed to Rome because they were involved in trade or commerce, or because they were imported as slaves, or because they were emigrating to the capital.[7] When Christianity expanded beyond the synagogues it naturally drew converts primarily from the foreign peoples of Rome among whom the early Christians resided.

The Foreign Population

Rome of the early imperial period was a densely populated city; its total population approached one million inhabitants with a density comparable to modern Bombay or Calcutta.[8] The enormous growth of the city during the republican and imperial periods is in large measure explained by the immigration of huge numbers of Italian and foreign peoples. No doubt many came for adventure or for economic and commercial reasons, as Seneca claims.[9] However, many others came against their will as the servile product of foreign wars and slave trade.[10]

Although familiarity with classical Roman authors had already alerted scholars to the presence of a sizable foreign population in Rome, attempts to quantify this element of the population awaited publication and analysis of the *Corpus of Latin Inscriptions,* particularly volume 6. These inscriptions, largely made up of simple epitaphs, promised scholars an opportunity to traverse the chasm that had long separated the historian — operating with sources representing the social situation and outlook of antiquity's elite — from the common person of ancient Rome. However, after decades of research the interpretation of these inscriptions remains problematic. A plethora of methodological issues have cast their shadow over the investigation making their interpretation among the most controverted issues facing historians of ancient Rome.

Tenney Frank's study of 13,900 of the inscriptions led him to conclude that perhaps 90 percent of the free plebeians on the streets of Rome "had Oriental blood in their veins."[11] Furthermore, he contended that the swelling of the foreign population was not due primarily to immigrants drifting into Rome of their own free will, but rather to the slave trade.[12]

Frank obtained his results by reading sepulchral inscriptions and isolating those representing foreign stock by considering the presence of a Greek cognomen as an indicator.[13] This obviously assumes that Romans of native stock did not favor Greek names. He defends his methodology by pointing out statistically that fathers with Greek names were prone to give Latin names to their children while the reverse was not true.[14] Since Roman plebeians avoided the Greek name and freedmen families often dispensed with it, Frank also considers the Greek name a good indication of servile or foreign stock.

Frank's conclusions regarding the Oriental provenance of the bearers of these names stem from what he sees as a "fairly uniform practice which differentiated between Greek and Latin names during the empire."

Bearers of Greek names are in general from the East or descendants of Eastern slaves who have been in the West; bearers of Latin names are partly captives of the North and West, partly, as we have seen from our Roman lists, Easterners and descendants of Easterners who have received Latin names from their masters.[15]

Frank's conclusions concurred with those of Bang, who concentrated on cases where slaves specified their origin as being outside of Italy. Bang also found that the larger portion came from the Orient, especially Syria and Asia Minor.[16]

Frank's findings, however, have been disputed, particularly his quantitative conclusions. M. L. Gordon raised serious questions regarding his method by seeking to demonstrate that the division between the East and West on the basis of the Greek cognomen does not hold.[17] L. R. Taylor, while respecting Frank's basic approach, warns of his failure to consider the motives of those who left such inscriptions and the effect this has on the sample.[18]

The strongest criticism, however, has come from F. G. Maier.[19] He challenged four areas of inquiry in which demographic conclusions had been postulated on the basis of Roman inscriptions: the number of inhabitants in imperial Rome; the proportion of slaves and freedmen in the population; the ethnic structure of the groups; and the social standing of the various groups including their economic significance.[20] The persistent theme of his criticism is that the inscriptions are sporadic in origin and consequently unrepresentative of the whole population. Therefore, in spite of their seemingly large numbers they are an unreliably small base upon which to project the population at large.[21]

The "most intractable problem in interpreting the pagan epitaphs of Rome," according to Duncan-Jones, "is that of why the freeborn population appears to make up such a small proportion of the whole."[22] Conclusions drawn from the epitaphs do not correlate easily with recent studies of late republican Rome that trace its population growth to the emigration of poor Italian peasants displaced by the absorption of land into large estates that increasingly utilized slave labor.[23] Many contemporary scholars argue that these large estates were the destination of the majority of slaves imported into Italy, not Rome.[24]

Huttunen, utilizing computer analysis of the epitaphs, concluded that the "low figure for 'freeborn' obviously cannot match their real position in the social structure." Consequently, he chose to assume that most of the inscriptions providing no accurate status indication represent freeborn.[25] This increased the ratio of freeborn to 60 percent versus 40 percent servile.[26] However, this represents an uncomfortable reversal of the figures for those of known status identified by Huttunen himself: freeborn 3.3 percent; slave stock 18.5 percent.[27] Hence, even when the Greek *cognomina* (surnames) are not taken as the sole indicator, the tension remains.[28] Moreover, Solin's conclusion that the freeborn at Rome did not usually have the Greek cognomen should remind the reader that with regard to the epitaphs few methodological issues have been settled.[29]

Even if Frank's original approach were accepted, his conclusions would have to be modified and stated in more general, conservative terms to leave room for the following ambiguities: the likelihood that westerners occasionally had Greek names;[30] the fact that the epigraphic record is not a uniform sample; finally, in spite of the large number of epitaphs, the fact that it is still a small data base from which to draw such definite conclusions.[31] Balsdon's interpretation of the evidence reflects the type of guarded approach that is warranted. Following mention of the methodological problems he writes, "Even so, it may well be true that by the end of the first century A.D. 'most of the Roman populace had the blood of slaves in their veins.'"[32] Juvenal's portrayal of the racial mix — for him Rome had become something of an Oriental bazaar — mirrors his own prejudices; nevertheless, most of the freedmen and slaves were probably of eastern Mediterranean extraction.[33]

The concerns of Juvenal and Tacitus that Rome was being inundated with Orientals were engendered not only by their numbers but also by the strength of their presence. Treggiari compares Juvenal's disapproving appraisal of the situation to that of modern attributions of prominence to the Jews in some societies; she explains the common exaggerations by noting: "They [the Jews] are a people who make themselves felt."[34]

Generally speaking, immigrants from the East tended to be more resistant to cultural absorption because of the greater strength of their Hellenistic cultures as compared to those of the northern and western parts of the empire.[35] They were decidedly un-Roman, a conclusion that was readily drawn from their language and customs.[36] To note the reaction this drew from conservative Romans one need only ponder the slower rate at which Easterners were admitted to the senatorial order when compared to their counterparts from the western provinces. It was more than two centuries after Egypt became a part of the empire before an Egyptian was admitted to the senatorial order.[37]

Persons from every corner of the empire had made Rome their home, or at least been made to have Rome as their home. Although data for determining precise ratios for various ethnic groupings are lacking, it is clear that Rome was a conglomeration of nations and peoples.

Rome possessed a remarkable ability to assimilate foreign stock into the native population, a policy of intermingling the conqueror and conquered that Seneca believed praiseworthy.[38] It should be recognized, however, that assimilation was slow, especially when the immigration of large numbers from the same region tended to develop a ghetto mentality and socialization. Many factors affected the immigrants' assimilation or resistance. Did they come voluntarily or by force? If slaves, what were their circumstances? Were they isolated from their fellow nationals or was contact possible? Were they forced by circumstance to learn Latin and/or Greek or could they survive with their native speech?[39] Cicero has his grandfather say, "The men of our generation are like Syrian slaves, the better they know Greek the more rascally they are," implying that many Syrians continued to be isolated by language.[40] Both Caesar and Augustus put on theatrical performances in various districts of the city in the native languages of the inhabitants.[41] Juvenal describes Syrian immigrants whose social practices reflect resistance to Rome's melting pot and suggest a socialization wherein maintenance of native language and customs was possible. Syrian presence is reflected, he says, by its "lingo and manners, its flutes, its outlandish harps with their transverse strings, its native tambourines, and the whores who hang out round the race-course."[42]

Of course, all traces of East or West might be obliterated in immigrants through social forces like intermarriage and the abnormal conditions of slavery making it inappropriate to describe them as Eastern or Western, or even Roman; they were the product of "Graeco-Roman civilization."[43] However, it should be pointed out that even in the case of a well-adjusted immigrant like Marcus Antonius Gaionas, a Syrian who obtained a minor civic office (*cistiber*), heritage continued to be important.[44] Inscriptions indicate that he was a devoted member of a cult society that met in the sanctuary of the Syrian gods on the Janiculum.[45] An illuminating picture of Rome's aggregate character — preserved in a summary of Athenaeus's reaction to Rome's ethnic diversity — is accessible in the *Deipnosophistae* (ca. 200 C.E.):

> Athenaeus speaks of Rome as "the populace of the world," and says that one would not shoot wide of the mark if he called the city of Rome an epitome of the civilized world; so true is it that one may see at a glance all the cities of the world settled there. . . . More than

one day would fail me if I tried to enumerate all the cities he counts within the heavenly city of Rome — nay, all the days numbered in the year would not be enough, so many are the cities there. Even entire nations are settled there *en masse,* like the Cappadocians, the Scythians, the Pontians, and more besides.[46]

The ethnic diversity of Rome impacted not only the demographic situation, but also produced a multifaceted and heterogeneous matrix for social, religious, and political developments of the period. Generalizations seldom reflect awareness of the radical differences that could exist with regard to the socialization of emigrants in Rome. The comments of Appian and Suetonius, both describing the events of 44 B.C.E., are instructive. One reports a universal mixture of foreign blood in the plebs,[47] while the other recounts different nationalities preserving their individual customs in the city.[48] Which one was right? Both were!

Resistance to assimilation was heightened when immigrants: (1) lived in a region where their ethnic group was concentrated; (2) participated in native cults and associations where ethnic grouping prevailed; and (3) maintained continuing relations with the land of their origin. Although these descriptive characteristics overlap at times, differentiating them allows the individual factors to be analyzed in terms of the evidence and their particular effect to be noted.

Regions of Ethnic Concentration

Both literature and archaeological data suggest the existence of pockets of ethnic concentration in Rome where immigrants were able to live in proximity to fellow nationals and maintain some semblance of their native way of life. Balsdon comments that the situation in Rome reflects what is universally the case:

> Foreign nationals tended to cluster together for comfort and security and often, as was particularly the case with the Jews, for the sake of having near-by shops which stocked their exotic foodstuffs. The Jewish settlements were in Trastevere and also — thirteen synagogues have been identified — in other parts of the city. There were settlements of Syrians on the Aventine (where the temple of Jupiter Dolichenus was built in the second century A.D.) and on the Janiculum, where the temple of Jupiter Heliopolitanus was

built at the end of the first century A.D. Egyptians lived largely in the Campus Martius, in the neighbourhood of the Pantheon.[49]

Evidence for Balsdon's synopsis of the situation comes from Philo, who mentioned that the Jews were gathered in the Transtiberine region,[50] and from conjectures based on the locations of temples of national deities erected by immigrants. It is reasonable to assume that such temples were built in areas where cult adherents lived and that following their construction new immigrants would tend to settle in the region around the temple.[51]

The Aventine hill was known as a residence for plebs and foreigners since the republican period.[52] The fact that it was somewhat isolated from the city and fell outside the *pomerium* (the religious boundary of the city) made it a natural location for immigrants who wished to settle in proximity to one another and to build sanctuaries to their native gods. Claudius eventually extended the *pomerium* to include this region.[53] However, by this time the gods whose temples rose in the area had been adopted into the state cult by the Senate and the character of the region had changed. It was crowded and could no longer provide space for newcomers.[54]

Trastevere, on the other hand, because of its physical disadvantages was settled later. Intensive settling became practical only after several bridges were built to span the Tiber. It was not until the Augustan reorganization of the city into fourteen districts that the region was included within the boundaries of the city of Rome: the Transtiberim, Rome's fourteenth district.[55] Its isolation and late settlement coupled with the fact that it was outside the *pomerium* determined its character as home to the foreigner and plebeian poor.

The description of Trastevere sketched above (based largely on literary materials and the region's socio-religious setting) is supported by archaeological evidence as well. This evidence includes not only the remains of foreign temples like the sanctuary of the Syrian gods on the Janiculum, but also epigraphic materials as well. Commenting on these, Savage writes:

> Foreigners, some of whom may have been traders, seem to have been preponderant in the population. Inscriptions from Trastevere, and especially epitaphs from the Via Portuense, almost invariably bear the names of freedmen with *cognomina* which indicate foreign origin. Orientals, predominantly Syrians and Jews, as well as free-born Romans contributed to the motley welter which was the population of Trastevere. Socially, they probably mingled, but in

religious life their dedications show that each nationality clung to the gods of its fatherland and asserted its right to independence in worship.[56]

To suggest that Egyptians were concentrated in the Campus Martius, while Jews and Syrians congregated in Trastevere does not mean that they were confined to these regions or resided nowhere else. In fact, there is considerable evidence of Jewish synagogue groups in various parts of Rome, though the community was most concentrated in Trastevere.[57] Likewise, besides the Iseum in the Campus Martius, material evidence for other Isis temples or shrines indicates Egyptian presence in the Augustan Regions II, III, V, VI, VIII, and XII.[58]

The development of these ethnic pockets resulted from the social dynamics of immigration observable even today. When foreign persons entered Rome they would have instinctively sought out fellow nationals from whom they could expect hospitality and help. They would have inquired after the street or quarter where their fellow nationals lived, and in some cases would search out a particular friend or family acquaintance who had made the transition sometime earlier.[59] Initially they would have stayed with some such person, possibly renting a room or portion of a room until they located a place of their own nearby.[60] The compulsion they felt to be near their ethnic peers was greatest during the initial transition.[61] The net effect of this on settlement patterns is predictable; moreover, it is borne out by the literary and material evidence.

What is important here is not the size of these pockets of ethnic concentration, the number of them, or even their location. Rather, it is critical that their existence is recognized; this fact alone suggests social contexts in the city of Rome where immigrants could find a cluster of fellow nationals whose distinct identity had not dissolved in Rome's melting pot.[62]

Foreign Cults

The maintenance of ethnic identity by immigrants in Rome was facilitated by Rome's attempts to deter Romans from participating in foreign cults. Certain Romans were understandably xenophobic about the influx of foreign populations into the capital — the Orontes flooding the Tiber, to quote Juvenal — and expressed their concern in legal and literary documents.[63] Anxiety over the foreign population of the city was inseparable from the apprehensions that Romans felt on account of the foreign cults that immigrants brought with them. Although Rome normally tolerated foreign religions, history records that it was at times a painful toleration. This was particularly true of the Oriental cults. Administrative action was often a compromise between the delicate balance of Roman fear and distrust on the one hand and the traditional practice of toleration on the other. Livy's account of the Bacchanal conspiracy of 186 B.C.E. reflects common fears that haunted both himself and his contemporaries during the Augustan period:

> Never for any assembly has this formal prayer to the gods been not only so suitable, but even so necessary, a prayer which reminds us that these are the gods whom our forefathers had appointed to be worshiped, to be venerated, to receive our prayers, not those gods who drive our enthralled minds with vile and alien rites . . . to every crime and lust.[64]

The threat that Livy and others saw in the unabating influx of foreigners with their respective deities was a real one to their Roman mores. The "vile and alien rites" of these cults were hardly compatible with Roman *gravitas* (seriousness of conduct). The well-known passage of Dionysius of Halicarnassus praising the conservative religious policy in Rome bears witness to an important convention: Even when Rome officially recognized a foreign cult, its worship in Rome by Romans was adapted according to traditional forms. Thus the practice of that cult by its native adherents remained exotic and essentially the business of the foreign groups themselves.[65] Moreover, La Piana has shown that in spite of Rome's attempt to domesticate these cults — through adopting some of them into the Roman pantheon and thereby eliciting compromise in their observance according to traditional Roman practice — their foreign character persisted.[66]

The assumption that foreign cults made numerous converts from native Romans — a view advocated by Franz Cumont — does not bear up under careful scrutiny. Jules Toutain, a contemporary of Cumont, made thorough use of inscriptions in his study of Oriental cults and concluded that generally the devotees of foreign gods were immigrants and not native Romans who were converted to the cults.[67] Although Cumont's view has been widely disseminated because of his enormous influence on the study of Oriental religions, the conclusion of Toutain has been followed by numerous scholars who have worked carefully with epigraphic materials.[68] Even in inscriptions listing members of collegia associated with the cult of Isis, the constituents are consistently Egyptians.[69] Reviewing the inscriptions of cult associations, Waltzing remarks, "During the first two centuries of the empire the oriental deities invaded Rome, and their adepts formed there special colleges, yet it seems that they did not recruit many members among the artisans."[70]

The cults of foreign groups in Rome continued to be dominated largely by immigrants who found in these cults not only a familiar ritual but also fellow nationals.[71] These native cults, along with their associated collegia, provided an opportunity to experience sacred aspects of their native cultures among peers. It was in worshiping their gods that immigrants celebrated their native identities, remembered their homeland, and passed their traditions down to their offspring. Such immigrants resisted Rome's melting pot; or, to be more accurate, their socialization placed them outside the melting pot.

Associations

The religious cults of foreigners in Rome were not the only social settings that fostered the maintenance of ethnic and religious identities of immigrants. Associations formed by foreign immigrants who shared trade, commercial, and religious ties also played a part. A. D. Nock defined an association as "a group which a man joins of his own free will, and which accepts him of its free will, and this mutual acceptance creates certain obligations on both parties."[72] The members of these clubs were generally from the humblest classes, including even slaves.[73] They often organized to provide for the burial as well as the subsequent memory of members.[74]

An inscription containing the by-laws of a burial society dedicated to Diana and Antinoüs gives first-hand insight into the nature and activities of such groups.[75] Their regular meetings were not for the discussion of business (though dues were probably collected), but rather for the pleasure that could be derived from a convivial meal: namely, social intercourse and the promotion of fellowship.[76]

The political involvement of many associations, combined with disturbances during the late republic, led to banning of collegia (64 B.C.E.) because they were deemed to be politically subversive.[77] However, through the efforts of Clodius, the restrictions were reversed (58 B.C.E.).[78] Subsequently, Julius Caesar banned all associations except those with ancient foundation.[79] Following the assassination of Caesar there was a period of chaos that resulted in a lapse in the enforcement of the ban.[80] Augustus instituted a new policy that required associations to be chartered by the emperor or Senate with a generally liberal policy toward burial societies of humble people (*collegia tenuiorum*) and those meeting for religious purposes.[81]

The administrative approach of Augustus apparently left the door open for the proliferation of associations during the early imperial period, a conclusion amply supported by the epigraphical record.[82] Augustus's division of the city into 265 *vici* spawned the formation of numerous collegia associated with neighborhood groups as well as the cult of the Lares at the crossroads (*compita*).[83] MacMullen thinks that at the height of the popularity of collegia in Rome (second century C.E.) a third of the urban male population would have been members of some type of association.[84] Waltzing suggests that some collegia utilized the cultic exception as a means of escaping controls, though cultic concerns were hardly the reason for the formation of all of these associations, nor the primary reason they came together.[85] Others, he believes, existed without authorization, maintaining a clandestine life. The number of such groups was so large that no measures were taken to disband them unless disorderliness drew attention to their presence.[86] This is what Peter Garnsey has called "tolerance by default," groups allowed by Rome to exist because there was no way of stamping them out, or at least a lack of resolve to do so.[87]

One interesting aspect of Graeco-Roman associations is the amount of energy that was focused on the pursuit and bestowal of honor. The clubs resembled the social context in which they found themselves and imitated it. Here humble people who had little hope of gaining status within society as a whole formed their own "little societies" within which prestige and honor could be found.[88] The case of Marcus Antonius Gaionas, a Syrian immigrant of the second century C.E., bears witness to these needs and demonstrates how immigrants could satisfy them. Although he managed to attain a minor civic office (*cistiber*),[89] he continued until his death to be a member of a cult society that met in the sanctuary of the Syrian gods on the Janiculum.[90] In the Roman civic sphere he could only boast of membership in the most humble of Roman offices.[91] However, among fellow worshipers of the Syrian gods he was able to a obtain a post of highest honor: *deipnokrites,* a cult official who apparently presided over the communal meal of the association.[92]

Ethnic concentrations were more common in groups that were formed for strictly religious purposes because they existed for the practice of national cults.[93] Nonetheless, the evidence for associations where ethnic grouping prevails is not limited to these. Trade associations whose memberships were largely or entirely foreign arose for the same reason that certain Roman *vici* were peopled with concentrations of foreigners of the same trade: Certain trades or crafts were specialties of particular provinces or towns from which craftsmen had come.[94]

The compulsion to become a member of an association was strongest among poorer immigrants who lacked resources that would have insured a proper burial: family or personal connections and the money for expenses relating to the funeral and cremation or burial.[95] The unthinkable prospect of being cast at one's death into a common grave moved great numbers of persons both native and foreign to seek the alternative burial societies offered.[96] Regardless of other benefits that may have been provided by the associations foreign groups formed, it can be assumed that the proper burial of its members was a service common to all of them.[97] In the urban society of Rome immigrants had to rely on fellow club members, unrelated by blood or marriage, for help in performing traditional burial rites. The peculiar rites of various immigrant peoples naturally led to the formation of burial societies concentrated with members of the same ethnic and religious connections.

Another type of association where persistence of ethnic identity is demonstrable consisted of persons who were directly involved in the importation of goods into the capital from other parts of the empire. It was the business of a commercial class of foreign stock, predominantly freedmen, to make the necessary arrangements for the delivery of goods to Roman markets. *Stationes* is the Latin term that was used to designate the establishments of these foreign merchants in Italy. These structures served as business locations where transactions could take place but were also used for social purposes.[98] Abundant evidence for the activities of foreign persons (usually from the East) who worked in these capacities is available from Rome's port cities of Puteoli and Ostia, as well as from the capital itself (though the evidence here is more limited).[99]

One such association that bears on the subject at hand was located in Puteoli.[100] The facility operated by the Tyrians had fallen on hard times, possibly due to the development of the harbor at Ostia.[101] On the other hand, the *statio* in Rome was prospering due to the increased commerce through Ostia. Hence, for some time the residents of Tyre in Rome had been paying the sum of a hundred thousand denarii per year to their co-nationals in Puteoli in order to meet the rent payments for their *statio*. When at some later date the Tyrians of Rome ceased contributing the funds, those in Puteoli appealed to the city of Tyre, encouraging its council to order their kinsmen in Rome to resume the payments. Interestingly, the council directed the Tyrians of Rome to pay up.[102]

This fascinating inscription not only illustrates the involvement of foreign groups in the commerce of Rome, but also vividly shows the level of social commitment that could exist among the residents themselves.[103] Furthermore, it implies that such groups functioned as representative bodies of the cities from which they came and were responsible for maintaining their ancestral worship.[104] Since the Tyrians of Puteoli claim in their letter that their *statio* is "superior to the others in beauty and size," it is reasonable to assume that this sort of foreign office was not unique to Tyre.[105]

The case of the Tyrians in Rome illustrates how powerful the connections to one's fellow nationals could be in a foreign setting. The Tyrian merchants lived as a concentrated ethnic group, participated in their native cult, and, because of their commercial activity, maintained ongoing relations with the land of their origin. The convergence of these social forces represented a conservative force, one that produced resistance to assimilation.

During the imperial period Rome was a great cosmopolitan city in which foreign residents sometimes lived as aggregate communities. Such groups would have been more common in areas where temples to their native gods stood or where *stationes* of their native cities were located. In these settings or through associations made up of persons of common heritage, immigrants often kept their national connections alive and persisted in their peculiar religious and social traditions. Hence, Rome was not only large, but also ethnically diverse. Athenaeus may not have been far afield when he called Rome the "epitome of the civilized world" where one "may see at a glance all the cities of the world settled there."[106]

The Jews of ancient Rome certainly formed one of these "collective cities" in the midst of Rome's diverse foreign population. The topographical connections between Christians, Jews, and other foreign peoples referred to at the outset of this chapter indicate not only geographical location, but also social circumstance. How did this context affect Roman Christianity's development? Because earliest Christianity took root in a Jewish context, a precise answer to this question cannot be given without carefully analyzing the socialization of Jewish communities in ancient Rome.

Jewish Socialization in Ancient Rome in Light of Recent Developments in the Study of Diaspora Judaism

During the past two decades the modern understanding of first- and second-century C.E. Judaism has increased significantly, resulting in modifications of previously held views.[1] It is the goal of this chapter to analyze the Jewish communities of ancient Rome in light of these developments. Consequently, the chapter is composed of two parts: First, we will briefly survey developments in the study of Diaspora Judaism that have a bearing on the interpretation of data from Rome; second, we will elucidate the situation of the Jews in ancient Rome, highlighting relevant social, religious, and political factors.

RECENT DEVELOPMENTS IN THE STUDY OF DIASPORA JUDAISM

Agrippa's claim before Gaius (as reported by Philo) that Jewish colonies have been established "in every region of the inhabited world — in Europe, Asia, Libya, on mainlands, on islands, both on the coast and inland" attests to the international character of Judaism in the early imperial period.[2] The Diaspora evidence suggests that individual Jewish communities responded in varying ways to the challenge of maintaining their identity and traditions in various gentile settings. Disregard for the diversity of acculturations exhibited by Diaspora Jewish communities throughout the regions noted above has resulted in historical reconstructions that distort rather than enlighten ancient texts that are read in light of them. Therefore, progress in the interpretation of specific documents can be made only when scholars treat particular socio-religious contexts, limited both geographically and temporally. Narrower, more contextualized interpretations of both literary and material remains from the Jewish Diaspora have challenged a number of traditional assumptions. Three of these assumptions bear directly on the study at hand and may be appropriately discussed under individual subheadings.

Syncretism and the Diaspora

Recent research indicates that the religion of the Jews in the Diaspora was not syncretistic in a way that marked it off paradigmatically from Palestine. However, the antithesis of this view functioned as something of a working hypothesis until the distinction between Palestinian Judaism and Hellenistic (Diaspora) Judaism eroded. Martin Hengel's monograph *Judaism and Hellenism* has played a key role in challenging this long-standing distinction. He demonstrated that Diaspora Judaism did not lack Palestinian elements and that Palestine itself was considerably Hellenized.[3]

Simplistic contrasts between Palestine and the Diaspora have all but disappeared. However, the recent use of the phrase "Palestinian Judaism" to indicate a kind of normative expression of the Jewish religion is an unfortunate choice of terms because it inevitably resurrects the old contrast.[4] Naive applications of such phrases can mask the diversity that existed both within and outside Palestine and ignore the flux of Judaism between the post-exilic and rabbinic periods. Judaism was no unified entity, but rather a cluster of movements engaged in self-definition. Jacob Neusner's well-known insistence on the term "formative" in place of "normative" remains a useful tool for stimulating greater regard for the diversity of Judaism prior to the rabbinic period.[5]

Assumptions of syncretism have influenced interpretations of data from the Diaspora.[6] Jews in the Diaspora, some historians presume, routinely minimized the differences between themselves and their neighbors in order to make Judaism more attractive to pagans and to lessen the cognitive dissonance the Jews felt as a minority group in an alien environment.[7]

Admittedly substantial evidence is extant indicating that the religious practices of certain Jews were influenced on occasion by pagan expressions of piety.[8] However, much of this evidence amounts to isolated cases where the connections of the individual to Judaism or a Jewish community are unknown. The excavations of synagogue buildings provide more dependable data because they offer first-hand information regarding the Judaism of particular communities whose members were expressing "their understanding of what it meant to be Jewish in that particular situation."[9] The comment of Seager and Kraabel concerning the Sardis evidence is apropos:

> But if syncretism among Jews was as widespread as we have been told, there should be clear evidence for it in the Sardis data. From Lydia and from Sardis itself there is abundant evidence for Sabazius and Dionysus: was any of it found in the Synagogue? The Sardis Jewish community can now be extensively documented; is there any indication that mixtures of traditional Judaism and pagan piety were being concocted there? The answer to both questions is no.[10]

Stereotypes like "the syncretistic Judaism of the Diaspora" do an injustice to the evidence; it is simply not the case that the Diaspora was syncretistic in a way that marked it off paradigmatically. Such judgments must be made only with regard to investigations of individual Diaspora communities.[11]

The objection raised above does not deny social differences between Palestine and the Diaspora, nor the implications these may have for the religious views and practices of a given community. It only challenges generalizations imposed on the ancient evidence or supposed in the absence of evidence. The bulk of Jewish literature that presents Judaism in Hellenistic attire did in fact emerge from the Diaspora where minority groups could not easily insulate themselves from cultural pressures and/or opportunities.[12] Yet, even here a range of responses is apparent: 3 Maccabees reflects strict observance of the law as a matter of ethnic solidarity with no apology even for dietary laws;[13] Philo represents a middle ground between literalists and allegorists — his framework is Hellenistic philosophy, but he utilizes it in exposition of the Torah, whose cultic laws are to be literally observed;[14] the Testaments of the Twelve Patriarchs ignore distinctive Jewish practices and present ethics only in the broadest moral terms.[15]

A spectrum of acculturations is indicated by the literature of Diaspora Judaism. Yet, the Torah continued to serve a foundational role in almost every form of post-exilic Judaism.[16] Even in cases where Jewish literature emphasized only monotheism, avoidance of idolatry, and sexual ethics, the practices of Jews within the communities that produced the documents was not necessarily limited to these.[17]

Anti-Judaism in the Graeco-Roman World

Jewish socialization in a given Graeco-Roman setting was influenced, if not determined, by options available to Jews as a consequence of majority opinions. Hence, assumptions regarding these majority opinions substantially affect reconstructions of extant evidence. In fact, few assumptions play a more formative role in the reconstruction of Diaspora Judaism than does the working hypothesis of scholars concerning whether or not Jews were generally disliked in antiquity.[18]

It must be kept in mind that the extent to which Jewish self-identity exhibited an "us-versus-them" outlook was governed not only by a tradition that emphasized Israel's "otherness," but also by the views and actions of their non-Jewish neighbors: The responses of non-Jews either reinforced or contradicted their view of reality.[19] Peter Berger's claim that "the individual becomes that which he is addressed as by others" clarifies the role that Graeco-Roman views of Jews and Judaism played in Jewish self-definition in late antiquity.[20]

Determining how the Jews were "addressed" by others has become a focal point for researchers in recent years. John Gager's 1983 monograph, *The Origins of Anti-Semitism*, reflects what in most quarters is called the "new approach" to this complex and highly controversial subject. Although Rosemary Ruether's book *Faith and Fratricide* is clearly Gager's point of departure, he traces the new approach back to post–World War II scholarly attention elicited by the Holocaust. His book, he argues, is only the continuation of a trajectory whose direction was marked off by Jules Isaac and Marcel Simon.[21]

Proponents of the "new approach" challenge the traditional reading of Greek and Latin writers that has led to generalizations like that of Meagher: "In general it may be said that the Jews were singled out for disdain."[22] In contrast, they point to the positive and neutral assessments of the Jews and their religion that are attested in the same literature. These texts coupled with the apparent attraction of many non-Jews to Judaism leads Gager to conclude: "The presumption of a universal anti-Semitism in antiquity, pagan or Christian, has been made possible only by suppressing, ignoring or misinterpreting the mass of non-conforming evidence."[23]

A perusal of Stern's *Greek and Latin Authors on Jews and Judaism* will quickly demonstrate that the evidence for pagan views of Jews and Judaism is ambiguous. Greek and Latin texts that speak disparagingly of the Jews have been well known for centuries. Meagher is not off the mark when he stresses the breadth of the sample: "The roster of ancient writers who expressed anti-Jewish feeling reads like a syllabus for a second-semester course in classics: Cicero, Tacitus, Martial, Horace, Juvenal, Persius, Dio Cassius, Marcus Aurelius, Apuleius, Ovid, Petronius, Pliny the Elder, Plutarch, Quintilian, Seneca, Suetonius."[24] However, some of these very texts by expressing disdain for Jews because of their proselytizing or the infiltration of their customs into Roman society, at the same time testify to the existence of more sympathetic opinions.[25]

The apparent ambiguity of the evidence is reduced somewhat when the provenance of data (particularly literary materials) is kept in view. Hatred of the Jews was widespread in Alexandria because of unique social and political circumstances that exacerbated tensions.[26] Sardis, on the other hand, seems to have been a place where Jews were influential, very much a part of the fiber of the city.[27] In Aphrodisias a list of donors to a Jewish building project included nine persons designated *theosebes* (godfearers) and honored with the title *bouleutes* (city council members).[28] In general terms, little more can be said than that attitudes toward Jews and Judaism during the early empire were mixed: Positive evaluations occur in the literature even though negative appraisals predominate.[29] Robert Goldenberg in a review of John Gager's book offers the following synopsis:

> With respect to the "origins of anti-Semitism," then, one can summarize by saying that Jews were by no means universally despised in late antiquity, but that certain more or less endemic issues did estrange them from their neighbors. Individuals might find these issues more or less critical, and might resist to varying degrees the temptation to hostility that they represented; but even if "antiquity on the whole" did not "dislike Jews" there must have been plenty of people who did.[30]

Even if Goldenberg's reading of the evidence is more balanced, it is of little practical help to those interpreting particular documents associated with specific locales. If "antiquity on the whole did not dislike Jews," who did? And under what circumstances? The success one enjoys in sorting out these narrower questions is obviously dependent upon sources that are often lacking or problematic.[31] These sources, however, must be tenaciously analyzed in their own contexts, not interpreted in light of Alexandria, or Sardis, or an imaginary mean.

One of the most important challenges that Diaspora Jews faced was that of maintaining their Jewish identity in a pagan environment. Yet, the assumption that the challenge was met with the same socio-religious response — segregation, religious and social — throughout the Diaspora is problematic. Excavations in Sardis indicate that the Jews of that locale were intimately involved in the life of the city while at the same time aware of their distinct Jewish identity.[32] The situation in Rome, however, was quite different as Kraabel admits:

> In the first century A.D. many Jews in Rome were slaves, products of successful campaigns in Palestine by Roman armies. Jews in Sardis were more prosperous and had a less direct tie with Jerusalem: their community had not come from the Holy Land but had been founded by Jews from Babylonia and Mesopotamia two centuries earlier.[33]

Indeed excavations of Jewish synagogues in the Diaspora (particularly Sardis) have challenged the old consensus and facilitated a needed corrective.[34] Nevertheless, Sardis must not become the new paradigm by which Diaspora data are deciphered and Jewish socialization predicted.[35] In his criticism of Sevenster's book — Sevenster had concluded that Jewish separateness was the root cause of anti-Semitism — John Gager writes, "Once we lift the veil of polemics, we find not 'a people apart, with their own customs and religion which admitted little intermingling with their Greek neighbors,' but a people both in and of their world."[36] Gager's generalization is as extravagant as those Gager endeavors to correct because the degree of separateness exhibited by a Jewish community depended on factors that cannot be applied across the board.[37]

Three factors should be kept clearly in view when interpreting data regarding the separateness of a given Jewish community. First, Shaye Cohen's comment:

> One of the characteristic themes of Jewish thought throughout the ages is the sense of contrast between the "us" and the "them," between Jew and gentile, between the ideas of Judaism and the ideas of the gentile world (whether paganism, Christianity, or Islam).[38]

Indeed the remarkable strength of Jewish self-identity through the centuries owes much to the boundaries that differentiated the Jew from the non-Jew. Second, how "separate" a particular Jewish community appeared in a given region depended to a large extent on social factors Jews did not control. Third, the precise boundaries between Jews and pagans were not always entirely clear. Although the "us-versus-them" outlook did play a paradigmatic role, the ambiguity of the boundaries and the spectrum of socializations represent variables that must be carefully weighed.

Diaspora Synagogues

Archaeological and epigraphic evidence from excavations of several Diaspora synagogue buildings has challenged assumptions regarding the development and function of synagogues in the Graeco-Roman world during the early empire.[39] Three different collections of essays have recently appeared suggesting the modifications that recent discoveries have prompted.[40] Cohen's synopsis reflects the more contemporary understanding: "The complexity of ancient Judaism is faithfully mirrored in the complexity of the ancient synagogue."[41] It is becoming apparent that the term "formative" is not only an apt description of Judaism during the Second Temple period but also of the synagogue of the same era.

Since 1930 at least six Diaspora synagogues have been excavated: Dura, Sardis, Priene, Delos, Stobi, and Ostia.[42] On the basis of analyses of the evidence collected from these sites, Kraabel offers nine conclusions that either correct or augment prior reconstructions. They may be summarized as follows:

1. No "canonical" pattern existed for early synagogue structures; local custom and conditions determined the plan.

2. Early synagogues cannot be described so narrowly as "varieties of a basilica plan" without forcing the evidence.

3. No chronological list of stages can be identified for the Diaspora buildings.

4. Diaspora synagogues cannot be dated by their plan.

5. Rabbinic statements about synagogue architecture and usage are irrelevant to the situation of the western Diaspora.

6. Diaspora synagogues may be concealed or deliberately inconspicuous due to the minority status of Jews in these areas.

7. The structure will be a complex of several rooms functioning as the community center for a minority group seeking to maintain its identity in a pagan environment.

8. Synagogues of the Second Temple period may be particularly difficult to identify because they lack Jewish symbols that developed

later and were not as differentiated in their usage as were later buildings.

9. In time the sanctity of the synagogue increases from a "prayer house" to a "holy place"; this process was exacerbated by the destruction of the Temple, though living without the Temple was a matter to be reckoned with in the Diaspora prior to 70 C.E.[43]

Although Kraabel's analysis is based on evidence that is generally later than the first century C.E., his conclusions are relevant because the lack of standardization in the architecture and function of synagogue buildings even during the third century underscores the formative character of the pre-rabbinic period. One must not read later rabbinic synagogal patterns back into the Second Temple period because evidence for such a consistent pattern is still lacking in the third century.[44] The study of early synagogue architecture suggests that the pre-70 C.E. synagogue should be conceived under the rubric of "assembly," not that of "institution" in the later Talmudic sense.[45]

The plurality of names used in antiquity to describe what today is called the ancient synagogue indicates in itself that the phenomenon was not as clearly defined an institution as the uniformity of modern terminology suggests.[46] A broad scope of activities took place in these gatherings according to the needs and desires of individual communities.[47] Levine summarizes the situation well when he writes:

> At the end of the Second Temple period the synagogue was still a relatively young institution, whose outward forms, patterns, rules, and rituals were far from crystallized. Throughout this period the synagogue was in the process of gradual development, and, as a result, its form and nature differed from place to place.[48]

Although no rigid pattern had yet emerged dictating the form of Jewish gatherings during this early period, Diaspora synagogues had at least one feature in common: function. These assemblies facilitated the maintenance of Jewish self-identity in alien pagan contexts. The label "community center" captures this function of the ancient synagogue better than other terms because it is broad enough to encompass the array of social and religious activities that may have expedited the preservation of Jewish identity in a particular locale.[49]

The use of ordinary homes for communal gatherings was common in antiquity. Eventually an association might acquire a house for their respective group (often through benefaction) and renovate it to serve their purposes for meeting. White draws attention to the pervasiveness of the practice by surveying the situation at Delos:

> A guild of professional scribes took over two houses and renovated them into a collegial establishment in the same block as the synagogue, also renovated from a house. Down the street in one direction stood the renovated *domus ecclesiae* [house-church] of the Christians; in the other direction was the house renovated to become a mithraeum. In case after case, year after year, these small religious associations adapted private domestic structures for public religious or collegial use.[50]

The initial use of a house for community meetings is impossible to detect in the archaeological record because the structure lacks distinguishing qualities. Functionally speaking it was a house, nothing more. Yet, when the structure was modified to facilitate group meetings, as in the cases cited above, the changes may stand out and bear witness to the transition.

Analyses of the six Diaspora synagogues mentioned above indicate that five were at one time private homes.[51] Only the structure at Sardis was clearly a public building, and even it was not originally designed as a synagogue.[52] The Delos synagogue, believed by many to be the earliest excavated synagogue structure, exhibits in its second stage an adaptation of a private dwelling according to the "style of other collegial halls on Delos."[53] Because early synagogues were gatherings of minority people seeking to preserve their identities in an alien setting, the homes of community members provided the natural locus for assemblies. Only later were synagogue buildings constructed specifically to serve the needs of the religious community.[54] Prior to 70, or even 135 C.E., synagogues met principally in ordinary or minimally renovated houses.[55]

Conclusion

The study of Diaspora Judaism is a complex endeavor, complicated by the diversity of Judaism and the sundry settings it called home. The Jews adapted a Graeco-Roman social form, the private association, to their own unique social and religious aims.[56] However, there was great diversity in the responses of different Jewish communities to the question of how one might "sing the song of the Lord in a foreign land."[57] These responses were not only a reflection of the religious convictions of the particular group, but also a derivative of the minority or alien status of the group; the community's station in a given setting affected the range of available options. This social-historical facet is especially relevant to the circumstances in Rome, a point noted by Kraabel:

> The Jews in Rome itself (where much of the gentile attitude was molded) were first of all a social or sociological datum: they were another of those ethnic groups streaming into the capital from the Greek world in what were for many Romans distressingly large numbers. It is for this reason that they were lumped together with the Egyptians frequently, and also with the Syrians, Lydians and other minorities.[58]

THE SOCIALIZATION OF JEWS IN ANCIENT ROME

It is to the situation of the Jews and their communities in ancient Rome that we now turn. Our goal in the second half of this chapter is to describe in more detail the "sociological datum" of the Jews that Kraabel referred to above in light of recent research in Diaspora Judaism. An analysis of the socio-religious situation of the Jews in ancient Rome will be followed by a consideration of political factors.

The Socio-Religious Situation

Our inquiry into the socio-religious situation of the Jews in ancient Rome highlights five areas: (1) origin and growth of the population; (2) Jewish neighborhoods; (3) social status; (4) synagogues; (5) Roman attitudes toward Jews and Judaism in Rome.

The Origin and Growth of the Jewish Population

Neither the date nor the circumstances under which Jews initially inhabited Rome are known. Nevertheless, by the time of the late republic and early empire it is clear that Jews were in the city in considerable numbers and were quite visible. The earliest reference to Jews in the city is the well-known Valerius Maximus text mentioning the expulsion of Jewish proselytizers along with certain astrologers.[59] However, it is a matter of debate whether they were permanent residents because they were compelled to "return to their homes."[60]

Information regarding the number of Jews residing in Rome during the first half of the first century B.C.E. and the circumstances that might account for their growing presence is sparse indeed. Nonetheless, their numbers must have increased significantly when Pompey returned to Rome with Jewish prisoners taken during the capture of Jerusalem in 63 B.C.E.[61] Philo corroborates this hypothesis when he says:

> The large district of Rome beyond the Tiber was owned and inhabited by Jews. The majority of them were Roman freedmen, who had been brought to Rome as prisoners-of-war and manumitted by their owners.[62]

Although Philo, writing in the early 40s C.E., does not indicate when they were brought to Rome, a process beginning with Pompey best fits the chronology. Moreover, Tacitus's account of the expulsion of Jews in 19 C.E. ordered by Tiberius specifies that "four thousand descendants of enfranchised slaves" were shipped to Sardinia.[63] Thus, in the mid-to-late first century B.C.E. the Jewish population of Rome swelled through the influx of a considerable number of slaves who had been brought to the capital from Judaea.

Although the early evidence might lead one to believe that the Jewish community was made up almost entirely of ex-slaves, other classes were no doubt included. Only four years after Pompey's return from the campaign in Judaea, Cicero, in his defense of Flaccus, referred to Jews as a large group, influential in public affairs.[64] Even when allowance is made for Cicero's trial rhetoric, the text still suggests the existence of a Jewish community during the late republic that consisted of more than a huddle of ex-slaves who had arrived in the city only a few years earlier.[65]

By the time of Augustus the Jews of Rome were both numerous and visible. Their conspicuous character is indicated by the references that crop up in literary works from the period.[66] The earliest data useful for quantifying the population comes from Josephus's record of a delegation sent from Jerusalem in 4 B.C.E. to petition the removal of Archelaus from the throne of Judaea. Josephus says that the Palestinian delegation numbering fifty was joined by more than eight thousand Jews from Rome.[67] This figure, along with Tacitus's account of the four thousand Jews conscripted into military service in association with the expulsion of Tiberius, has significantly influenced the common Jewish population estimates of forty to fifty thousand.[68]

Jewish Neighborhoods in Ancient Rome

Philo's observation that the Transtiberine region (Augustus's fourteenth region) of Rome was an area of Jewish concentration has been confirmed by excavations of the Jewish catacombs. Based on inscriptions from the catacombs and the proximity of the burial places to the region, Leon estimates that seven synagogues in the capital were located in the Transtiber, modern Trastevere.[69] Furthermore, the Monteverde catacomb, the largest and oldest of the cemeteries, was situated just outside this area.[70]

Some scholars have referred to this portion of Rome as a Jewish "ghetto." Reinach, for example, called Persius's depiction of Roman Jews a "lively and picturesque sketch of a Roman ghetto on a Sabbath afternoon."[71] Nonetheless, the term "neighborhood" is preferable since neither literary nor archaeological evidence substantiates the notion that Jews resided here because it was compulsory, a condition often associated with the use of the term "ghetto."[72]

Jews initially settled across the Tiber because it afforded one of the few locations where foreign immigrants could find housing during the late republic, and because living in proximity to one another facilitated the observance of their religion and native customs. Yet there is evidence that Jews lived in other parts of the city as well. The Campus Martius and the Subura are both areas for which synagogue communities were named, obviously indicating a Jewish presence in those regions.[73] Juvenal's comment that Jewish beggars had taken over the sacred grove of Egeria suggests that Jews lived in the Porta Capena area as well.[74] The location of two catacombs along the via Appia also intimates a concentration in that region of the city and possibly along the via Appia outside the city.[75] Suzanne Collon, utilizing literary and epigraphic materials, published a map depicting the locations of the Jewish synagogues of Rome.[76] Although there is literary and epigraphic evidence for many of her choices (at least the general regions), most scholars have been more cautious in their specifications.[77]

Because of evidence indicating a wider distribution, some scholars have doubted Philo's assertion that the Jews were principally concentrated in Trastevere.[78] However, Philo's comment need not imply that Jews lived only in that region. Even in Alexandria, where the evidence for Jewish quarters is clear, sources indicate that Jews also lived in other parts of the city and formed synagogues outside the regions known to have been strictly Jewish.[79] Solin does not believe it is possible to make out whether there was in Rome an entirely Jewish quarter as was the case in Alexandria.[80] However, it is safe to say that the Transtiber was the location of the highest concentration of Jews in Rome during the late republic and early empire.[81]

Social Status

The Jews of ancient Rome were not uniquely poor, but their social context was by and large that of Rome's impoverished and humble masses. Philo's comment that the Jewish population in Rome was concentrated in the Transtiber and made up of recently manumitted freedmen entails two indicators: servile status and a social context among the poor of the Transtiberine region.[82] Because of its physical disadvantages, particularly the problem of access, the Transtiber was settled late. It was one of the few areas where space was still available to accommodate the large numbers of immigrants who came to Rome during the late republic. Modern references to this region as a "slum" depend not only on settling patterns but also on the preponderance of mass housing in the area indicated by the ratio of *insulae* (tenement) to *domus* (house).[83] Stambaugh's synopsis reflects this approach:

> There was relatively little mass housing either in the lower Campus Martius, with its plethora of public buildings, or in the more exclusive neighborhoods atop the Oppian, Esquiline, and Aventine. The number of *insulae* was proportionately higher in the valleys between the hills, in the eastern, non-monumental part of the Campus Martius along the Via Lata, on the slopes of the Palatine, and in the slums of the Trans-Tiber section.[84]

The servile background of many Jews in ancient Rome is indicated not only by the statement of Philo noted above but also by Tacitus's record of the conscription of four thousand Jewish freedmen during the reign of Tiberius.[85] Gradually Jews who were brought to Rome as prisoners of war gained their freedom, just as non-Jews did.[86] The *mitzvah* to redeem captives may have hastened the process for some Jews.[87] Once set free, however, these Jews could do little more than take their place among the mass of poor citizenry in the bulging capital.[88] Philo fills out the picture further when he mentions Augustus's policy that allowed an alternate date for the distribution of the grain dole for the poor if the scheduled date fell on a Sabbath.[89] Since the grain dole was limited to Roman citizens, this text demonstrates that by the time of the early empire many Jews had gained citizenship but had not escaped poverty.[90]

Almost a century ago Lazare described the Jews of Rome as "a powerful and rich colony" in spite of his awareness that they lived in the poorer section of the city beyond the Tiber.[91] During Lazare's era the supposed dominance and power of Jews in the economy of the ancient world was a standard explanation of anti-Semitism. Blaudau specifically identified the "Reichtum der Juden" (the wealth of the Jews) as the catalyst for hostility towards the Jews in gentile cities.[92]

Contrary to this picture, ancient sources are more prone to malign the Jews for their poverty than their wealth. This was certainly the case in Rome.[93] Among the beggars of Rome Juvenal refers to are Jewish squatters inhabiting Egeria's grove who possess only a "Sabbath haybox."[94] In his description of the fortune-telling rabble of the city Juvenal stresses the bargain to be found among Jewish diviners: "Jews will sell you whatever dreams you like for a few small coppers."[95] Martial singles out a "Jew taught by his mother to beg."[96] Sevenster's comment is apropos: "If the Roman authors were our only source of information, we would be inclined to assume that the Jews were nothing more than a group of miserable paupers."[97]

For the most part, the poverty and lowly status of the Jews of ancient Rome, exploited by Roman authors, are borne out by the evidence from their cemeteries. Leon in describing the Jewish tombs writes:

> Thousands of these are plain loculi, many of them marked, it seems, by no epitaph at all, others by a brief notice, crudely scrawled with paint or even just scratched on the stuccoed closures, or unskillfully carved with ill-shaped letters and in faulty grammar on pieces of discarded marble. The language of the inscriptions also . . . points to a generally low degree of literacy.[98]

When one pauses to consider that it is the rich and powerful who normally stand out in the ancient sources, the indications of poverty and lowly status from Roman Jewish evidence is even more striking.

The socio-economic status of Roman Jews, however, was not as monolithic as the data surveyed thus far suggest. Although the Jewish population was concentrated in the Transtibernum, Jews resided in other parts of the city. Moreover, though many of the Jews were manumitted slaves or their descendants with little hope for upward mobility or economic prosperity, some clearly were not. Material evidence from the Jewish catacombs in Rome bears witness to these exceptions. Although limited in number, private decorated tomb chambers, elaborate sarcophagai, and marble slabs attest that some Jews in imperial Rome were more prosperous.[99]

Admittedly, the circumstances of other Diaspora communities (i.e., Sardis) were somewhat different. However, analogies to these must not be allowed to obscure the interpretation of the data from Rome. The Jewish population in the capital was made up of individuals who were as a rule neither rich nor powerful. Exceptions existed, but they were clearly exceptions.[100]

The socio-economic status of the Jewish communities of Rome did not distinguish them from other foreign groups nor from the poor Roman masses. Due to the upheavals of the late republic and the limited economic opportunities in the capital, poverty was widespread.[101] Yet, the Jewish population exerted influence in the city of Rome out of proportion to its status. This was due to the size of the Jewish population and because "their religion kept them together and did not permit them to become assimilated in the citizen body as other groups did."[102] The Jews in Rome lobbied to protect their own interests and even rallied in support of Jews from other parts of the empire.[103] The level of ethnic and religious solidarity evidenced by the Jews was an anomaly to the Romans, sometimes a threat. The concessions that were made for the Jews were a source of frustration to many non-Jews precisely because this group seemed to be accorded inappropriate privileges, status that did not match their station in life.[104]

Synagogues

No architectural remains of any Jewish synagogue building have been unearthed in Rome. Moreover, neither Jewish nor Roman authors from antiquity offer information about the various synagogue groups that existed among the Jews of ancient Rome. Shaye Cohen's comment regarding the silence of pagan authors regarding the ancient synagogue is especially pertinent to Rome because the Roman Jewish community was large and many of the literary references to Jewish practices originated there:

> Pagan authors commented on many of the beliefs and practices of Judaism — notably circumcision, the Sabbath, the fasts, the food laws, the avoidance of images, and the ethos of separation — but none of them commented on the synagogue, and only a few of them even bothered to mention it.[105]

One is less likely to be surprised by this omission if the formative nature of the synagogue during the pre-70 C.E. period is appreciated. Jews in Rome probably met in the homes of community members.[106] Some of these houses eventually may have been adapted for community use according to the patterns already discussed. Because these meetings took place in homes located in Jewish neighborhoods, the gatherings did not necessarily attract the attention of outsiders. Furthermore, because the meetings of other religious cults and associations often took place in similar domestic settings, the Jewish meetings were simply part of the social fabric of society; they were not outstanding, architecturally or socially.[107]

Although no architectural remains have been discovered for a community structure where Jewish gatherings took place in ancient Rome, references to at least eleven different Jewish synagogues have been found in epitaphs from the Jewish catacombs in Rome.[108] The catacomb inscriptions afford limited but helpful data regarding Jewish communities during the first few centuries C.E. Yet, because funerary inscriptions are seldom datable within narrow limits, in most cases it is impossible to sort out the epigraphs that belong to the third century C.E. from those of the first century.[109] Therefore, care must be taken not to read later developments back into the earlier period.[110] Data drawn from the inscriptions coupled with the locations of the various catacombs suggest that at least seven of the synagogues were located in the Transtibernum, confirming the assertion of Philo that the Jewish quarter was to be found in this region. Monteverde, the largest and oldest of the cemeteries, was situated just outside this area. The number of synagogues located across the Tiber confirms the earlier observation that the Jews of ancient Rome lived among the poor, less assimilated immigrant population of the city.

Analysis of the names of the various synagogues sometimes indicates what differentiated the groups from one another. Three were named for patrons or benefactors, the Agrippesians, Augustesians, and Volumnesians; three were called after the districts where they were headquartered, the Campesians, Siburesians, and probably the Calcaresians;[111] two, the Tripolitans and maybe Elaeans, were named for the city from which their founders emigrated; the Hebrews and the Vernaclesians were named for characteristics of their members;[112] one, that of the Secenians, has not been successfully deciphered.[113]

Other information relevant to the synagogue groupings of the Roman Jews may be couched in the language of the inscriptions themselves.[114] Leon has shown that those who buried their dead in the Appia catacomb were the most Romanized, since a far greater percentage (36.4) of inscriptions from that burial place are in Latin. Conversely, the epitaphs of Nomentana are almost exclusively Greek. The preponderance of Greek inscriptions throughout the catacombs is striking. Leon tabulated that 76 percent of the catacomb inscriptions were Greek while only 23 percent were Latin.[115] Denali Poliakoff, in her study of Jewish acculturation on the basis of evidence from burial places, explains that the persistence of Greek among the Jews in Rome "indicates the strong cohesiveness of the Jewish community in Rome."[116] If Greek had not been the lingua franca among the Roman Jews it is extremely doubtful that such a preference for Greek would have continued into the third century C.E.[117]

Although Semitic epitaphs are rare, nearly all of them come from one catacomb, Monteverde. Moreover, proportionately, almost twice as many Semitic names are found in the inscriptions of Monteverde when compared with the other two large catacombs, Appia and Nomentana.[118] It is a reasonable conjecture that the Monteverde catacomb, located just outside the Transtibernum region, served synagogues that were more resistant to acculturation.[119] Michael White speculates that such differences likely "had an impact on the relations of individual groups to the Roman culture and, consequently, on theology as well."[120]

The catacomb inscriptions also provide a window into the organization of the Jewish communities of ancient Rome. Although numerous synagogue officials are honored in the various inscriptions, the evidence does not support the view that Roman Jews were organized under a central authority (an ethnarch or *gerousia*) who represented the entire city as was the case in Alexandria.[121] Although La Piana and Juster argue otherwise, funerary inscriptions from Rome indicate a "decentralized organization" because offices are consistently linked to the names of individual synagogues within which honorees served.[122] Millar has drawn attention to the differences between the two cities by setting them in contrast:

> Two extremes are represented by Alexandria and Rome. In the former a united corporation of Jews, numbering many thousands, with significant political power, in the latter, in spite of considerable numbers, only isolated private associations without special political rights.[123]

The differences between the socializations of Jews in Rome and Alexandria are best explained by noting the relative youth of the Jewish population in Rome and its lack of involvement in the political life of the city as compared to the Jews of Alexandria, who were there in numbers from the fourth century B.C.E.

Individual synagogue communities in Rome were organized independently with their own leaders.[124] It is apparent that some of these communities had their own *gerousia* (council) because inscriptions refer to persons of importance within a particular *gerousia:* A *gerousiarches synagoges Augustesion* (gerousiarch of the Augustan synagogue) and a *gerousiarches synagoges Agrippesion* (gerousiarch of the Agrippa synagogue).[125] The title that occurs most frequently in the catacomb inscriptions is not *gerousiarch* but *archon.*[126] The precise function of the *archon* is nowhere indicated, but the recurring title *dis archon* (twice archon) suggests they were elected officials who served for limited periods.[127]

Inscriptions from the Jewish catacombs intimate that the law exercised a dominant place in the lives of the Jews in Rome and that great importance was attached to synagogue membership. References to the law and the deceased person's faithfulness to the law occur with great frequency. On this basis Frey asserts that the law was "the primary object of its [the synagogue's] worship and its piety."[128] The two most characteristic items found in the epitaphs of the Roman Jews are the use of Greek and identification with the synagogue.[129] In Rome 54 percent of the inscriptions are synagogue related (12 percent of the total collection contain textual references to particular synagogues) whereas only a few synagogue connections are mentioned in the Beth She'arim inscriptions, and none is noted in Egypt.[130] Jewish self-definition in Rome was closely tied to synagogue affiliation, a phenomenon best explained by the estrangement Roman Jews felt in the capital and the strong sense of group identity that emerged as a result.[131]

For many Jews in the Graeco-Roman world Jerusalem and Palestine continued to play an important role in their self-definition. Kraabel has noted that the Jewish world community found a common tie in the "Homeland, not necessarily the Palestine of their own times, but the biblical Israel elevated to mythical status."[132] Yet, the ties that existed between the Jews of Rome and Jerusalem were not limited to the "symbolic" or "mythical." Because much of the early growth of the Jewish population resulted from the forced immigration of Judaeans, strong connections between the Roman Jews and Jerusalem naturally persisted.[133] Josephus's account of eight thousand Jews from Rome who took a stand with an embassy from Palestine to express resistance to the appointment of Archelaus as ruler of Judaea confirms these expectations.[134] Moreover, the Jews of Rome, like other Diaspora Jews, sent the half-shekel to Jerusalem.[135]

Roman Attitudes toward Jews and Judaism

Information presented earlier in this chapter emphasized that although anti-Judaism was widespread in antiquity it was not a universal response. Consequently, conclusions must not be drawn until narrower investigations are conducted into the socialization of Jewish communities in particular locales during limited time periods. Under this heading we will isolate Roman authors and limit the list to those whose comments regarding Jews and Judaism are relevant to the late republic or early empire.[136] The relevant authors include: Cicero, Horace, Ovid, Valerius Maximus, Seneca, Persius, Petronius, Quintilian, Martial, Juvenal, Tacitus, Suetonius, and Dio Cassius.[137]

In these writers references to the Jews take different forms. Tacitus includes the most extensive description of the Jews as a people, while Juvenal treats one specific aspect of Judaism in some detail. Suetonius and Dio Cassius generally mention the Jews in their historical surveys only when they are the object of some administrative action. The remainder of these authors allude to the Jews only in passing, often with glancing blows that exploit some facet of Jewish life or religion they find stupid, anti-social, or humorous. The critique of Tacitus offers a rather comprehensive catalogue of social practices that could be exploited by a Roman fault-finder: They export their money to Jerusalem; they separate themselves from all other peoples and practice circumcision in order to distinguish themselves; they proselytize non-Jews; they are misanthropic, god-haters, un-Roman, and anti-family.[138] The conservative Roman prejudices of Tacitus are evident in almost every line of his discussion of the Jews. Judaism, like Egyptian superstitions, is a threat to the Roman society to which he is committed. Nevertheless, the practices or characteristics Tacitus exploits are not unique to his caricature. Other Roman authors utilize many of the same topics in critiques that censure the Jews for their strangeness, exclusivity, or proselytizing.

A brief survey of allusions to Jews or Judaism by authors who lived or had experience in Rome will demonstrate the array of opinions that existed among these writers and the audiences for which they wrote. Cicero, in his defense of Flaccus, refers to the Jews of Rome as influential in politics and even vicious in lobbying for their cause. He accuses them of practicing sacred rites that are "at variance with the glory of our empire, the dignity of our name, the customs of our ancestors."[139] Horace mentions personal inconvenience caused by Sabbath observance among Romans and compares the recruiting zeal of a band of poets to the Jews: "We, like the Jews, will compel you to make one of our throng."[140] Ovid mentions the "foreign Sabbath" as an excuse one should not use to avoid a needed but undesirable journey.[141] The Valerius Maximus text (published ca. 31 C.E.) states that Jews were expelled from Rome in 139 B.C.E. on account of their contamination of Roman customs.[142] Seneca faults the Jews for wasting a seventh of their lives and expresses outrage at the infiltration of Jewish customs into Roman practice: "Meanwhile the customs of this accursed race have gained such influence that they are now received throughout all the world. The vanquished have given laws to their victors."[143]

Persius was aware of Jewish celebrations in Rome of Herod's birthday and of daily Jewish practices: "Floppy tunnies' tails are curled round the dishes of red ware, and the white jars are swollen out with wine, you silently twitch your lips, turning pale at the sabbath of the circumcised."[144] Habinnas, writes Petronius, owned a slave who was perfect except for two faults: "He is circumcised and he snores."[145] Petronius knows the central importance attached to circumcision among Roman Jews: "The Jew may worship his pig-god and clamour in the ears of high heaven, but unless he also cuts back his foreskin with the knife, he shall go forth from the people and emigrate to Greek cities, and shall not tremble at the fasts of Sabbath imposed by the law."[146] Quintilian refers to the Jews as a "race which is a curse to others."[147] Martial focuses his satire primarily on circumcision. He tells of an unfortunate man whose enormously large sheath fell off in the middle of the exercise ground revealing that "he was circumcised!"[148] He also attacks a Jewish poet who criticized his work, referring to him four times in seven lines as "circumcised poet."[149] With his characteristic glancing blows he cites a "Jew taught by his mother to beg" as contributing to the unbearable noise of the city of Rome, and in a list of the most hideous items he can think of — which he still prefers to the stench of a certain Bassa — he includes the "breath of fasting Sabbatarian women."[150]

Juvenal has a lengthy passage in which he chastises those who by adopting a few Jewish practices bear the responsibility for their children's proselytism. However, other aspects of Jewish practice that he finds contemptuous also surface in the text:

Some who have had a father who reveres the Sabbath, worship nothing but the clouds, and the divinity of the heavens, and see no difference between eating swine's flesh, from which their father abstained, and that of man; and in time they take to circumcision. Having been wont to flout the laws of Rome, they learn and practice and revere the Jewish law, and all that Moses handed down in his secret tome, forbidding to point out the way to any not worshiping the same rites, and conducting none but the circumcised to the desired fountain. For all which the father was to blame, who gave up every seventh day to idleness, keeping it apart from all the concerns of life.[151]

Similar, but even more harsh, is the description of the Jewish people offered by Tacitus. According to Tacitus, the Jewish rites are:

sinister, infamous, and based on depravity. For every very evil person abandoning the religion of his ancestors has brought contributions and money to them, as the result of which the resources of the Jews have increased; and among them there is an obstinate sense of integrity, also pity that is ever ready, but enmity and hatred against all others. Separate in their table, and sleeping apart, it is a people very prone to lust, but they abstain from sleeping with alien women, while among themselves nothing is illicit. They have established the custom of circumcision, so as to recognize themselves by this distinction. Proselytes to their way of life adopt the same custom, and they are at once imbued with despising the gods, rejecting their own country, and considering parents, children, brothers without value.[152]

Tacitus, Suetonius, and Dio Cassius add information that is political and administrative in nature.[153] They report the evictions of the Jews during the reigns of Tiberius and Claudius, the relationship between Titus and Bernice, as well as the stern measures of Domitian.[154]

Interpreting the evidence for pagan attitudes toward the Jews would appear at first glance rather elementary. Yet, it is clear that if Tacitus and Juvenal spoke for every Roman there would have been no proselytism problem against which to banter. Nonetheless, there is considerable evidence of anti-Jewish sentiment in Rome during the period under consideration. The references cited above show that anti-Jewish views in Rome were elicited by the separateness of the Jewish community, its foreign character, alien cult, and the negative reactions on the part of some

Romans to the attraction of other Romans to Jewish religion and/or customs.[155] Roman administrative actions against the Jewish communities of Rome under the Julio-Claudian emperors indicate that these opinions were not limited to Roman authors. Such administrative actions did not stem from the opinions of a few intellectuals nor were these views read only by the elite and literate.

The Socio-Political Situation of the Jews in Rome

To divide the socialization of Jews into socio-religious and socio-political factors is somewhat artificial because the political issues were largely a consequence of socio-religious issues. Nonetheless, the division helps to clarify the relationships between the factors and to underscore the significance of the political factors. The historical circumstances of the Jews in ancient Rome were affected to a considerable degree by relations with political administrators in Rome, particularly the emperors themselves. However, the case of the Jews was not unique. Their situation politically was part of a bigger picture: the administration of foreign, non-Roman religions. In order to understand properly Roman administrative actions with regard to the Jews, it is important to view such actions in the context of this broader picture.

Roman Administration and Non-Roman Religions

The religions of the Roman empire can be grouped according to three main types: the traditional civic gods of the state religions; the Oriental cults from the Middle East, Persia, and Egypt; and the exclusively monotheistic religions, Judaism and Christianity.[156] These existed side by side in many communities, and they were all represented in the city of Rome itself. Although Ferguson describes ancient religions as generally accommodating, it would be misleading to typify the Roman approach to religion as intrinsically cosmopolitan.[157] Rome was the political center of a vast, pluralistic empire. Not surprisingly, it soon became the religious center of that empire as well. Because the gods and cults of Rome's subject peoples came with the territories the Romans conquered, they were forced politically to deal with religions that were very different from their own.[158]

Because the official religious outlook of the Romans was starkly conservative, assimilating non-Roman religions could be problematic.[159]

North highlights three features of Roman religion that demonstrate its conservative character: Institutions existed that made conservation or continuity possible; the Romans practiced a punctiliousness over ritual detail that encouraged, if not insured, precise repetition from year to year; and rituals were preserved even after they no longer made sense to the participants.[160] For the Romans, experience had proven the validity of their religion: They had won battles and the empire had prospered. The continuation of their prosperity depended on preserving the purity of the ritual; it simply had to be done correctly.[161] However, in times of distress the search for what was lacking in their ritual sometimes opened the door for non-Roman religions. At the Senate's request the Sibylline Books were consulted for remedies. Interestingly, the solution sometimes involved the importing of a foreign cult or some action on behalf of one of these cults. In fact, during the early and middle republic foreign deities were "summoned" to Rome (Asclepius, Magna Mater) and tutelary deities of enemy states were on occasion "captured," summoned out, and brought to the capital.[162]

A fascinating anomaly confronts the student of Roman religion: The religion of the Romans was both conservative and innovative.[163] Because Roman religion was essentially polytheistic, the incorporation of new deities presented no theological obstacle. However, as foreign cults became more common and their practices more apparent, the Romans became increasingly troubled about the effect of these cults on traditional Roman religion. Under the empire no new gods were added to the Roman pantheon as official gods of the Roman state until Isis and Serapis were admitted during the reign of Caracalla (third century C.E.).[164]

Oriental cults, with their exotic rituals and expanding numbers, posed a particularly ominous threat.[165] Their emphasis upon the individual (conversion, salvation, ritual purification, etc.) threatened to "undermine rather than supplement the ancestral religion."[166] The attraction of women to these cults coupled with allegations of improprieties fostered concern that Eastern religions also undermined the Roman way of life.[167] The immigration of large numbers of people from the East during the middle and late republic only heightened the tension between the conservative and innovative aspects of Rome's religion. One way of managing the growing conflict was to endure the religious pluralism of the capital but to discourage Romans from dabbling in non-Roman religions. This was a natural approach because the Romans felt that people were entitled to worship their native gods with only limited exceptions (i.e., when law and order were threatened or when the rites observed were starkly un-Roman as in the case of the Druids).[168] When Hannibal invaded Italy, Magna Mater was summoned to Rome in an attempt to mitigate the crisis.[169] Nevertheless, participation in the Phrygian practices of the cult by Romans was disallowed.[170] Cicero objected to the involvement of Romans in foreign rites even when performed privately; Romans were to worship only traditional Roman deities:

> No one shall have gods to himself, either new gods or alien gods, unless recognized by the state. Privately they [Romans] shall worship those gods whose worship they have duly received from their ancestors.[171]

The intensity of these apprehensions is starkly demonstrated by Roman actions during the Bacchanal crisis of 186 B.C.E.[172] The continuation of these anxieties into the Augustan period is evidenced by Livy's long and detailed account of the Bacchanal conspiracy. Because the events took place almost 150 years before Livy wrote, the text mirrors Livy's own concerns and those of his contemporaries.[173]

Not all foreign cults were viewed by the Romans with equal concern. According to Suetonius, "Augustus showed great respect towards all ancient and long established foreign rites, but despised the rest."[174] In spite of Rome's discomfort with certain foreign cults, Hugh Last is correct when he observes: "Nowhere is there any cogent proof that a cult was attacked merely because it was not Roman."[175] Roman policy toward foreign religions was clearly one of toleration. However, exactly what would be tolerated was determined by a complex set of factors that included a mix of the tradition of toleration, Roman fear of non-Roman religions, and an array of social and political settings within which particular administrative actions had to be contemplated. There was no elaborate policy by which Rome managed the religious affairs of the empire, no over-arching strategy that was broken down into logical divisions and executed on the local level according to set patterns and precedents. As a matter of fact, Roman criminal law lacked even a general category of *laesa religio* (behavior injurious to religion) or *sacrilegium* (profane or impious behavior).[176] Such terms were normally applied only to the protection of sacred property.[177]

Roman administration was characteristically passive in nature.[178] One should not conclude, however, that Rome was uninvolved or unconcerned about the administration of religious matters. Instances of Roman intervention abound, but on a case-by-case basis.[179]

The gap between policy and the actual business of administration can be ascertained by surveying particular cases of Roman intervention involving Eastern cults. During a span of approximately a century the Isis cult in Rome was subjected to a baffling series of conflicting decisions. In 64 B.C.E. all clubs and associations were banned in Rome because the political activities of such groups were deemed subversive. Administrative actions against the Isis cult followed in 59, 58, 53, 50, and 48.[180] However, in 43 B.C.E. a temple of Isis was built by the triumvirs. Heyob notes that this decision "is in marked contrast not only to the persecution of the cult in the two previous decades but also to the severity of Augustus towards the Egyptian cults some years later as emperor."[181] Augustus ordered the removal of the temple from the *pomerium*, and in 19 C.E. Tiberius expelled Isis devotees from the city on moral grounds in the same order that evicted the Jews.[182] Nevertheless, by the time of Nero the cult was visible in the city once more.[183]

Do these reversals demonstrate policy shifts on the part of the Romans with regard to Oriental cults or merely administrative reactions to concerns prompted by the actions of particular groups? Rome's response to the problem of magicians and astrologers suggests the latter. Astrologers and magicians were expelled from the city numerous times. Although technically illegal, magic was tolerated as long as the craft was not used to injure.[184] Likewise, astrologers were endured provided they steered clear of forbidden areas such as the health of the emperor.[185] Of course substantiation of charges that would arouse Roman officials required investigations and legal proceedings. This required hostile or otherwise motivated parties who would bring the problem to the attention of the authorities and press for administrative action. Although Roman practice regarding foreign cults was tolerant, the actual task of keeping order both in the empire and in a city drove officials to act in social situations where ferreting out dangerous groups and individuals was problematic.[186] The notion that astrology was an illicit activity was one thing; an actual and effective expulsion of astrologers was another, as Tacitus well knew: "A decree of the Senate was then passed for the expulsion of the astrologers from Italy, stringent but ineffectual."[187] Administrative action required both policy and the will to act on it. Rome's will to act in such cases was motivated by civil disturbances or the lobbying of concerned parties (e.g., informants).

The passive administrative approach of the Romans is perhaps best illustrated by the famous Pliny-Trajan correspondence concerning the Christians.[188] Pliny sought counsel because he had limited experience dealing with Christians and several cases involving them had come before him during a recent assize tour. After explaining in detail how he had handled various cases, he requested certain clarifications and solicited additional information concerning the emperor's policy. In his rescript, Trajan upheld Pliny's actions. Yet, the emperor refused to be specific in articulating a policy for dealing with such matters; rather, he left discretion to the governor. Trajan's statement is instructive for the point at hand: "It is not possible to lay down any general rule which can be applied as the fixed standard in all cases of this nature." In keeping with the administrative approach already described in this study, Trajan instructed Pliny not to seek out the Christians but, rather, to deal with them case by case as they were brought before him by accusers.[189]

The Jewish religion posed problems for Roman administrators unlike those posed by other foreign religions. On the one hand, Judaism was clearly a national religion with a long tradition; on the other hand, because of its strict monotheistic convictions, the Jewish cult could not be Romanized. Scholars have illustrated the problem by pointing out that when Vespasian defeated the Jews in 70 C.E., he could have introduced the Jewish cult into the Roman pantheon or destroyed it.[190] Yet the former was quite impossible, while the latter was complicated because of the wide dispersion of Jews throughout the empire with their own synagogue communities. Consequently, Vespasian opted to do neither; instead, he set up the *fiscus Judaicus* (the Jewish tax) and used the revenues for the temple of Jupiter Capitolinus in Rome.

The unique national and international character of Judaism presented two quite different situations for Roman administrators. In theory Rome's policy toward the two groups, Palestinian Jews and the Dispersion, was the same: toleration. Nevertheless, in practice there were significant differences.[191] In Judaea, toleration was largely a matter of whether Rome would avoid taking steps that it knew beforehand would be offensive to the Jews. Outside Judaea, toleration had more to do with Rome encouraging local administrators to protect Jewish rights when hostile opponents interfered with Jews and the observance of their native religion and cultural practices.

Although Rome's administrative options varied from Palestine to the Diaspora, Roman actions in either setting were more the product of local crises than imperial policies. Sufficient evidence of Claudius's dealings with the Jews has survived to illustrate the occasional nature of his approach. Claudius inherited a troubled situation in Alexandria from the reign of Gaius. In order to calm the intense friction between Alexandrian Jews and Greeks, Claudius wrote a letter in November of 41 C.E.

In this communication Claudius protected the Jewish right to practice their religion but ordered them to accept their alien status in Alexandria and to desist from attempts to gain the same social privileges as the native Greeks. Toward the end of the letter Claudius warned that further trouble would precipitate his acting against the Jews as a group guilty of "arousing a sort of common plague for the whole world."[192] At about the same time Claudius restricted synagogue assemblies in Rome because of disturbances.[193] In 44 C.E. he reversed the order of the governor Fadus and permitted the Jews of Palestine to retain custody of the high-priestly vestments.[194] But in 49 C.E. Claudius expelled Jews from Rome because of synagogue riots.[195]

At first glance such a diversity of responses to the same religion by a single emperor might seem incredible. However, in view of the stimulus-response nature of Roman administration the differences are explicable.[196] Roman toleration of foreign religions should not be taken to mean that the Romans steered clear of cults when the interests of the state were thought to be jeopardized by some religious group's conduct. However, action was prompted by destabilizing behavior among reckless members of a cult or through the lobbying of opponents hostile to the cult. Crackdowns were not the result of routine audits conducted by officials with responsibility of keeping tabs on cults according to well-articulated guidelines. A catalyst was required to trigger Roman intervention; nevertheless, during times of high tension regarding Oriental religions small catalysts could occasion disproportionate reactions.

The Jews in Rome under the Julio-Claudians

The Julio-Claudian period was a tumultuous era for the Jews of ancient Rome. The vicissitudes of the Jewish communities during this interval paralleled a heightened concern over the effects of Oriental cults on Roman life and religion. As Roman administrators became more alarmed by the spread of Oriental cults in the capital, the likelihood of confrontations with the Jewish communities increased. A synopsis of each emperor's dealings with the Jews will illustrate the relation between these two factors and demonstrate that, especially under Tiberius and Claudius, isolated events could bring about a response out of proportion to the catalyst itself.

The shrewd politics of the Herodians, particularly their support of Caesar during his struggle for power, produced a favorable climate for Roman-Jewish relations at the end of the republic.[197] The exemption of the Jewish communities from Caesar's ban on associations and the grief expressed by the Jews of Rome following his assassination are evidence of amiable relations.[198] Caesar's administrative actions on behalf of the Jews — especially the precedent his actions set — played a determinative role in defining the political status of the Jews vis-à-vis the Romans.[199]

When Augustus assumed control of the empire, he inherited not only a large community of Jews in Rome but also a tradition for ruling them. The influence of Caesar's policies was due largely to the normal force of precedent; yet his influence was heightened in this case by the conservative tendencies of Augustus — he had particular regard for the *mos maiorum*, "the way our ancestors did things."[200] Michel Malaise characterized Augustus's religious policy by highlighting three areas: faithfulness to the Roman gods, attachment to Magna Mater, distrust towards foreign cults not under the control of the state.[201]

Although Augustus was concerned about the infiltration of foreign religions, he sought to address the problem by restoring Roman religion rather than by censoring non-Roman cults.[202] There is no indication that this emperor ever attempted to suppress the Jews or their religion. On the contrary, the Jews in Rome — or at least part of the community — perceived his administration to have been benevolent. This conclusion follows from the evidence of the catacombs that synagogues in the city were named after both Augustus and Agrippa, the emperor's son-in-law, co-emperor, and designated successor.[203] Moreover, Augustus's policy of allowing an alternate date for distribution of grain and money for the poor, if the scheduled date fell on a Sabbath, supports the same deduction.[204]

Tiberius, on the other hand, used repressive measures to check the spread of non-Roman cults that continued to make inroads into Roman society.[205] Josephus, Tacitus, and Suetonius all report his attack on the Jewish and Egyptian cults in Rome in 19 c.e.[206] In each writer the censorship of Judaism and the Egyptian cults is closely associated, suggesting that they were not isolated events but indicative of a more aggressive approach to the problem of foreign cults under Tiberius. Tacitus introduces the discussion by writing: "Another debate of the Senate dealt with the proscription of the Egyptian and Jewish rites."[207] Josephus prefaces his remarks by saying:

> About this same time, another outrage threw the Jews into an uproar; and simultaneously certain actions of a scandalous nature occurred in connection with the temple of Isis at Rome. I shall

first give an account of the daring deed of the followers of Isis and shall then come back to the fate of the Jews.[208]

Josephus recounts that the actions against the Isis cult were prompted by the sexual exploitation of a Roman woman of noble rank by a frustrated lover with the assistance of priests of the Isis cult. The suffering of the Jews, according to Josephus, was precipitated when a Jew, passing himself off as a teacher of the law of Moses, procured the assistance of three other men in a scheme to embezzle funds from a Roman noblewoman who had been proselytized to Judaism. They convinced her to donate gold and purple for the temple in Jerusalem but appropriated her contribution for themselves. Josephus concludes the passage by pointing out specifically that the Jews were banished from the city because of the wickedness of four men. Josephus attempted to put the best possible face on this episode by placing the blame on four individuals and intimating that the Jews of Rome were merely caught in the crossfire of Rome's punishment of embezzlers.

It should be noted, however, that the Isis incident as well as the one involving the Jews entailed the repression of an Oriental cult because of an offense against a female adherent of the respective cult who was Roman and of noble rank. The explanation offered by Josephus may contain the cause that served as a catalyst for Roman intervention, but the severity and breadth of the response were motivated by the advance of these Oriental cults in Rome, particularly among Roman women.[209] A fragment of Dio Cassius includes a reference to Tiberius's expulsion of the Jews that makes the connection to proselytizing explicit: "As the Jews flocked to Rome in great numbers and were converting many of the natives to their ways, he [scil. Tiberius] banished most of them."[210]

A further indication that Tiberius acted out of concern regarding the influence of foreign religions in Rome can be seen in Tacitus's comment that those who give up "their outlandish rites by a certain date" could avoid punishment.[211] Seneca's rationale for suspending his vegetarianism is concomitant:

> I was imbued with this teaching, and began to abstain from animal food; at the end of a year the habit was as pleasant as it was easy. Do you ask how I came to abandon the practice? It was this way: The days of my youth coincided with the early part of the reign of Tiberius Caesar. Some foreign rites were at that time being inaugurated, and abstinence from certain kinds of animal food was set down as a proof of interest in the strange cult. So at the re-

quest of my father, who did not fear prosecution, but who detested philosophy, I returned to my previous habits.[212]

Because his avoidance of animal food would have included meats that were avoided by Jews, an observer could have drawn the potentially harmful conclusion that his practice was Jewish.[213]

Philo attempts to explain the anti-Jewish measures under Tiberius by blaming Sejanus. Since Philo's *Embassy* serves to indict Gaius Caligula, it is important that Gaius's conduct be portrayed as exceptional when compared to the "sane" behavior of Tiberius. Therefore, Philo does not mention the 19 C.E. expulsion and explains that if the Jews suffered under this emperor it was only because of the wicked Sejanus.[214]

Sejanus contributed to the repression of the Jewish population in Rome, but only in the latter portion of Tiberius's reign.[215] His role does not account for the problems the Jews encountered for well over a decade. The Jews suffered under Tiberius because intense apprehension regarding Oriental cults in Rome produced an administrative climate within which a lesser stimulus could evoke a greater response.

It is unclear when the expulsion edict was lifted; however, Philo's remark — that after the death of Sejanus (31 C.E.) the emperor recognized that the accusations that he had brought against the Jews of Rome were groundless — offers a plausible hypothesis.[216] This would be in line with Dio Cassius's comment about the large number of Jews once again in the city by 41 C.E.[217]

The traumatic standoff involving Gaius Caligula and the Jews of Palestine accounts for much of what we know regarding Roman relations with the Jews during Gaius's reign. Both Josephus and Philo include accounts of the incident, though they differ on details as well as the chronology of the episode.[218] The gist of it, however, is apparent. The emperor Gaius ordered that a statue of himself in the guise of Jupiter should be set up in the temple at Jerusalem.[219] The order was sent to Petronius, the legate of Syria, with instructions to position troops so that all who attempted to interfere would pay with their lives. Petronius was overwhelmed by the directive and the difficult position into which it placed him. According to Philo, Petronius knew that his life was in imminent danger whether he opposed the order or followed it. Eventually, the legate determined to obey the order because a Jewish revolt appeared less certain than the vengeance of Gaius.[220] Petronius met with the Jewish leaders privately and explained Gaius's intentions. When the Jews confessed their willingness to die before submitting to this outrage he adopted a program of bureaucratic procrastination. Gaius ordered Petronius's execution because of his hesitation in carrying out the order, but the legate was saved because news of the emperor's assassination arrived before the execution order.

Although Barnett is correct in pointing out that the incident was resolved without bloodshed, the six-month ordeal must have strained relations between Rome and Palestine.[221] There is no indication, however, that Diaspora communities suffered as a result of the confrontation. The conflict between Gaius and Jerusalem was precipitated by the Jews' destruction of an imperial image that had been set up by the gentile population of Jamnia. Hence, it was a stimulus-response situation limited basically to that locale, not a program of Jewish repression.

The lack of evidence regarding Gaius's relationship to the Jewish communities of Rome leaves historians to speculate. Gaius did not share the anti-Oriental views of Augustus and Tiberius.[222] On the contrary, the festival of Isis was established in Rome during Gaius's reign and, according to Josephus, this emperor donned female garb and participated in the mysteries he instituted.[223] Because the persecution experienced by the Jews in Rome under Tiberius was related to anti-Oriental biases, it is probable that under Gaius the Jews, as well as other Oriental cults, enjoyed improved conditions.

The actions of Claudius relative to the Jews of Rome have been a matter of considerable scholarly debate. Most of the controversy surrounds the relationship between what ostensibly appear to be two edicts against the Jews, and with the possible association of Christianity with the disturbances that stand behind the action(s).[224] Dio Cassius, in a report involving activities early in Claudius's reign, noted the following administrative crackdown:

> As for the Jews, who had again increased so greatly that by reason of their multitude it would have been hard without raising a tumult to bar them from the city, he did not drive them out, but ordered them, while continuing their traditional mode of life, not to hold meetings.[225]

Suetonius, on the other hand, described not a restriction of assembly privileges but an expulsion: "Since the Jews constantly made disturbances at the instigation of Chrestus, he [Claudius] expelled them from Rome."[226]

H. J. Leon has condensed the fundamental issues of the debate by posing four questions:

1. Was there actually an expulsion of Jews under Claudius?

2. If there was an expulsion, did it include all the Jews or only the rioters?

3. Did the episode, whatever its character, occur in the first year of Claudius or several years later?

4. Do the words *impulsore Chresto* indicate disputes in the Jewish community with regard to the new Christian gospel or do they simply refer to the leading troublemaker, one named Chrestus?[227]

The first question must be answered in the affirmative. The statement of Suetonius is corroborated by Acts 18:2, which mentions two Christian Jews who had recently arrived in Corinth, having left Rome when Claudius expelled the Jews. Scholars who question whether there was actually an expulsion attempt to silence the statement of Suetonius by setting it over against the letter of Claudius to Alexandria. For them the intervention of Claudius in the Alexandrian conflict indicates that his general policy toward the Jews was favorable. Hence, they interpret accounts of Claudius's actions against the Jews in Rome in light of a reputed empire-wide approach to the Jews. Consequently, the Suetonius text is read with skepticism: There may not have been an expulsion; if there was one it must have been very limited.[228]

Two problems with this reading of the evidence are apparent. First, the letter of Claudius to Alexandria is not as favorable toward the Jews as is often assumed, particularly when one reads the papyrus version rather than that of Josephus. Claudius did indicate that Rome would enforce the rights of the Jews to practice their native religion but he rejected the Jewish designs of equal rights with Greeks in Alexandria that lay behind the whole conflict.[229] Second, in view of the stimulus-response character of Roman administration already noted, it is extremely hazardous to extrapolate from Alexandria what Claudius could have done in Rome.

The independent witness of Acts 18:2 — that Claudius expelled the Jews from Rome — cannot be overturned by appeal to Claudius's general policy. In fact, Claudius's actions regarding religious groups, particularly in Rome, provide a coherent background against which to interpret the censorship of Jewish communities in Rome during his reign. Claudius was a student of Roman and Etruscan history who sought to restore the conservative ideology of Augustus.[230] Scramuzza's explanation of Claudius's outlook is instructive:

Let us recall that it was a revolution that placed him on the throne. Gaius owed his death partly to reaction against his design of orientalizing the West. Claudius, then, was bound to repudiate that design. In religion that meant a return to the old practices. In sum, temperament, self-interest, and circumstances combined to make Claudius the champion of the Roman gods.[231]

The religious practices of Claudius are well-documented and a clear pattern emerges when the evidence is collected. In 47 C.E. Claudius restored the college of Haruspices in order to provide a Roman alternative to Oriental astrology.[232] The following year he elevated several leading men to the patriciate in order provide the priestly colleges with the required number of members.[233] In 49 C.E. he reintroduced the *Salutis Augurium*[234] and enlarged the *pomerium*.[235] During the next few years several persons, including Lollia Paulina, were prosecuted for consulting astrologers, and in 52 C.E. Claudius expelled practitioners of astrology from Rome.[236] According to Scramuzza, two things worried Claudius: "public indifference to the sacred lore bequeathed by antiquity and the intrusion of foreign superstitions."[237] The Jewish communities in Rome found themselves once again conducting their affairs under the scrutiny of an anti-Oriental administrator.

Although the evidence for an expulsion of Jews under Claudius is compelling, the scope and date of the eviction remain problematic.[238] Syntax would allow a reading of Suetonius that restricts the reach of the eviction to the Jews involved in the riots; however, the Acts version states that "all" of the Jews were commanded to leave. One might argue that the absence of the episode in Tacitus or Josephus would indicate that its effect was limited, hence not worthy of mentioning, but such reasoning is hardly conclusive. Nevertheless, the administrative burden involved in removing the entire Jewish population would have been notorious. Consequently, even if all the Jews were commanded to leave Rome, it is unlikely that all did.

In order to date the expulsion it is necessary to clarify the relationship between the texts of Suetonius and Dio. Dio Cassius's reference occurs in his account of the earliest acts of Claudius's reign. The Suetonius passage is not datable on the basis of internal evidence. However, Orosius quotes Suetonius and cites Josephus in dating the event in the year 49 C.E. Because no such text from Josephus is extant and because Orosius is not the most reliable source, his testimony is not generally accepted as conclusive. However, Acts 18:2 corroborates Orosius's date. The Acts text has Aquila and Priscilla "recently" arriving in Corinth from Italy as a consequence of the Claudian eviction. On the basis of the well-known Gallio inscription, Paul's sojourn in Corinth is the most datable event of his ministry: 51–52 C.E. An expulsion in 49 C.E. corresponds best to the arrival of Priscilla and Aquila in Corinth just prior to Paul's sojourn there.[239]

E. Mary Smallwood doubts whether the Dio and Suetonius texts can be harmonized, asserting with other scholars that they must represent separate episodes.[240] She surmises that a prohibition of assemblies in 41 C.E. (the Dio Cassius text) was followed by an expulsion in 49 C.E. (the Suetonius text) because of continued disturbances. This reconstruction is preferable because rather than artificially harmonizing the references it offers a plausible explanation of their relationship to each other.[241]

The question as to whether *impulsore Chresto* refers to disputes caused by the propagation of the Christian gospel involves two problems. The first has to do with the obvious misspelling of "Christus" if that is who was intended by "Chrestus." However, the pervasiveness of this spelling error in antiquity all but erases the difficulty. Because "Christus" was unknown as a proper name while "Chrestus" was very common, it was inevitable that writers would make the substitution knowingly or unknowingly. Tertullian complains that "Christian" is often incorrectly pronounced "Chrestianus," at which point he adds, "you do not even know accurately the name you hate."[242] Likewise, Lactantius writes of "the error of the ignorant, who by the change of a letter are accustomed to call him Chrestus."[243]

The other objection arises from the apparent implication that "Chrestus" was present in Rome, instigating the disturbances. Suetonius may have in fact thought so because of limited information on his part or simple misunderstanding of the Christian claim that Jesus was still alive.[244] Smallwood's contention that "the only reasonable interpretation of Suetonius's sentence is that the reference is to Christianity, though he was apparently under the misapprehension that 'Chrestus' was a rabble-rouser present in person," has certainly been the consensus of scholars.[245]

Early in his reign, Claudius dealt with Jewish disturbances in both Rome and Alexandria.[246] Restrictions on the Jewish assemblies designed to contain the problem were not ultimately effective. Continuing disturbances were repaid by an expulsion of Jews from Rome; whether the eviction dislodged the Jewish population in general or only a subset of troublemakers is unclear. It is clear, however, that the Jews faced repression once again under a conservative emperor with anti-Oriental views.

Public disturbances served as the catalyst, but administrators were poised for action because of heightened concern for the preservation of Roman religion and the Roman way of life.[247]

Nero's fourteen-year reign seems, on the whole, to have been tranquil for the Jews. The Jewish cause was probably aided by court connections with Nero through Poppaea and a Jewish actor, Alityrus.[248] However, the lack of conflict under this emperor was more directly due to Nero's openness to Eastern religions than to court connections.[249] Nero was less a champion of Roman tradition and religion than his predecessor had been.[250] Hence Oriental cults did not operate under the same scrutiny and suspicion as before. Isolated disturbances were not as likely to result in repression of the cult. In this regard the reign of Nero has more in common with that of Gaius than Augustus, Tiberius, and Claudius.[251]

The persecution of Christians under Nero resulted not from a general policy against foreign cults but rather from the necessity of the moment. Whether or not the search for scapegoats was a matter of special urgency because of rumors that ascribed responsibility for the fire to Nero, Tacitus's claim that public opinion demanded scapegoats is reasonable.[252] The exemption of the Jews from Nero's outburst against the Christians in 64 C.E. not only indicates that Rome had already begun to distinguish between Christians and Jews; it also mitigates the conclusion that the event evidences a general anti-Oriental program.

Under the Julio-Claudians the Jews of Rome were not singled out for contempt by the Romans. However, it is hardly coincidental that the repressive measures occurred under Tiberius and Claudius. Although misdeeds may have triggered the administrative actions, more than police measures were involved. The vicissitudes of Rome's Jewish population under the Julio-Claudians were related to the level of distress felt by emperors over the expansion of Oriental religions in the capital: The greater the fear, the more likely the conflict.

CONCLUSION

When the evidence regarding the Jewish communities of ancient Rome is analyzed in light of recent scholarly investigations, important comparisons and contrasts with other Diaspora sites emerge. Although the Jews of Sardis had a place on "main street," the Jews in Rome were concentrated in the Transtibernum. They were largely poor and of low status in a city where the distance between the other bank of the Tiber and "main street" could indeed be considerable. The Jews of Rome had no official representation before city officials comparable to what one finds in Alexandria. No inscription from the Jewish catacombs honors a deceased person with a title reflecting any position of importance within the city of Rome during a period of time spanning over three hundred years. The lack of significant Jewish involvement in the public affairs of the city indicates the limited options that were available to Jews in Rome and suggests a socialization wherein Jews would have been keenly aware of their "Jewishness." In such a situation considerable resistance to assimilation would be expected. Like the Tyrians of Puteoli, the Jews of Rome lived in a concentrated ethnic setting, participated in their native cult, and maintained ongoing relations with their homeland. Consequently, resistance to the urban melting pot was considerable.

Jews in Rome met in synagogue groups, eleven of which are named by catacomb inscriptions. However, our perception of Jewish socialization in Rome should not be unduly influenced by our knowledge of the names of these eleven groups. Even if all of them existed during the first century C.E. — an unlikely assumption — they alone could not have provided a social network for the entire Jewish population of Rome. This is all the more apparent when one considers that even if specific buildings for synagogue meetings existed in Rome during the first century C.E., they would likely have been adapted houses, not expansive basilicas. Informal gatherings within homes of Jews in particular neighborhoods, streets, or *insulae* were basic to the maintenance of Jewish self-identity in ancient Rome because they were the common settings for Jewish life, instruction, fellowship, and worship. Many, probably most, groups were unnamed and lacked any developed organization during this formative period of the ancient synagogue's emergence.

The Transtiberine area, Augustus's fourteenth district, was something of a foreign quarter that accommodated the bulk of Rome's immigrants during the late republic and early empire. The Jews of ancient Rome were one among many foreign peoples concentrated primarily in this region. Here the Jews were not distinguished by their foreign provenance, by their poverty, or by their tendency to gather together in communal meetings with fellow nationals. However, they were distinguished by the intensity of their resistance to assimilation, by daily customs that delineated pronounced boundaries between themselves and other peoples, and by an intolerant monotheism that refused to honor the gods of others. For other foreign groups these distinguishing marks may have occasioned only limited negative reactions. After all, these foreign groups had their own gods and customs as well. However, from the vantage point of conservative Romans, Jewish resistance to Roman acculturation and Roman gods made the Jews appear anti-Roman, aloof, misanthropic, and dangerous for Roman mores. Roman emperors who were particularly disturbed by the spread of Oriental religions in Rome inevitably interpreted the Jews as a threat. Tiberius and Claudius took repressive measures against the Jews when isolated incidents pushed the anxiety level over the brink and gave occasion for Roman intervention. These measures communicated to the Jews the importance of avoiding behavior that would endanger the Jewish population of Rome. The emergence of Christianity in Rome represented just such a threat, one that would prove determinative for the relationship between these communities.

Christians and Jews in Rome
between 49 and 64 C.E.

The relationship between the Jews and Christians in Rome during the middle of the first century C.E. was decisively affected by the Romans. Marcel Simon — in the introduction to a chapter dealing with the relations between Judaism and Christianity in antiquity — emphasizes the determinative role of the Romans when he writes:

> If we are to produce a satisfactory picture of the relations between Judaism and Christianity it is vital to see the two religions in their setting within the Roman empire. The attitude of the Roman authorities to the two cults was not without influence on their attitudes to one another. Conversely, it is a priori unlikely that once Christianity had been recognized for what it was, a separate and distinct religion from Judaism, its rapid progress and widespread dissemination did not have some repercussions on Roman policy toward the Jews. And by the same token, if we wish to understand the anti-Christian measures taken by the imperial authorities, it is vital not to forget the Jewish factor.[1]

Simon demonstrates his thesis by analyzing evidence from a later period (135–425 C.E.); however, even during the first century C.E. the Romans were key players in the developing self-definitions of these cults in relationship to one another. Two episodes documented by Roman historians, the edict of Claudius (49 C.E.) and the persecution of Christians under Nero (64 C.E.), bear witness to the involvement of the Romans during the earlier period. Moreover, these two events provide a unique opportunity for assessing the changing relationship between Christianity and Judaism during the middle of the first century C.E. The dramatic changes that occurred during this fifteen-year interval — and the temporal relationship of Paul's Roman letter to the events that bracket the interval — are illustrated in the following chart:

49 C.E.	55–58 C.E.	64 C.E.
CHRISTIANS ARE:	PAUL'S LETTER ARRIVES	CHRISTIANS ARE:
• Synagogue based • Predominantly Jews and gentiles who live like Jews • Jewish in their socialization		• No longer synagogue based; meeting in house-churches of their own • Mostly gentiles • Distinct from Jews in certain pronounced ways

This chapter sketches a trajectory between these events that will account for the dramatic changes that transpired and will assess their effects.

The Effects of the Claudian Edict

"A study of the edict of Claudius ca. 49 and its consequences is a logical beginning point for reconstructing the situation of Roman Christianity when Paul wrote."[2] So reads the advice of Harry Gamble who — in a study of the textual history of the Roman letter — concluded that it was an occasional letter intended for Rome. Gamble was by no means the first to suggest that the Claudian edict played a role in precipitating the Jew-gentile problems Paul addressed in Romans.[3] However, attempts to correlate the edict with the content of the Roman letter have failed to assess the effects of the edict with sufficient precision to account for the peculiar argument of Romans.[4] The present discussion attempts to appraise the consequences of the edict by concentrating on three effects: Persons were expelled from Rome; Jewish and Christian self-definition was affected; and the unity of Christians in Rome was threatened.

Persons Expelled from Rome

Obviously the most direct consequence of the edict was that some who lived in Rome and were part of the Jewish community before the expulsion were no longer present after it. As indicated earlier, the number of Jews affected by the expulsion is debated. Some, including Smallwood, Leon, and Lampe, feel that the number was limited to those actually involved in the incident; others believe that the edict was more far-reaching.[5] Whichever view is accepted, the result has ostensibly the same effect upon early Christianity because Christian Jews were no doubt involved. This conclusion is substantiated by Acts 18:2, which reports that Priscilla and Aquila, Christian Jews, were evicted under the edict.

Another, more difficult, problem involves the edict's effect upon gentile Christians who maintained some measure of attachment to Jewish communities. Were they considered "Jews" by the Romans and expelled, or was the expulsion strictly ethnic? Wolfgang Wiefel, in an influential article dealing with the results of the episode, treated it in rigidly ethnic terms: The expulsion meant "the end of the first Christian congregation in Rome which up until now had consisted of Jewish Christians."[6] Hence for Wiefel and those who have been influenced by his work, Jews and Jewish Christians returned to Rome in great numbers after the reign of Claudius. When the Jewish Christians arrived they found house-churches organized independently of the synagogues and shaped under the influence of gentile Christianity.[7]

Although Wiefel's reading of the evidence is insightful, it treats the scope of the edict simplistically. It is more likely that gentile Christian adherents to the synagogue were expelled as well, particularly if they were involved in the disruptive behavior that occasioned the intervention. It is true that the only persons evicted whose ethnic identity is known, Aquila and Priscilla, were Jews.[8] However, the Romans characteristically defined a "Jew" not in merely ethnic terms but rather by observing the person's manner of life: To live like a Jew was to be counted as a Jew.[9] For example, the Jewish apostate Ti. Julius Alexander, though circumcised as an infant, is described by Tacitus as a distinguished Roman knight of Egyptian origin.[10] Although Jewish by origin, he did not live the life of a Jew. The other side of the matter is reflected in a text from Dio Cassius:

> The country has been named *Ioudaia* and the people *Ioudaioi*. I do not know how this name came to be given to them, but it also applies to all other people who, though of different ethnicity, follow their customs. . . . This people is distinguished from the rest of mankind in practically every detail of life and especially in that they do not honour any of the usual gods but show extreme reverence for one particular god.[11]

Although for Dio Cassius the Jews seem distinguished by "every detail of life," it was circumcision, dietary habits, and Sabbath observance that especially demarked the life of a Jew for non-Jews.[12] Epictetus reflects this emphasis on lifestyle when he writes:

> Do you not see in what sense the term Jew (or Syrian, or Egyptian) is applied? When we see a man hesitating between two belief-systems we usually say "He is not a Jew; he is only play-acting the part." But when he has adopted the mentality of the baptized person and has thus made his choice, then he is a *de facto* Jew and is appropriately called by that name.[13]

Similarly, in determining whether Jews should be exempted from military service it is apparent that the Romans did not simply consider the ethnic origin of the individuals but rather whether or not they lived the life of a Jew.[14] Finally, in his description of Domitian's zeal for collecting revenue Suetonius related how the emperor dealt with those who had evaded the *fiscus Iudaicus*. Suetonius's depiction of the scene illustrates the type of criteria that was used to determine whether the person in question was to be counted a "Jew":

> Domitian's agents collected the tax on Jews with a peculiar lack of mercy; and took proceedings not only against those who kept their Jewish origins a secret in order to avoid the tax, but against those who lived as Jews without professing Judaism. As a boy, I remember once attending a crowded court where the imperial agent had a ninety-year-old man inspected to establish whether or not he had been circumcised.[15]

Such texts make it apparent that during a police crackdown on disorderly behavior in Rome the label "Jew" would have been applied to those who lived the life of a Jew. In other words, the Romans would be concerned with the troublemakers, the group, those belonging to the cult, not chiefly with the national origins of the individuals. Certainly the unique national-international character of Judaism led to ambiguities. Nonetheless, the quotations cited above show that the Romans were well aware that not all Jews were Judaeans. Hence, the edict of Claudius removed Christian Jews as well as gentile Christians who lived like Jews, either a subset of the troublemakers or all the "Jews."[16]

Jewish and Christian Self-Definition

The most significant consequence of the edict of Claudius for Christianity in the capital was its influence on the self-definition of the group vis-à-vis Judaism. The edict accelerated the evolution of Christianity's self-definition as a cult distinct from Judaism. In addition, the edict made it necessary for Jews to clarify their distinction from Christians in order to avoid censorship for disturbances caused by Christians. Therefore two forces were simultaneously operating to alter the relationship between Christianity and Judaism in ancient Rome.

In order to assess the edict's impact on the self-definition of Christianity in Rome we must focus on how the expulsion affected the composition of earliest Roman Christianity. Under the previous heading we demonstrated that the effect of the edict could not be evaluated in strict ethnic terms. Admittedly, the ratio of Jewish adherents of the Christian faith to gentiles was affected by the edict. However, a careful interpretation of the edict's scope suggests that the shift was more socioreligious than ethnic. When Christian Jews, like Aquila and Priscilla, and gentile Christians who lived as Jews were driven from Rome, the ratio of gentile Christians without Jewish socialization increased. Because the self-identity of these Christians was not shaped in a Jewish context they were less likely to conform to Jewish practices. Roman Christianity lacked significant "Jewish" presence for about five years, until the death of Claudius (54 C.E.), when the edict lapsed and the "Jews" returned.[17]

Because of early Christianity's initial Jewish socialization, the self-identities of the early Christians were molded within Jewish boundaries. However, the content and implications of the Christian message coupled with the attraction of gentile God-fearers, and especially gentiles without synagogue ties, introduced dissonance that was destined to play a formative role in the developing self-definition of Christianity in Rome. Segal's explanation of the conflict that was occasioned by Paul's attempt to unite Jew and gentile in his mission reflects proper attention to the social dynamics that were operative:

> From a legal perspective Paul may not have startled the Jewish Christian community so much by saying circumcision was unnecessary for gentile salvation per se, as claiming that the saved Jews and gentiles could form a single new community and freely interact. The issue was not how the gentiles could be saved but how to eat with them and marry them.[18]

Of course, these problems were not unique to Roman Christian communities. The Lukan version of the Noahide Commandments in Acts 15 evidences the pervasiveness of the problem of Christianity's emerging self-definition in relation to Judaism. The minimum practices required of gentiles in Acts 15:20, 29 reflect elements found in the covenant with Noah (Gen. 9:1ff), but they must be read together with the rules governing the lives of gentiles dwelling among Jews in Leviticus 19–26 (esp. Lev. 17–18).[19] After comparing the Lukan version of the Noahide Commandments with the version in Jubilees and in later rabbinic materials, Segal concluded that the Christian version was stricter than the other Jewish versions but more positive in its outlook toward gentiles. He explained the former by noting:

> It is possible that the reason the Christian version of the rules is stricter than the other Jewish versions is that a large section of the church was allowed to remain uncircumcised, thus bringing possible sources of pollution much closer to the table.[20]

On the other hand, the more positive outlook was "due to the Christian necessity to face this issue more squarely than any other Jewish group. The Christian group had a larger percentage of gentile converts than the other groups."[21]

Christian beliefs and practices invariably jeopardized the boundaries that maintained the ethnic integrity of the Jewish communities and protected them from foreign invasion.[22] For Jews the process of resocialization within Christian communities that did not maintain traditional boundaries was tumultuous and painful. In Rome, the dramatic changes in Christian self-definition that were occasioned by the edict of Claudius determined that a characteristically difficult process would be even more difficult for Roman Christians.

Suetonius says that Claudius expelled the Jews because of riots that took place "at the instigation of Chrestus." Although the statement of Hoerber that the disturbances resulted from heated discussions concerning the "acceptance of Jesus as the Christ" represents the common synopsis, such claims, at least on a theoretical level, would have prompted little concern or resistance from the Jews.[23] However, the implications of the Christian message for Jewish self-definition and the threat it represented to the boundaries of Judaism were quite capable of stirring violent opposition.[24]

Was Christianity only a way of being a Jew, or was it something else?[25] The Claudian edict affected not only the answers Christians would have given to this question, but also the responses of Jews. Theological issues that could have continued to be discussed indefinitely took a back seat to the social crisis: Christians were a threat to the integrity of Judaism in Rome and to its already delicate relations with administrators in the capital. Hence, although Christians may have already begun meeting in homes of fellow believers prior to the edict, the expulsion played a decisive role in detaching Roman Christianity from synagogue communities in the capital.[26] Following the edict, Christians and Jews in Rome had to define themselves separately from one another and ultimately formed distinct social networks.

The evolution sketched above is corroborated by the actions of Nero against Christians in Rome in 64 C.E.[27] Nero's persecution presupposes that Roman administrators could distinguish between Christians and Jews when sufficiently motivated to do so. This in itself indicates a significant transition in the self-definitions of the groups relative to one another.[28] In 49 C.E. the government made no such distinction; consequently, both Jews and Christians who lived like Jews came under pressure from the Claudian edict.[29] During the time span separating these two events, Christians clearly became more visible and, consequently, more exposed.[30]

Without the shelter of Judaism, the Christians were in danger of Roman censorship as a superstitious, non-national foreign cult of recent origin with riotous tendencies. The Jewish communities, in all likelihood, consciously lobbied Roman administrators in order to distinguish themselves from the Christians.[31] The Jews had nothing to lose and everything to gain by making their autonomy clear.[32] They had already endured an expulsion order because of turmoil precipitated by Christians, whom the Romans did not distinguish from Jews. The fact that in the persecution of 64 C.E. the Romans had no difficulty distinguishing Christians from Jews indicates both the attainment of the Jews' objective and its disastrous consequences for the Roman Christian communities.[33] Though the problem of Jews stirring up Roman magistrates against the Christians is not a new theme — for the author of Acts every brush with the Roman authorities begins with a Jewish catalyst — never before were the Christians in so vulnerable a position.[34] Regardless of the other effects that the Claudian edict may have had on Jews and Christians in Rome, it is apparent that the episode decisively affected the relationship between the two communities and generated the distinctions that made Nero's attack on Christians a possibility. The edict escalated the already-under-way process of self-definition and precipitated the separation of the communities as fundamental differences between community boundaries became more apparent and as Jews attempted to distance themselves from the Christians because of the Romans.

The Unity of Christianity in Rome

Wayne Meeks sets up an important contrast concerning the relationship between Pauline Christian communities and Judaism:

> Theologically it is correct to say that the scriptures and traditions of Judaism are a central and ineffaceable part of the Pauline Christians' identity. Socially, however, the Pauline groups were never a sect of Judaism. They organized their lives independently from the Jewish associations of the cities where they were founded, and apparently, so far as the evidence reveals, they had little or no interaction with the Jews.[35]

Readers of Romans must be bear in mind, however, that the circumstances of the Christian communities in Rome and their relationship to the Jewish communities of that city cannot be reconstructed by analyzing Paul's missionary practice and his routine of establishing house-churches. The Roman house-churches were not Pauline churches. Herein lies an interesting situation for Paul. He was addressing Christian house-churches in the throes of a transition that was unlike that of any church he had established. The changes in Rome had more in common with Paul's own personal life than with any paradigm that can be reconstructed from his apostolic career.[36] Paul's conversion involved a radical reorientation and resocialization that was not experienced by Jews who had merely become messianic adherents within their synagogue communities. Hence, Christian Jews in Rome in the aftermath of the Claudian edict found themselves in an exceedingly painful situation: Being a Christian involved changes that were more radical than they could have previously imagined. The resocialization they once expected of gentiles who wished to enter the Jewish community was now being required of them.[37]

The unity of Jew and gentile in Roman Christianity was destined to be a problem because of the heterogeneous make-up of the communities coupled with their roots in the Jewish synagogues. However, the potential for conflict was increased by the Claudian edict and the changes it prompted. When Jewish Christians and gentile Christians (who lived like Jews) returned to Rome after the edict lapsed, they encountered Christian groups whose socialization had changed profoundly.[38] Not only were Christians becoming more independent of the synagogues structurally, they were moving in the direction of increasing autonomy from Christianity's Jewish roots.[39] During the intervening years between the expulsion and the lapse of the edict, gentile Christians in Rome would have attracted other gentiles who had not previously been involved with Judaism.[40] Moreover, anti-Jewish sentiments that were common among some Roman residents were easily intensified by the Christian message itself.[41]

The turmoil that Jewish Christians and God-fearing gentiles experienced was compounded in the aftermath of the edict; not only were they separated from their *ethnos,* but they had at the same time to deal with the heightened dissonance caused by changes in the Christian communities.[42] Because the Christian community in Rome originally developed around a Jewish Christian nucleus drawn from the synagogues, the leaders of the community would in all probability have been (at least primarily) Jewish. In any case, the edict would have caused a considerable shift in roles of authority in the community. Either there would have been a complete reversal — assuming the previous leaders were Jewish — or a notable shift — assuming that some of the previous leaders were Jewish.[43] Gentile Christians, free from the scrupulous consciences of their law-abiding comrades, were no longer observing dietary laws and were not optimistic about renewing old practices.[44] If they were willing to accept returning "Jewish" Christians into their household meetings, they would have resisted attempts by these returning Christians to make the "life of the Jew" compulsory for all community members. Following the edict the stage was set for a mirror version of the famous Antioch episode when gentile Christians were pressured to follow Jewish norms. In Rome, because of the edict of Claudius and the growth of gentile Christianity, those advocating freedom had the upper hand and gentiles would not be "forced to live like Jews" (Gal. 2:14). The pressure that law-abiding Christians felt under these conditions must have been enormous. Consequently, these circumstances posed a serious threat for the unity of Jew and gentile in Roman Christianity.

Roman Administration and Paul's Letter to Rome

There is evidence in Paul's letter to the Romans itself that Roman administrative intervention had impacted early Christians in Rome and that Paul was aware of the delicacy of the situation. In Romans 13:1–7 Paul admonished the Roman Christians to submit to their Roman administrators without exception. Scholars have had great difficulty explaining this text in light of the characteristic structures of Paul's theology. Furnish communicated the issue eloquently when, after discussing other Pauline texts that should allow one to predict Paul's posture regarding the state, he wrote:

> Can there be any question, then, about the implications of this for one's obligations to earthly rulers? Christians belong to another world, to the one Ruler above all earthly rulers, to the One to whom all earthly powers shall be put in subjection. Does not Paul himself show us what kinds of practical consequences follow from this when he tells the Corinthians not to take their disputes to the secular courts (1 Cor. 6:1–6)? It would seem so — until one reads Romans 13:1–7 with its explicit admonition to "be subject to the governing authorities." Is this not a monumental contradiction of what seems, from other texts, to be a fundamental Pauline principle?[45]

In view of this apparent inconsistency some have argued that the text is an interpolation, others have maintained that Paul was pressed to the fringes of his theology by an occasion that demanded a strong statement, while still others have concluded that though Paul was moved by a particular crisis, his handling of it can be resolved within the main lines of his theological outlook.[46]

Although Paul may not have been on the outer fringe of his theology in this pericope, he was dealing with a rather uncharacteristic topic and addressing a community where circumstances were anything but ordinary.[47] The passage should be viewed as the communication of a missionary intervening in a crisis, not that of a theologian composing a systematic doctrine.[48] Consequently, Romans 13:1–7 should not be interpreted as "Paul's Theology of Church and State," nor should it be utilized as subject matter for constructing such a theology without careful reflection on its function.[49]

When Paul wrote Romans, the Christians were in an extremely vulnerable position. This pericope addresses the altered circumstances of Roman Christianity following the edict of Claudius. Previously the Christians operated under the umbrella of the synagogue, but now they must survive independently, as small house-churches, alienated from the synagogues and lacking the greater tolerance Rome afforded to ancient religions. The best course of action would be for Christians to keep their heads down by living "peaceably with all men." This would be facilitated by avoiding disruptive encounters of any kind; a painful lesson from experience (the Claudian expulsion) should have already suggested this strategy. Moreover, they should stay clear of politically charged controversies such as the tax resistance movements of that period.[50] Instead, they must be subject to the governing authorities as ordained protectors of the divine order, thereby illustrating the non-subversive nature of the Christian congregations.

Conclusion

The crucial events of 49 and 64 C.E. provide a useful trajectory along which we can track the relationships of the Jewish and Christian communities to one another. By the earlier date, intramural disputes were reaching such levels that the conflict gained the attention of city administrators. By the later date, the Romans moved against the Christians as members of a despised foreign cult, distinguishable from the Jews.

Paul's letter to Rome provides a vista between these two events. It addressed Roman Christianity along the trajectory sketched above precisely during the period when the relationship between Christianity and Judaism was an unavoidable topic of consideration. As the communities moved further apart, Jewish Christians found themselves under increasing pressure. The self-understanding that might be tagged "Christian Jew" was becoming impossible to maintain. Being a "Jewish Christian" was beginning to be the only option available short of abandoning the Christian community altogether. A middle ground was no doubt sought by many Jews and some proselytes through maintaining their fidelity to dietary laws as well as festival and Sabbath observances. However, the refusal of others in the Christian house-churches to follow suit jeopardized this intermediate option. Hence, the pressure persisted. As the self-definition of Christianity in Rome continued to be hammered out, the question of the gospel's continuity with Judaism was both pressing and unavoidable. Christianity's Jewish origin raised the question, a large Jewish community in Rome provided a setting for its debate, the Claudian edict animated it, and the Neronian persecution indicated its ultimate answer. The Roman letter arrived in the midst of this process. It is hardly coincidental that the letter's central concern involves the place of Jews and Judaism in the gospel.

CHAPTER FOUR

Ethnic Issues in Romans

A ffinity between the historical reconstruction posited in this study and the actual content of Paul's letter to the Romans cannot be simply presumed. A. J. M. Wedderburn in a recent monograph dealing with the occasion(s) of Romans suggests three criteria by which the likelihood or credibility of a given hypothesis may be tested:

1. Is the situation presupposed inherently plausible? Does it provide a coherent picture of the life of the Christian community in that place?

2. Is this picture compatible with what we know from other sources concerning the history of the earliest church? Is it similar to anything else we know happened elsewhere in the church of that day?

3. Does it fit in with what Paul's text says? Does it make good sense of that text?[1]

Earlier portions of this study have attempted to establish the first two criteria. The present chapter will continue to fill out that picture by using information contained in the letter to the Romans itself. However, primary attention will be focused on Wedderburn's third criterion: Does the letter address problems or concerns consonant with those one would expect under the circumstances that have been described? I demonstrated at the conclusion of the previous chapter that Paul was aware of the political dangers that Christianity faced in Rome. Analysis of other texts in Romans will make it apparent that the apostle was also cognizant of the crisis of self-definition that the Roman Christian communities faced.

The correlation of the socio-historical context outlined earlier in this study with the content of Romans will be demonstrated by analyzing Paul's treatment of ethnic issues in the letter. Three major arguments developed by Paul in Romans are applied by the apostle to ethnic relationships: the impartiality of God; the priority of Israel; the coexistence of the weak and the strong.

The Impartiality of God

In the opening argument of Romans Paul attempts to establish as much common ground as possible between Jews and gentiles. The central premise of Paul's argument is that God is impartial, an affirmation that functions rhetorically to minimize perceived distinctions between Jews and gentiles. In the first four chapters Paul exposes the implications of this premise for Christian self-definition by examining God's judgment by works as well as God's justification by faith. Paul makes his aim of establishing common ground explicit when he writes:

> ...is God the God of Jews only? Is he not the God of gentiles also? Yes, of gentiles also, since God is one; and he will justify the circumcised on the ground of their faith and the uncircumcised through their faith. (3:29, 30)

The dogmatic category "justification by faith" has long functioned as a rubric within which investigations of the rhetorical function of Romans 1–4 have been carried out. In light of the key role these chapters played in Reformation and post-Reformation theologies it is little wonder that scholars have found it difficult to view these chapters from any other perspective. There is, however, a compelling reason to suggest a different interpretive framework: In discussions of Paul's teaching regarding justification by faith as advanced in Romans 1–4, chapter 2 is consistently neglected or treated negatively — analyzed in terms of what it could not be saying in view of justification by faith.[2]

If Romans 1–4 is a section where Paul was chiefly concerned with explaining that all people must be justified by faith, chapter 2 is an anomaly. Why would Paul have introduced a discussion that would seem to weaken his central point? The solution to this apparent anomaly can be found only by rethinking the aim of Paul's argument. His goal in chapters 1–4 was not to explain justification by faith, but rather to break down distinctions between Jews and gentiles, as 1:16 announced. Stendahl pointed scholars in the right direction when he wrote:

Paul was not chiefly concerned about on what terms we are to be saved (justification by faith), but rather about the relation of Jew to gentile and justification by faith was one of his arguments.[3]

Justification by faith and judgment by works both contribute to Paul's reevaluation of the relation between Jews and gentiles. Although Nils Dahl did not resolve the tension between chapter 2 and chapter 3, he did account for it by pointing out what the two discussions have in common:

> There is indeed a problem here, but apparently Paul did not pay much attention to it. The most obvious reason for this is that Paul stressed the same point in both cases. There is no distinction between Jew and Greek, because God shows no partiality, neither when he justifies the ungodly nor when he renders to every man according to his works.[4]

Jouette Bassler, building on Dahl's work, has insisted that Romans 2:11 is the "pivot" of Paul's opening argument.[5] Her observation not only underscores the importance of chapter 2 but also shifts the interpretive framework of 1:16–4:25 in the direction suggested by Dahl.

Utilizing J. A. Fischer's criteria for determining the limits of a thought unit (introductory formulae, inclusions, and word chains), Bassler argues for the unity of 1:16–2:11 and then proceeds to show that the theme of impartiality persists through chapter 4.[6] Paul's assertion that "God shows no partiality" functions rhetorically as a summary of the argument from 1:16–2:10.[7] This conclusion depends upon two preliminary interpretive observations concerning the literary development of Paul's argument: The apostrophe of 2:1 represents no radical shift in the argument; the condemnation of the hypocritical judge (2:1ff) is based on a retribution formula that is structurally significant in chapter 1.

The abrupt shift to the second person at 2:1 has figured prominently in the traditional breakdown of the argument whereby 1:18–32 condemns the gentiles while chapter 2 indicts the Jews.[8] Yet, when scrutinized, this interpretive stance has problems. Stowers demonstrated that the abruptness of the apostrophe at 2:1 is characteristic of the diatribe.[9] Moreover, he explained its literary function:

> The function of 2:1–5 is to bring home, to concretize and to sharpen the indictment in 1:18–32 (especially verses 28–32) for Paul's audience. It takes the indictment of "them" in 1:18–32 and makes it into a personal indictment of any of the audience to whom it might apply.[10]

Unless one looks forward in the argument, it is difficult to explain rhetorically how it follows that if the gentiles are under sin the Jews are without excuse if they judge. Scholars aware of this problem but committed to the traditional outline attempt to discount the normal inferential force of *dio* (therefore) at 2:1 or sidestep the problem by postulating a gloss or interpolation.[11] The variety of suggestions put forward to explain away the *dio* of 2:1 is itself an indication of the difficulty scholars have encountered in dismissing its normal function. It is better to assume that *dio* functions in the usual manner but that the logical conclusion being drawn is simply not what scholars have come to expect.

If there is no major break in the argument at 2:1 and if *dio* has its usual inferential function the indictments of chapter 1 should be read in the most inclusive sense.[12] The recurring use of the word *pas* (everyone) in key texts throughout Romans 1:16–2:11, contrasted with its absence from the remainder of chapter 2, also supports the inclusive nature of the argument prior to the apostrophe at 2:17.[13] True, the indictment of 1:18–32 utilizes a standard Hellenistic Jewish polemic against pagan idolatry; however, it contains unmistakable allusions to Israel's idolatry as well.[14] Paul does not use the terms "gentile" or "Greek" anywhere in the argument of 1:18–32; instead, the term *anthropos* (person) appears in 1:18; 2:1, 3, 9, 16. It is most reasonable to conclude that Paul was being deliberately inclusive, intending to cast a wide net that would encompass "the Jew first and also the Greek" (1:16; 2:9, 10).[15]

It should not be concluded from this analysis that Paul was thinking of humanity in general, oblivious to Jew-gentile distinctions. Cranfield is probably correct when he observes that Paul "primarily" had gentiles in mind in 1:18–32, though he recognizes that they were not "exclusively" in mind.[16] Moreover, Bassler after denying the traditional division of the argument grants that "even the Jews would recognize themselves behind the description in Chapter 2 of the one who judges immoral actions."[17] However, Paul intentionally frames the indictment in the broadest terms possible: *o anthrope pas o krinon* (whoever judges) (2:1). He refuses to focus on those distinctions until after 2:11; they are left underneath the surface. The effect of this is clear: In an argument whose goal is to show that ethnic distinctions do not count, Paul refuses even to admit the categories into the argument; they are irrelevant.

Once it is granted that 2:1 represents a continuation of the argument of 1:18–32, the logical relationship between the chapters still awaits explanation. Bassler explains the connection by drawing attention to a retribution formula in the condemnation of the hypocritical judge that links the indictment structurally to chapter 1.[18] Here she builds on the work of Klostermann, who argued that the notion of corresponding or exact retribution governs the structure of the first chapter.[19] The three-fold repetition of the phrase *paredoken autous ho theos* (God gave them up) (1:24, 26, 28) prompts Klostermann to divide the argument into three periods. Paul supports his thesis that the wrath of God is righteous judgment by focusing on human sins. Paul divides the sins into three groups with their corresponding punishments: Their failure to *honor* God resulted in God giving them up to *dishonor* their bodies; their exchange of the truth of God for a lie (worshiping the creature instead of the creator) resulted in abandonment to sexual immorality; their failure to acknowledge God (*edokimasan*) resulted in God giving them over to a base mind (*adokimon*).[20]

Bassler augments Klostermann's analysis by proposing a continuation of the pattern into chapter 2: "The theme of *paredoken ho theos* (God gave them up) is mirrored in the *hos apodosei* (who will repay) of 2:6."[21] An indication that corresponding retribution is still operating in chapter 2 is found in the statement that the one who judges (*krinon*) condemns himself (*katakrineis*). The cogency of this proposition is highlighted by the movement of the argument in 2:6–10. God's judgment (2:5) is demonstrably righteous in that God recompenses to all according to their works (2:6–10). In other words, God's judgment corresponds to the sins (or virtuous conduct) of individuals: "God shows no partiality" (2:11). Justifiably, Bassler declares that 2:11 "functions as a terse summary of the entire preceding unit."[22]

This, however, does not exhaust her claim. She maintains that 2:11 is not only a summary of what precedes but the "pivot" of Paul's argument.[23] Ostensible references to God's impartiality in chapters 3 and 4 indicate that the claim of 2:11 casts its shadow over the discussion that follows the assertion. Meeks, commenting on Bassler's thesis (2:11 as "pivot"), presses the point:

> The human implication of that "theological axiom" is that "there is no distinction, for all have sinned and are lacking the glory of God, yet they are justified as a gift by grace, through the redemption that is effected in Christ Jesus" (3:22–23). Paul's summation in 3:27–31 of his first, foundational argument shows that in fact the axiom of 2:11 is pivotal of the whole argument, not only the first part. For the appeal here, again in vivid diatribal style, to the even more fundamental axiom, "God is one," recalls for the reader

again the impartiality of the one God, who is obviously therefore not the God of Jews only but also of the gentiles and "will justify circumcision on the basis of faith and uncircumcision through faith" (3:30).[24]

The scope of the axiom's role does not even find its outer limit with the concluding summary of chapter 3. The lengthy treatment of Abraham as the paradigm for faith in chapter 4 sits firmly on it as well. This conclusion can be drawn from the links between the end of chapter 3 and the beginning of chapter 4.[25] By using the example of Abraham and by means of a complex argument based on Genesis 15:6, Paul is able to deal with the interlocutor's concerns expressed in the dialogical exchanges of 3:27–31.[26] Here Paul presents Abraham not merely as an illustration of a justified sinner, but as the "first of the people of God."[27] The details of Abraham's existence relative to circumcision, works, and the promise allow Paul to show that Abraham was justified by faith. Yet, the goal of the apostle's argument was not reached until he pressed one step further: Because Abraham was justified by faith, he is "the father of us all" (4:16). Indeed, justification by faith is grounded in scripture (Gen. 15:16), and "the impartiality that removes the distinction between Jews and gentiles was already anticipated there."[28]

Clearly the assertion of divine impartiality at 2:11 casts a lengthy shadow.[29] However, the function of Paul's claim that God is impartial stands out most clearly when one recognizes the relation of 2:12–29 to the pivot. This pericope anticipates a rather obvious objection to the thesis that God's judgment is impartial: Even if works are the criterion the Jews still have the advantage because they were given the law. The special revelation of the law would seem to represent an element of favoritism. Paul guards this vulnerability by affirming that God will deal with those under the law and those without it by judging according to standards appropriate to each group (2:12–16). Because gentiles will be judged by "what the law requires," not by the law itself, they are ostensibly in the same situation as the Jews.[30] God's impartiality remains intact.

Furthermore, any suggestion that the Jews enjoy a favored position before God's tribunal is dismissed by an argument from experience (2:17–24). Merely possessing the law represents no advantage.[31] The apostrophe of 2:17 introduces an indictment quite in keeping with the style of the diatribe.[32] Although the Jews possess the law and assume the role of teaching the gentiles, they are guilty of breaking the law themselves.[33] Hence, the criterion of 2:6 rules out any perceived advantage.

Finally Paul takes the ethnic categories themselves and challenges their prevailing definitions (2:25–29). As we saw earlier, the transition in self-identity experienced by Christian communities in Rome during the period occasioned conflict over such definitions. An indication that Paul would ultimately address the question "Who is a real Jew?" was suggested by the ambiguity of the address at 2:17 — "if you call yourself a Jew." Hence 2:12–24 not only functions to defend the impartiality of God's judgment but also lays the groundwork for Paul's discussion of what being a "real Jew" involves. It is hardly surprising that Paul focuses his attention on circumcision at this crucial juncture; it was the fundamental boundary marker between Jews and non-Jews.[34] By linking the value of circumcision to keeping the law Paul is able to draw from his previous analysis of the situation of gentiles and Jews vis-à-vis the law (2:12–16 and 2:17–24, respectively). If gentiles "do the things of the law," as 2:14 argues they can, circumcision will be attributed to them, i.e., they will be considered circumcised though lacking the physical marks. On the other hand, if Jews do not keep the law, as 2:17–24 summarily claims, they will be considered uncircumcised even though they possess the physical marks.[35] Because God impartially renders to "every man according to his works" (2:6), ethnic distinctions do not count. Paul's emphasis on the deeds of Jews and gentiles demonstrates the common ground on which they stand and relativizes their ethnic differences.[36]

A consideration of Paul's general rhetorical strategy clarifies further the goal and function of the theme. The thesis that "God shows no partiality" was a claim Paul could assume would command wide acceptance from his readers. Consequently, the apostle can use it as a rhetorical lever to force a reevaluation of prevailing Jew-gentile distinctions based on the law and circumcision.[37] If on the basis of this axiom Paul could challenge ethnic distinctions drawn from current Jewish practices, his argument would legitimate the self-definition he is proposing for Christianity in Rome: The people of God are not (nor have they ever been) merely those who possess the law and are circumcised; rather, the people of God are (and have always been) those who *do* what the law requires and are "circumcised."

The force of Paul's argument rests on his willingness to challenge commonplace definitions in current Judaism on the basis of divine impartiality alone, not on the basis of Christian faith. The gentile of chapter 2 is no gentile Christian; the Jew of chapter 2 is no Jewish Christian.[38] It is true that justification by faith corroborates the claim (3:22, 30); nevertheless, it is not the basis of it. Dunn is correct to warn commentators against tendencies to squeeze Paul's argument into a "later dogmatic mold."[39] The subject in chapter 2 is judgment, not justification. Furthermore, interpreting the gentiles as Christian gentiles creates as many tensions as it resolves. Would the apostle have described gentile Christians as those who "have not the law"? Romans 13:8–10 suggests otherwise. Would Paul have said Christians "do by nature what the law requires"?[40] Once again interpreters need not go beyond Romans to discover that for Paul Christians do what the law requires by the Spirit, not by nature:

> ... in order that the just requirement of the law might be fulfilled in us, who walk not according to the flesh but according to the Spirit. (8:4)

Moreover, when Romans 2:12–16 is viewed from the vantage point of the reader it is difficult to imagine how Roman readers, prior to Paul's explanation in chapter 3, could have understood these gentiles as "justified."[41] In addition, pursuit of "the good," the activity of the conscience, and the existence of inner moral conflict were commonplace topics for pagan moralists.[42] Paul knew it and so did his Roman readers. They would have made this connection immediately without lingering to contemplate dogmatic issues.[43]

If the gentile of Romans chapter 2 is a Christian, Paul's argument would imply that divine impartiality was an innovation that came with faith in Jesus.[44] This, however, would be out of character with the apostle's rhetorical approach in the letter. In Romans Paul characteristically argues his case theologically rather than christologically because the former facilitates the apostle's emphasis on the continuity of the present with the past and makes broader common ground possible between Jews and gentiles.[45] By stressing this continuity, Paul calms the fears of Jewish Christians in Rome; they have apprehensions that the evolving self-definition of Christianity in Rome involves accommodations that are novel and compromise the boundaries of covenantal identity. Hence, issues are consistently approached in terms of what God has done, is doing, and will do. Paul Sampley has drawn attention to the theocentric character of Romans by contrasting it with Galatians:

> Galatians sets many matters forward more christologically than theologically and Romans tends to reverse the pattern. Romans

centers about questions and claims concerning God; Galatians focuses on issues concerning Christ.[46]

Paul emphasizes Christianity's continuity with Judaism in Romans because the circumstances in Rome require a re-evaluation of Christian self-understanding in terms of that continuity. Paul's emphasis on continuity inevitably blurs the distinctions between Christians and pre-Christians: This is true for gentiles (2:14–16) and Jews (2:29), as well as Abraham (4:1–5) and David (4:6–8). However, by advancing the theme of God's impartiality without reference to Christian faith Paul legitimates the common ground he is advocating while avoiding the conclusion that Christianity is a departure from God's purposes with Israel. The result is that Paul makes room for gentiles but not at the expense of Jewish Christians who in Rome are finding it increasingly difficult to feel that as Christians they are remaining faithful to their election.

Conflict regarding what Paul could have said about non-Christian persons — gentiles doing what the law requires and Jews experiencing spiritual circumcision — is not unique to Romans 2. Paul makes comments concerning the Jewish "people" (*ethnos*) in Romans 11 that raise similar questions.[47] Because the rhetorical approach Paul uses in these two contexts is parallel, comparing the arguments will elucidate Paul's strategy in chapter 2. In both contexts Paul attacks pretension and arrogance that stem from ethnic identities. In Romans 11 Paul is concerned with gentile Christian attitudes toward Jewish Christians (see 11:18). However, the argument attacks gentile Christian opinions of Jews as Jews (11:11–36). Likewise in Romans 1–4 Paul is chiefly concerned with Jewish Christian attitudes toward gentile Christians; however, he deals with gentiles as gentiles. There is no distinction between Jews and gentiles before God: Both are equally under the power of sin, both stand before God as an impartial judge of human works, both are dependent on divine mercy. This type of argument is rhetorically suited to the situation because it does not assume that the reader is viewing the matter from a well-defined Christian self-understanding. The assumptions of the argument are broad enough to move a spectrum of readers toward the common ground Paul hopes to establish.

The practical goal of Paul's opening argument in the Roman letter is suggested by the apostle's censorship of the judgmental person in 2:1. Wayne Meeks has recently drawn attention to the parallels between the apostrophe at 2:1 and those in 14:4, 10, 22. After a brief discussion of the function of these abrupt shifts to the second person in Romans 14, Meeks writes:

> Once we recognize how central and forceful these apostrophes are in this last of Paul's admonitions in Romans, it becomes surprising that commentators, as far as I can see, have paid no attention to the striking parallel in form, substance, and function with the apostrophe that startles every reader in the middle of the first argument in the letter, 2:1.[48]

Paul's theological claim that God is impartial, coupled with this warrant not to judge one another, indicates that Paul expected his argument to undermine the ethnic assumptions upon which judgment was being exercised in Rome.[49]

Analysis of Paul's use of the diatribe in Romans also indicates that Paul's fundamental aim was to create common ground between Jewish and gentile Christians. Stowers in his study of the diatribe in Romans found that "all the texts which clearly address imaginary persons in Romans react against pretension and arrogance." He attributes this phenomenon to three factors, the third of which he considers the most crucial for the interpretation of Romans:

> It is clear that the apostle perceives *alazoneia* (pretension) and *huperefania* (arrogance) as types of behavior which prevent Jews and gentiles from uniting in God's plan. Paul censures the pretentious and arrogant gentile (or all men?) in 2:1–5, the pretentious Jew in 2:19–24, the pretentious and arrogant gentile Christian in 11:17–24 and the pretentious Christian in 14:14 and 10.[50]

Paul, in Romans 1–4, was not constructing a theological treatise in defense of his gospel of justification by faith. There are too many elements of the discussion in these chapters that run counter to justification by faith for that theme itself to have been Paul's primary concern. If Paul was introducing himself to the Romans by expounding his message of justification by faith, why did he press judgment by works in chapter 2? If he was only concerned to show in 1:18–3:20 that all humanity was under sin, why did he introduce the reader to gentiles who will be acquitted because they "do by nature what the law requires" (2:14), or to pre-Christian characters like Abraham — the first of those justified by faith (4:1–5) — and David — against whom God did not count sin (4:6–8).

What Paul did in Romans 1–4 was to construct an inclusive argument on the basis of a theological maxim he assumed of all his readers — the impartiality of God. Both justification by faith and judgment by works demonstrate the impartiality of God. Paul's application of the maxim is designed to highlight the implications of this truth for Jew-gentile relations in Rome: "Therefore you have no excuse, O man, whoever you are, when you judge another" (Rom. 2:1).

The Priority of Israel

Under this heading I will attempt to show that the theme of Israel's priority is ubiquitous in Romans and that the theme's occasion is best explained in light of the changing self-definition of Christianity in Rome. Although some attention will be given to a range of texts that suggest or declare Jewish priority in the gospel, the focus of the discussion will be on chapters 9–11 because these chapters offer both an extended treatment of the subject and clues concerning its occasion.

Before completing the first paragraph of Paul's letter to the Romans the reader is already introduced to the issue of Israel's priority. Two phrases in Paul's description of the gospel signal his intention to emphasize the special relationship that exists between the gospel and Israel: The gospel was "promised beforehand through his prophets in the holy scriptures," and this gospel concerns "his Son, who was descended from David according to the flesh" (Rom. 1:1–3). Paul's definition of the gospel in Romans stands out when compared to other Pauline formulations in the extant letters. Only here (in the undisputed Pauline letters) does the apostle appeal to the Davidic descent of Jesus, a move that signals Paul's intention to emphasize the special relationship that exists between the gospel and Israel.[51]

Israel's priority in the gospel is announced or alluded to numerous times in the letter. In 1:16 Paul declares that the gospel is "the power of God for salvation to every one who has faith, to the Jew first and also to the Greek."[52] This formula, unique to Romans, recurs in chapter 2 when Paul asserts that divine retribution and reward are likewise "to the Jew first and also to the Greek" (2:9, 10).[53] To the question "... what advantage has the Jew?" Paul answers, "Much in every way" (3:1, 2). In Romans 9:4–5 Paul details the advantages: "They are Israelites, and to them belong the sonship, the glory, the covenants, the giving of the law, the worship and the promises; to them belong the patriarchs, and of their race, according to the flesh, is the Christ." Paul trumpets his own Jewish credentials in 11:1 without even a single disclaimer: "I myself am an Israelite, a descendant of Abraham, a member of the tribe of Benjamin."[54] He follows this ethnic self-portrait with a stark claim: "God has not rejected his people whom he foreknew" (11:2). In 11:17ff he deflates gentile Christian arrogance toward the Jews by pointing out that the roots of the olive tree into which the gentiles have been grafted are Jewish and support the whole tree: "Remember it is not you [gentile] that supports the root, but the root that supports you" (11:18). Likewise it is the Jews who are the "natural branches"; gentiles can be grafted in, but "contrary to nature" (11:24). In 11:26 Paul announces that "all Israel will be saved" and defends the apparent unlikelihood of his claim by asserting that, "As regards the gospel they [the Jews] are enemies of God, for your [gentiles'] sake; but as regards election they are beloved for the sake of their forefathers" (11:28). In 15:4 Paul maintains that Christians have hope through the encouragement of Israel's scriptures. In the closing paragraph of the letter's body Paul declares that, "Christ became a servant to the circumcised to show God's truthfulness, in order to confirm the promises given to the patriarchs" (15:8).

The theme of Israel's priority extends to the concluding portions of the letter where Paul announces his travel plans and encourages the Romans to greet one another. In his explanation of the journey to Jerusalem with the collection Paul avows that it is proper for the gentile churches to contribute to the poor saints in Jerusalem because the "gentiles have come to share in their [the Jews'] spiritual blessings" (15:27). When Paul mentions the names of acquaintances in Rome, those who are Jewish are distinguished. All of the "churches of the gentiles give thanks" for the Jewish couple Priscilla and Aquila (16:4). Andronicus, Junias, and Herodion are greeted as Paul's "kinsmen," a means of recognition that is unique to Romans.

The circumstances of earliest Christianity in Rome, detailed earlier in this study, help to account for this pervasive theme.[55] The evolution of self-identity among Roman Christians in the aftermath of the detachment of Christianity from the synagogues precipitated tensions between Christians who lived like Jews and those who did not. The Jewish communities in Rome were seeking to differentiate themselves from Christians for their own protection. At the same time, some of the gentile Christians in Rome were responding with autonomy ambitions of their own.

Romans 9:30–33 summarizes the contemporary situation with which Paul had to contend: Gentiles have attained righteousness by faith, Jews have stumbled. Kaylor describes the matter aptly: "The gospel was working out to be not 'to the Jew first and also to the gentile' (Rom. 1:16) but to the gentile instead of to the Jew!"[56] The conclusion that God had rejected Israel (11:1) was already being drawn by gentile Christians in their bid to claim special status (11:17–24). At one time it may have appeared that God's promises to Israel would be realized within the Jewish communities at Rome. However, in the aftermath of the Claudian edict, as the Jewish and Christian communities moved farther and farther apart, such expectations would have been hard to sell, especially to gentile Christians whose own status was enhanced by the failure of the Jews.

Jewish Christians were under unique pressure as the Christian and Jewish communities increasingly defined themselves in contrast to one another. As the breach between the communities expanded and as Christianity drew more of its members from non-Jewish residents of Rome, the self-definition of Christianity in the capital was increasingly determined by gentile Christians in a non-Jewish setting. If anti-Jewish feelings among these gentile Christians were allowed to go unchecked, the Jewish character and roots of Christianity would continue to recede, forcing Jewish Christians to make a decision to be Jewish or to be Christian.

It is in Romans 9–11 that Paul's intended application of the theme of Israel's priority is most evident.[57] In fact, the argument of chapters 9–11 was constructed to deal with the tensions noted above. Romans 11 contains a direct address to gentile Christians (11:13) which associates Paul's claim regarding the priority of Israel with a specific circumstance, viz., gentile Christian boasting. Even scholars who are reluctant to stress the circumstances of Roman Christianity in their analyses have recognized the connection of chapter 11 to anti-Jewish tendencies in Rome.[58] It is possible, however, not only to account for chapter 11 against this setting but also to recognize the integral part that chapters 9 and 10 play in Paul's argument and the conclusion he reaches in chapter 11.

Before we survey the literary development of these chapters, Paul's general rhetorical strategy in chapters 9–11 should be noted. Paul's affirmations of the faithfulness of God at the conclusion of chapter 8 lead naturally into an argument where the assumption of that faithfulness is the ground of the discussion. Chapters 9 and 10 do in fact underscore key themes already treated in Romans 1–8, but they especially serve to set two components of the query in stark relief: God has promised; Israel has failed. Paul's own language indicates that he desired to exploit the tension created by juxtaposing God's promise with Israel's failure. Notice how blatantly he makes the contrast in 11:28: "As regards the gospel they are enemies . . . as regards election they are beloved."[59]

The rhetorical value Paul saw in this strategy — explaining Israel's situation vis-à-vis the gospel in terms of a radical tension — can be demonstrated by comparing chapters 9–11 with 3:1–8. Scholars generally recognize the relationship between these texts because chapter 3 brings up an issue that is not treated in detail until chapter 9.[60] In 3:1ff Paul set out to list the advantages of Israel because his argument in chapter 2 had left the implication that none existed. However, the list was truncated when Paul broke off to answer the supposed objection that Israel's unfaithfulness had resulted in the cancellation of God's commitments to the Jews. This led back, though clumsily, to a synopsis of the previous argument: Both Jews and Greeks are under sin's power.

Although the discussion of Israel's priority in chapter 3 was cut short, Paul went far enough to expose his strategy. Paul was willing to discuss the status of Israel's priority only within the framework of God's faithfulness in spite of Israel's failure.

> Then what advantage has the Jew? Or what is the value of circumcision? Much in every way. To begin with, the Jews are entrusted with the oracles of God. What if some were unfaithful? Does their faithlessness nullify the faithfulness of God? (3:1–3)

The significance of this is highlighted upon comparison with chapters 9–11, where Paul sets up the same framework for his more extended discussion of the issue. After affirming the faithfulness of God at the close of chapter 8, Paul writes:

> I am speaking the truth in Christ, I am not lying; my conscience bears with me in the Holy Spirit, that I have great sorrow and unceasing anguish in my heart. For I could wish that I myself were accursed and cut off from Christ for the sake of my brethren, my kinsmen by race. They are Israelites, and to them belong the sonship, the glory, the covenants, the giving of the law, the worship, and the promises, to them belong the patriarchs, and of their race, according to the flesh, is the Christ. God who is over all be blessed for ever. Amen. But it is not as though the word of God had failed.

Beker's stress on the interrelation between Israel's priority and God's faithfulness is warranted:

> It is essential for Paul to maintain the priority of the Jew in the gospel, not only for the sake of the Jew, but especially for the sake of

the Christian. What is at stake is nothing less than the faithfulness of God.[61]

It should be observed, however, that the faithfulness of God was not "at stake" in the sense that it was weighing in the balances for either Paul or his Roman readers. Paul's handling of the interlocutor in chapter 9 by using the analogy of the potter and the pot indicates that questions regarding the integrity of God were not open to discussion. As Stowers notes, "Such questions are unthinkable for Paul."[62]

There is no evidence that Paul's readers were questioning the faithfulness of God. In fact, it would have been rhetorically foolish for Paul to have leaned his entire argument for Israel's priority on the faithfulness of God if God's faithfulness were in doubt. Not only would his argument have had little force, but he would have risked destroying what little confidence in God's trustworthiness remained by wagering it against a position gentile Christians were reluctant to grant — the priority of Israel. What gentile Christians were questioning was the place of Israel vis-à-vis the gospel, not the faithfulness of God. Hence, Paul wishes his readers to understand that a denial of the continuing priority of Israel can persist only by denying the faithfulness of God.

Paul brings up both items (the priority of Israel and the faithfulness of God) because one forces the proper conclusion regarding the other, not because they were both in jeopardy. Hence, rhetorically Paul uses the fundamental conviction of God's faithfulness as rhetorical leverage against those who would doubt the continuing priority of the Jews.[63] Confirmation that this analysis is consistent with Paul's argument is found in the application he makes in chapter 11. Here, in a direct address to the gentile Christians, Paul presses them to accept the priority of Israel and desist acting arrogantly toward the "natural branches" (11:17–24) no matter what hardships have befallen them.

Although Paul's fundamental aim in chapters 9–11 was to challenge gentile Christian attitudes toward Jews by focusing on the implications of Israel's election and God's faithfulness, a survey of the development of Paul's argument suggests that more was involved. After juxtaposing the advantages of Israel with the faithfulness of God (9:1–5), Paul presses the claim that God's election has never been based on physical descent or works.[64] By citing the examples of Isaac/Ishmael and Jacob/Esau, Paul "deduces that God's promise and election matter, and not ancestry or merit."[65] These examples function to protect the common ground Paul had already won in the Roman letter from being jeopardized by conclusions that could be drawn from Paul's affirmation of Israel's priority. Paul must be sensitive to how Jewish readers will respond to this emphasis on Israel's priority lest old boundaries re-enter and wreck the common ground that has been established. Hence, Paul must show that the priority of Israel is not the result of an ethnic judgment based on "God's valuation of peoples."[66] In order to place emphasis on God's faithfulness, Paul must describe God's actions in terms of promises God made to Israel. In order to guard the common ground he fought for in chapters 1–4 the apostle must show that promises are not dispensed on the basis of ethnicity or works (9:6–13).[67] Though this runs the risk of making God appear arbitrary,[68] it is a risk Paul is willing to take because he must dissociate ethnicity and works from God's promises if he is to maintain the impartiality of God while defending the priority of Israel.[69] Of course Jewish history as recounted in Israel's scriptures illustrates that the Jews in fact do have a notable priority when it comes to God's promises. Nevertheless, God's promises include not only Jews but also gentiles, a crucial corollary to the argument of Romans and a conclusion also supported by Israel's scriptures (9:24–29).

With Israel's election tied to promise (independent of ethnicity or works) and promise undergirded by God's faithfulness, Paul could face Israel's failure head on. Gentile Christians reasoned that the failure of the Jews indicated that God had rejected Israel. Paul was willing to grant the gentile Christian contention that the Jews had failed (9:30–32).[70] Not only this, he was willing to explain how they went wrong (in terms that reinforce earlier affirmations in Romans) and to hold them, not God, responsible for their failure (10:1–21).

What Paul was willing to grant in his argument indicates where his argument rested.[71] In 9:30–10:21 Paul blatantly exposed the failure of the Jews because he knew it was irrelevant.[72] Therefore, he took away from gentile Christians the foundation of their boasting against Israel by admitting it.[73]

Although Paul was willing to grant Israel's failure, he refused to grant the conclusion that gentile Christians drew from it: namely, that God had rejected the Jews (11:1). Paul's confidence in God's faithfulness was clearly the fundamental premise by which he dismissed the gentile conclusion. However, in the remnant of Jewish believers he found further evidence that God had not rejected Israel.[74] This remnant indicated that God was still at work in bringing to fruition the promises made to Israel. Yes, most of Israel had stumbled (as the gentile Christians argued) but they had not "stumbled so as to fall" (11:11a). Paul claimed in chapter 11 that the promises to Israel had not been rescinded; on the contrary, they were continuing to be fulfilled.[75]

In support of his claim that God's work with Israel is not over, the apostle offers a current status report of that work and a glimpse of its prognosis. Paul can account for the current hardening of most of Israel within God's purposes as parallel to Pharaoh's hardening that resulted in the deliverance of Israel. This time, however, it is the gentiles who have benefited (11:7–12): "Through their [Israel's] trespass salvation has come to the gentiles" (11:11). The hardening, however, is not permanent. After the benefits are realized for the gentiles, the rest of Israel (i.e., those hardened, see 11:7) will be remembered because "the gifts and the call of God are irrevocable" (11:29).[76] Paul maintains that the current situation of the disobedient Jews is the same as that of gentile Christians prior to their conversion (11:30–32).[77] This fundamental analogy is accented in Meeks's summary of the conclusion of Paul's argument:

> Just as, contrary to all "natural" expectation, gentiles have been grafted into the people of God, so also, contrary to what now seems evident to gentile Christians, "all Israel will be saved." If the Jews are now disobedient (to the righteousness of God revealed in Messiah Jesus), then they are in just the same position as the gentiles before that revelation, and again the impartiality of God will triumph: "For God confined all to disobedience, that he might enact his mercy to all" (11:32). Precisely how God is going to bring that about, Paul does not tell us, for the way is hidden in the "unsearchable judgments (*krimata*) of God" (11:33).[78]

The goal of the apostle's argument in these chapters is most clearly evidenced by one paragraph in chapter 11 that stands out because it does not really contribute to the development of Paul's point. Regarding 11:17–24 Stowers has remarked:

> The main purpose of the analogy [the olive tree] is not to advance the argument. The real answer to the question, "Have they stumbled so as to fall?" in vs 11 is only given in vss 25–32. In vss 23–24 the metaphor does make the point that God is more willing to graft the natural branches back on if they come to faith, but the real emphasis in addressing the branches is hortatory.[79]

The nature of the exhortation is clear: God had not rejected Israel and the gentile Christians in Rome must not either. Paul's rebuke of the gentile believers is transparent: They are proud (11:20), latecomers

(11:24), branches unnaturally grafted on (11:24).[80] Being Jewish should certainly represent no disadvantage for a Christian in Rome. On the contrary, Israel remains special not on the basis of ethnicity or works but rather because of the promises of God. Gentile believers should not be arrogant toward their Jewish counterparts but thankful because they, as gentiles, enjoy the riches of an olive tree whose roots are clearly Jewish.[81]

In Romans 9–11 Paul argues that the common ground that exists by virtue of the gospel's power (Rom. 1:16) must not be realized at the expense of God's promises to Israel. The Christian self-definition that Paul advances in Romans does not require gentiles to become members of the Jewish *ethnos* in order to be saved. However, because gentile Christians in Rome were rewriting the self-definition of Christianity in the capital under the supposition that God had rejected Israel, it was necessary for Paul to underscore that the "natural" and "unnatural" branches have *Jewish* roots in common.

The "Weak" and the "Strong"

Ostensibly, Romans 14:1–15:13 deals with conflict between Christians over the proper boundaries of the Christian community: "One believes he may eat anything while the weak man eats only vegetables" (14:2); "One esteems one day as better than another, while another man esteems all days alike" (14:5).[82] The boundary-keeping function of the practices is apparent in Paul's corrective admonitions and questions: "Welcome him" (14:1); "Let not him . . . despise . . . , and let not him . . . pass judgment?" (14:3); "Who are you to pass judgment" (14:4); "Why do you pass judgment on your brother?" (14:10); "Why do you despise your brother?" (14:10); "Let us no more pass judgment on one another" (14:13); "Welcome one another" (15:7).

Paul straightforwardly rejects foods and special days as boundaries for the Christian community and presents alternative markers:

> For the kingdom of God is not food and drink but righteousness and peace and joy in the Holy Spirit; he who thus serves Christ is acceptable to God and approved by men. (14:17–18)

However, Paul introduces a consideration that mitigates an out of hand dismissal of food and calendar restrictions. Christians who restrict their diet and daily activities in this fashion are "weak in faith" (14:1); and "he who has doubts is condemned, if he eats, because he does not act from faith; for whatever does not proceed from faith is sin" (14:23).[83]

Paul's concern for the faith of the weak person and the unity of the community account for the remainder of the exhortations in the pericope: "Let everyone be fully convinced in his own mind" (14:5); "Decide never to put a stumbling block or hindrance in the way of a brother" (14:13); "Do not let what you eat cause the ruin of one for whom Christ died" (14:15); "Do not let your good be spoken of as evil" (14:16); "Let us then pursue what makes for peace and for mutual upbuilding" (14:19); "Do not, for the sake of food, destroy the work of God" (14:20); "The faith that you have, keep between yourself and God" (14:22).

Although the admonitions Paul delivers in the passage appear straightforward, the relationship of the pericope to the larger document and its concrete occasion are often debated. Regarding these ambiguities, Meeks has written:

> On the face of it, this topic thus seems remote from the epistolary situation of Romans and from the letter's main themes, although those who see the "weak" as "Jewish Christians" and the "strong" as "gentile Christians" obviously recognize some connections between the two parts of the letter. Those connections are in fact much tighter than is commonly perceived, and they remain intact even if one calls into question the simple identification of the two factions just mentioned.[84]

Nonetheless, the "tightness" of these connections is often disputed because of three fundamental problems with the correlation: (1) Vegetarianism and abstinence from wine were not characteristic Jewish dietary practices; (2) the equations "weak" = Jewish Christians / "strong" = gentile Christians do not hold; (3) the passage appears to be a generalized version of a position Paul worked out in relation to a concrete problem in Corinth; therefore it requires no specific historical referent in Rome.

The first objection raises a question that has long plagued researchers who have attempted to use the history of religions to unravel the passage. Not only is it difficult to associate vegetarianism and observance of special days with common Jewish dietary practices, attempts at correlating the Romans text with any known group from antiquity have been fraught with problems. Suggestions range from Jewish Christians who had been influenced by ascetic Jewish or pagan sects to gentile Christians who abstained from meat because of prior experience with gnostic mystery religions.[85] The lack of consensus is not because evidence of vegetarianism and special days in antiquity eludes historians, but because no correlation can be established between the evidence and the text and argument of Romans. Robert Karris finds Rauer's work on the history of religions the most compelling but finally dismisses it because for his thesis — the vegetarians were pagan Christians with gnostic mystery religions in their past — "he [Rauer] has to resort to conjectures not founded in the text of Romans."[86]

The only circumstance of dietary restrictions in antiquity that has any prospect of correlation with the content of Romans is one that involves common Jewish dietary practices.[87] Yet, this identification appears doubtful at first glance because Jews were not generally vegetarians.[88] Some have suggested that Jews in Rome resorted to vegetarianism because of difficulty obtaining meat that was ritually pure and uncontaminated.[89] They are compared to the priests mentioned by Josephus who were imprisoned in Rome during the reign of Nero: They ate only fruit and nuts, thereby illustrating that they "had not forgotten the pious practices of religion."[90] It is doubtful, however, that obtaining meat that met Jewish requirements would have been a problem in a city with such a sizable Jewish population as Rome.[91] Furthermore, assuming that a shortage of acceptable meat resulted from continuing effects of the Claudian edict exaggerates the scope of the edict.[92] Even if the availability of acceptable meats was interrupted by the edict and the disruptions it caused, it is highly improbable that the supply problem would have persisted after the death of Claudius when Jews were clearly back in Rome in large numbers.

Vegetarianism and special days can be explained without resorting to unlikely historical conditions if one recognizes in Paul's approach a deliberate intention to be inclusive in his description. The suggestion of Sanday-Headlam that Paul intended by using "vegetables" to be inclusive, covering all cases of dietary abstinence, is in my judgment correct.[93] That does not mean, however, that the discussion is general and therefore unrelated to any real situation in Roman Christianity. Harry Gamble issued a warning regarding the interpretation of Romans that is important here: "It is altogether possible that we have mistaken an obliqueness of approach for a generality of content."[94] Wayne Meeks accounts for the generality of Paul's language in Romans 14:1–15:13 by highlighting the rhetorical aims of the apostle in a fashion that reflects Gamble's caution:

> To be sure, the way Paul characterizes the issue between strong and weak does embrace specifically Jewish categories, and those

are probably the starting point in his mind. Nevertheless he avoids halakic language, for example, about *kashrut* (dietary laws) and Sabbath.... Furthermore, Paul takes pains to state the issue in terms general enough that a former Jew is not necessarily on one side and a former gentile on the other.... Thus, throughout the argument, Paul is describing concerns that every diaspora Jew faced, but using language general enough to include gentiles, too.[95]

Two benefits of the oblique approach are evident for Paul's purposes: (1) The strategy lets readers move from common understanding to self-application; (2) it avoids a direct attack upon any group whose ultimate integration into the community might be thus hampered. By formulating his argument in an oblique fashion, Paul is able to treat a delicate Jew-gentile problem without exacerbating the tensions in Rome.[96] Being unnecessarily specific could polarize and crystalize conflicting views.[97] Paul wishes to approach this conflict as an issue of diet and special days, not as an ethnic problem. To set the discussion specifically in terms of Sabbath and *kashrut* (dietary laws) would have made of the matter an ethnic issue that would reflect negatively on Jews and Judaism, the very thing Paul takes pains to avoid because of the situation in Rome.[98]

The second objection — the equations "weak" = Jewish Christians / "strong" = gentile Christians do not hold — also disappears when Paul's oblique approach is factored into the analysis. It should be apparent that Paul does not supply these equations for the reader, nor do they fit his case: He is a Jewish Christian, but includes himself among the "strong" (15:2). Furthermore, at least some gentile converts to Judaism and God-fearers would have continued to observe special days and dietary restrictions after they became Christians.[99] Therefore, it is obvious that the matter cannot be puzzled out according to strict ethnic categories. However, Paul's discussion does not demand strict categories. As long as the conflicting self-definitions of Jewish and gentile Christians are addressed within the parameters of vegetables and special days the argument is effective. By utilizing an oblique approach Paul was able to speak to the issue at hand in terms of appropriate behavior in Christ without respect to the ethnic origin of the convictions.

Paul's approach in this pericope is oblique, not vague or ambiguous. If an oblique approach is to be effective in achieving a writer's purpose, the author must present the case broadly but in a manner that insures that the reader will draw the proper conclusion. Hence, the argument should be opaque enough for the readers to sense that the conclusion is their own, but transparent enough to insure that the conclusion is the desired one. Consequently, Paul's primary aim in Romans 14:1–15:13 should be indicated in the text by items that are transparent for the conclusion Paul seeks. The terms "clean" (*katharos*) and "unclean" (*koinos*) in Romans 14:14, 20 are in fact transparent:

> I know and am persuaded in the Lord Jesus that nothing is unclean in itself; but it is unclean for any one who thinks it unclean. . . . Do not, for the sake of food, destroy the work of God. Everything is indeed clean, but it is wrong for any one to make others fall by what he eats.

Katharos was commonly used of Jewish dietary distinctions in antiquity; the use of *koinos* for a dietary category has never been attested outside of Jewish usage.[100] These terms indicate that the boundaries Paul was chiefly concerned about were those that separated Jews from gentiles.

A further sign that the "weak" and "strong" bear some relation to Jewish Christians and gentile Christians is found in the last paragraph of the pericope.[101] The summary appeal for mutual acceptance in 15:7 is followed by a direct reference to the benefits of Christ's ministry for the Jews ("the circumcision") and the gentiles (15:8, 9):

> Welcome one another, therefore, as Christ has welcomed you, for the glory of God. For I tell you that Christ became a servant to the circumcised to show God's truthfulness, in order to confirm the promises given to the patriarchs, and in order that the Gentiles might glorify God for his mercy.

By presenting the current status of these two ethnic groups in light of God's faithfulness in fulfilling the promises made to the patriarchs, Paul associates the issue of the "weak" and "strong" with the theme of Israel's priority. This link not only binds the discussion to the larger document, it also supports Paul's contention in the previous paragraph that "the strong ought to bear with the failings of the weak." Meeks, commenting on 15:7–13, states the connection succinctly when he writes:

> Christ accepted the gentile Christians by being a *diakonos* (servant) of the Jews, in order to fulfill promises made in the Jewish scriptures to Jewish patriarchs about gentiles. This extraordinarily compact statement constitutes a reprise of the themes Paul has developed in chaps. 9–11.[102]

The third objection to reading 14:1–15:13 in light of Jew-gentile conflicts in Rome stems from the generalized character of the pericope and the parallels with the discussion of weak consciences in 1 Corinthians 8. Victor Furnish raised questions about the validity of reading the Romans text in light of a historical referent in Rome when he wrote: "Romans is addressed to a church of which Paul has no first-hand knowledge, and his discussion of 'the strong' and 'the weak' in 14:1–15:13 reads like a generalized adaptation of a position he had earlier worked out respecting an actual, known situation in Corinth."[103] Hence, the similarities between the passages are understood by Furnish to result from Paul's recycling of the central premises of the Corinthian passage. Karris has produced a detailed comparison of the two passages in which he draws attention to impressive verbal parallels between them.[104]

The similarities between the passages are undeniable. However, it is the differences that should be highlighted in order to test the occasional character of the text.[105] One obvious difference between the texts is their length: The Romans pericope is almost three times as long as the Corinthian text (thirty-six verses compared to thirteen). Karris, who shares the viewpoint of Furnish, admits the difference and attempts to explain it: "If Paul is dealing with a generalized adaptation of a previous position, why does he expand his generalized adaptation?"[106] Karris attempts to account for the expansions as primarily the result of Paul inserting scripture quotations to bolster his points.[107] This, however, does not sufficiently account for the Romans text's decided emphasis on the problem of judging and the admonitions to accept one another. Both Romans and 1 Corinthians share Paul's conviction that the strong should defer to the weak and that behavior should be governed by the desire to edify. However, the discussion in Romans is bracketed by carefully placed exhortations to "accept one another" (14:1; 15:7) with intervening apostrophes that disallow judging (14:4, 10; see also 14:13).[108] Furthermore, in the Romans passage reciprocal responsibilities are enjoined: The "strong" are to accept the "weak" while the "weak" are admonished not to judge the "strong" (14:1–4). In 1 Corinthians only the "strong" are admonished. These important differences suggest a function for the Romans passage that is distinct from that of the Corinthian text and well suited for the Roman situation. What Furnish mistook for a "generalized adaptation" that rendered a Roman situation irrelevant was in fact the oblique approach that Paul utilized to address the situation in Rome.

The common objections raised against reading Romans 14:1–15:13 in light of Jew-gentile conflicts in Rome disappear when Paul's oblique strategy is recognized. Earlier portions of this study have demonstrated that the Christian communities of Rome were ethnically diverse; gentiles were in the majority but the Jewish contingent was strong as well. The origin and early association of Roman Christianity with the Jewish communities of Rome insured that the boundary markers that contributed to Jewish self-definition influenced early Christian self-understanding as well. In fact it is likely that before the edict of Claudius those who "lived like Jews" were in a position to exert considerable sway over the practices of the wider Christian community, even the gentile Christians.[109] As noted earlier in this study, however, rapid changes in the relationship between Judaism and Christianity took place as a consequence of the Claudian edict. The detachment of Christianity from the synagogue communities coupled with the eviction of many Christians who had the strongest ties to Judaism precipitated an evolution in Christian self-definition in the capital that heightened tensions between Christians "who lived like Jews" and those who did not. These tensions would have been most keenly felt by Jews who returned to the capital after the edict expired and suddenly encountered the changes.[110]

It is important to view discussions that relate to Jewish dietary laws in light of the great importance attached to dietary observances in the aftermath of the Maccabean crisis. Evidence that these laws became crucial norms for Jewish identity is found in literary materials that routinely portray loyalty to God by a hero's refusal to eat the food of gentiles.[111] Dunn highlights the socio-religious function of such practices when he writes:

> For Jews, not least in the diaspora, the boundaries which marked them off in their distinctiveness as the elect people of the one God were most emphatically and visibly drawn in the daily lifestyle expressed in diet and festivals.[112]

As we have seen, negative views on the part of Romans toward Jews and Judaism often developed because dietary practices emphasized the separateness of the Jews, making them appear aloof. Abandonment of Jewish dietary observances would have been of little consequence to gentiles in the Christian communities who lacked prior Jewish socialization. In fact, it would have eased tensions between themselves and non-Christians who viewed them as strange and exclusive because of such restrictions. Neither would the neglect of these laws have posed significant problems for Jewish Christians who shared an outlook similar to Paul's or a socialization more open to Hellenism. However, for other

Jews the changes were radical. The old yardsticks of covenant loyalty had been rejected. What was at stake was "nothing less than the whole self-understanding of the new movement."[113]

When the content of 14:1–15:13 is analyzed in light of these circumstances and in relation to the argument of the rest of the letter, a number of striking connections emerge. Throughout Romans Paul endeavored to create as much common ground between Jewish and gentile Christians as possible. The content of 14:1–15:13 seems a fitting climax for his program. In light of what Paul said earlier in the letter, it is natural that he would exhort Christians in Rome to "welcome one another" (14:1; 15:7), not "despise" or "pass judgment" (14:3,4), but "bear" with one another (15:1). According to Wayne Meeks, in 14:1–15:13 the reader is confronted with how Paul wishes to see the theological themes of chapters 1–11 "work out in the everyday life of the Roman house communities."[114] Meeks supports his claim by showing the numerous linkages that exist between 14:1–15:13 and earlier themes in Romans.[115] He especially emphasizes the similarity between the apostrophe at 2:1 censoring the judgmental person and those of 14:4 and 14:10.[116] In both parts of the letter it is God's impartial judgment that relativizes human judgment:

> It is the just, impartial judgment of the one God, therefore, that eliminates the distinction (or separation, *diastole*) between Jew and gentile within the community of faith and, as we learn from Rom. 9–11, in God's ultimate plan, though without abolishing the special gifts and promises which the Jew received (3:1; 9:4–5; 11 passim).[117]

It is difficult to determine with certainty whether differences over dietary laws and observance of special days were responsible for some of the separate house-church groupings reflected in Romans 16. However, because of the tendency for such practices to serve as boundaries it is likely that some house-churches in Rome were more law observant than others, especially in the aftermath of the Claudian edict and the return of expelled law-observant Christians.[118] If so, by curbing human judgment on the basis of foods and days and by advocating mutual acceptance, Paul would be attempting to check the development of separate "Jewish" and "gentile" versions of Christianity.[119] In this light Paul's request in chapter 16 for greetings to pass between the house-churches would be a practical suggestion that would initiate new or renewed relations. Also indicative of this goal is the apostle's comment that "all the churches of the gentiles give thanks" for the Jewish couple Priscilla and Aquila. The statement immediately precedes his request that the readership greet the church in their house.

Paul's admonitions in 14:1–15:13 reflect his desire for greater harmony between Christians who "live like Jews" and those who do not. Throughout Romans Paul has appealed to both sides of the conflict in an attempt to create as much common ground as possible. The pericope at hand continues the pattern by admonishing both groups with specific responsibilities and by interpreting those responsibilities in light of Israel's priority.

It is Paul's prayer for the Christians in Rome that they discover such "harmony" among themselves that God may be praised with "one voice" (15:5–6). In his letter to the Romans Paul makes it clear that this "voice" must be a unified voice but not at the expense of God's promises to Israel. Consequently, the burden is placed on the "strong" to make room for the "weak" (15:1). Hence, in this pericope Paul demonstrates in practical terms his commitment to protect the priority of the Jews against presumptuous gentile Christians who are prepared to claim possession of the olive tree.

The Purpose of Romans in Light of the Ethnic Issues It Treats

A history of the interpretation of the ethnic issues addressed in Romans could be carried out by analyzing the lengthy debate over the occasion and purpose of the letter.[1] This avenue exists because decisions regarding the occasion and purpose determine the setting against which scholars read the Jew-gentile discussions, and conversely, decisions regarding the setting of the Jew-gentile discussions determine conclusions with regard to the occasion and purpose of the document. Now that the three major ethnic issues treated in Romans have been analyzed in light of the social context of Roman Christianity, it is in order to ask why Paul wrote this letter.

I submit that the Roman letter was occasioned by Paul's desire to press westward in his mission to the gentiles with the support of the Roman congregations.[2] Because of Paul's avowed commitment not to build on the foundations of others (Rom. 15:20), it is unlikely that he would have written the Roman Christians if they did not incorporate into his mission of preaching the gospel where Christ had not been named.[3]

However, this rather straightforward occasion gave rise to an elaborate document because of the complexity of the contexts, both Paul's and Rome's. This study has detailed the complexity of the situation in Rome, but not specifically as it relates to Paul's westward mission. Romans 1:8–13 and 15:14–29 certainly indicate that Paul hoped to secure Roman support for his mission to Spain; however, such a statement involves a rather bold assumption: that there was a unified Roman Christian community to which Paul could appeal for support.[4] This study has demonstrated that Roman Christianity was undergoing a critical change in its self-definition when Paul wrote. Christianity in Rome was not unified and the issue threatening it was the very one that made Paul's mission controversial among Jews from Jerusalem to Rome: Insufficient regard for Jewish practice and identity in the gospel. Hence, in Romans Paul must expound the righteousness of God in such a manner that both the universality of the gospel and the priority of Israel are protected.[5] If successful, his argument would deflate gentile Christian boasting and quiet Jewish Christian concerns regarding his gospel, thereby creating a more unified and sympathetic base of support for his westward mission.

Paul's context was similarly complex. He wrote the Roman letter at a critical nexus in his missionary career. In the letter itself the apostle informs his readers that his work in the East (from Jerusalem to Illyricum) is finished. His much-anticipated journey to Rome and points west represents a new missionary horizon. However, Paul's trip to Rome must be routed through Jerusalem because the apostle to the gentiles has too much at stake in the Jerusalem collection to entrust its success to others. Because this relief project symbolizes Paul's commitment to one church of Jews and gentiles (Rom. 15:26–27), the Jerusalem church's acceptance or rejection of the gentile Christian gift will be tantamount to a verdict on Paul's ministry.[6]

Hence, whether interpreters look east to Jerusalem, west to Rome, or farther west to Spain, the ethnic issues Paul faces at this juncture in his ministry are amazingly similar. In order for Paul's ministry to be acceptable in Jerusalem common criticisms of his gospel must be apologetically engaged and the continuity of his gospel with God's purposes for Israel must be demonstrated. In Rome the same are required if common ground is to be established between "Jewish" and gentile Christians. Furthermore, a successful mission to Spain demands that Paul present the Roman Christians with a clearer picture of his missional enterprise; otherwise, he risks another mission plagued by the same uncertainty he now faces in Jerusalem.

The convergence of these factors has led to a growing conviction among scholars that interpreters should cease their efforts to discover *the* occasion and purpose of Romans and recognize instead an array of "reasons for Romans."[7] Indeed, the complexities of the Roman letter mirror the complexity of Paul's missionary situation as well as the complexity of Roman Christianity. However, to read the letter without regard for the Roman situation is surely a mistake. The fundamental question facing interpreters is not so vague as, Why did Paul write Romans? The real question is, Why did Paul write *this* letter to the Roman Christians?

Notes

Abbreviations

CIG	*Corpus Inscriptionum Graecarum*
CIJ	*Corpus Inscriptionum Iudaicarum*
CIL	*Corpus Inscriptionum Latinarum*
CPJ	*Corpus Papyrorum Judaicarum*
IGRR	*Inscriptiones Graecae ad res Romanas pertinentes*
ILS	*Inscriptiones Latinae Selectae*
MAMA	*Monumenta Asiae Minoris Antiqua*
OGIS	*Orientis Graeci Inscriptiones Selectae*

Foreword and Introduction

1. See the discussion in J. Christiaan Beker, *Paul the Apostle* (Philadelphia: Fortress, 1980), 23–36.

2. Ibid.

3. Gary Porton's comments regarding apocalyptic Jews underscores the problem with Robert Karris's approach: "To date, no one has convincingly argued that apocalyptic Jews formed a unique segment of the Jewish community. Apocalyptic thought was widespread and probably affected a number of different Jewish groups" (Gary G. Porton, "Diversity in Postbiblical Judaism," in *Early Judaism and Its Modern Interpreters*, ed. Robert Kraft and George Nickelsburg [Philadelphia: Fortress, 1986]: 57–80).

4. Wayne Meeks, *The Moral World of the First Christians* (Philadelphia: Westminster, 1986), 11–12.

5. The definitions of "reality" and "knowledge" offered by Berger and Luckmann are helpful in clarifying an important distinction that is basic to their outlook. Reality is "a quality appertaining to phenomena that we recognize as having a being independent of our own volition." Knowledge, on the other hand, is "the certainty that phenomena are real and that they possess specific characteristics" (Peter L. Berger and T. Luckmann, *The Social Construction of Reality* [Garden City, N.Y.: Doubleday, 1967], 1). The knowledge that these sociologists seek is not the theoretical knowledge of social elites. On the contrary, Berger explains, "the sociologically most relevant knowledge is that of the

man in the street, that is, 'commonsense knowledge,' rather than the theoretical constructions of intellectuals" (Peter L. Berger, *The Sacred Canopy: Elements of a Sociological Theory of Religion* [Garden City, N.Y.: Doubleday, 1969]).

6. This is a modest goal but it respects the charges of critics that approaches informed by the social sciences are guilty of reductionism. I do not claim that this is the only perspective through which to view a text, but one way that should not be overlooked. See Gerd Theissen, *The Social Setting of Pauline Christianity,* trans. John Shultz (Philadelphia: Fortress, 1982), 195. For a discussion of the common objections raised against the use of social sciences in historical inquiry, see Wayne Meeks, *The First Urban Christians* (New Haven: Yale University Press, 1983), 2–7.

7. For an extensive bibliography of the interaction between New Testament studies and the social sciences, see Daniel J. Harrington, "Second Testament Exegesis and the Social Sciences: A Bibliography," in *Biblical Theology Bulletin* 18 (1988): 77–85. Although distinctions are very fluid, several authors have attempted to categorize approaches to the social history of the New Testament based on whether they use sociological theories and models and if used how they apply them: Jonathan Z. Smith, "The Social Description of Early Christianity," *Religious Studies Review* 1 (1975): 19–25; Daniel J. Harrington, "Sociological Concepts and the Early Church," *Theological Studies* (1980): 181–90; Robin Scroggs, "The Sociological Interpretation of the New Testament: The Present State of Research," *New Testament Studies* 26 (1980): 164–79; Cyril S. Rodd, "On Applying a Sociological Theory to Biblical Studies," *Journal for the Study of the Old Testament* 19 (1981): 95–106; John Gager, "Shall We Marry Our Enemies? Sociology and the New Testament," *Interpretation* 36 (1982): 256–65; Thomas Best, "The Sociological Study of the New Testament: Promise and Peril of a New Discipline," *Scottish Journal of Theology* 36 (1983): 245–61.

8. John Gager, for example, claims that an entire sociological model can be applied to a society even when the evidence is not available for all of the parts. In such cases Gager maintains that one may be able to extrapolate the existence of the data and account for their absence in the historical record by appealing to chance; they simply did not survive (John Gager, *Kingdom and Community: The Social World of Early Christianity* [Englewood Cliffs, N.J.: Prentice-Hall, 1975], 21).

9. See Stanley Kent Stowers, "The Social Sciences and the Study of Early Christianity," in *Approaches to Ancient Judaism,* vol. 5, ed. William Scott Green, Brown Judaic Studies 32 (Atlanta: Scholars Press, 1985), 149–81.

10. Philip Francis Esler, *Community and Gospel in Luke-Acts* (Cambridge: Cambridge University Press, 1987), 6.

11. My reservations are similar to those expressed by Abraham Malherbe, although I would grant that because of the horizon of the interpreter the distinction he makes between "social facts" and "sociological theory" is not always clearly marked: "Sociological description of early Christianity can concentrate

either on social facts or on sociological theory as a means of describing the 'sacred cosmos' or 'symbolic universe' of early Christian communities. Even though new historical information may be assimilated within old paradigms, we should strive to know as much as possible about the actual social circumstances of those communities before venturing theoretical descriptions or explanations of them" (*Social Aspects of Early Christianity* [Baton Rouge: Louisiana State University Press, 1977], 20).

Chapter One
The Socialization of Foreign Groups in Rome

1. George La Piana, "Il Problema della Chiesa Latina in Roma" (Rome, 1922), 20, quoted in translation by the same author in his "Foreign Groups in Ancient Rome," *Harvard Theological Review* 20 (1927): 184.

2. Peter Lampe, *Die Stadtrömischen Christen in den ersten beiden Jahrhunderten* (Tübingen: J. C. B. Mohr, 1987), 37.

3. Suet. *Claud.* 25.4; Acts 18:2. For a discussion of the Claudian edict and its interpretation, see pp. 57–64 of the present study.

To affirm that Christian beginnings in Rome should be traced to the Jewish synagogues of that city by no means denies gentile Christian presence. One does not have to venture outside the Jewish communities of ancient Rome to discover potential gentile Christian devotees. In fact, it is likely that synagogue gentiles, the so-called God-fearers, were common in Rome and supplied many of the Christian converts. See Walter Schmithals, *Der Römerbrief als historisches Problem* (Gutersloh: Gutersloher Verlagshaus Gerd Mohn, 1975), 83–91.

4. Acts 18:2; it is almost certain that Aquila and Priscilla were already Christians before arriving in Corinth. If they were Paul's converts, Luke would not have passed up the opportunity to make the matter explicit. Furthermore, as Haenchen notes: "That a Jewish couple expelled because of the conflict with Christians in Rome deliberately gave a Christian missionary work and shelter is far more improbable than that Paul found lodgings with Christians who had fled from Rome" (Ernst Haenchen, *The Acts of the Apostles,* trans. R. McL. Wilson, et al. [Philadelphia: Fortress, 1971], 533).

5. Ibid., xlvi; Wayne Meeks, *The First Urban Christians* (New Haven: Yale University Press, 1983), 26–28. E. A. Judge and G. S. R. Thomas argue that Roman Christianity was an intra-Jewish affair until Paul arrived in the city early in the 60s (E. A. Judge and G. S. R. Thomas, "The Origin of the Church at Rome," *Reformed Theological Review* 25 [1966]: 81–93). See arguments for Romans being addressed to Jewish converts in T. Fahy, "St. Paul's Romans Were Jewish Converts," *Irish Theological Quarterly* 26 (1959): 182–91. The Jewish character of early Christianity in Rome is pointedly emphasized in the prologue to Ambrosiaster's fourth-century commentary on Romans:

It is established that there were Jews living in Rome in the times of the apostles, and that those Jews who had believed passed on to the Romans the tradition that they ought to profess Christ but keep the law.... One ought not to condemn the Romans, but to praise their faith; because without seeing any signs or miracles and without seeing any of the apostles, they nevertheless accepted Christ, although according to a Jewish rite. (Quoted in F. Watson, *Paul, Judaism and the Gentiles: A Sociological Approach*, Society for New Testament Studies Monograph Series 56 [Cambridge: Cambridge University Press, 1986], 93. The Latin text = *Corpus Scriptorum Ecclesiasticorum Latinorum LXXXI: Ambrosiastri qui dicitur Commentarius in Epistulas Paulinas. Pars. I. In Epistulam ad Romanos* [Vienna, 1966], 5–6)

The modern reader of this text is left wondering from what source Ambrosiaster derived this information. Cranfield is suspicious that his conclusions are based on "either his own inferences from the epistle or the influence of Marcion's preconceptions" (C. E. B. Cranfield, *The Epistle to the Romans*, 2 vols., International Critical Commentary, ed. J. A. Emerton and C. E. B. Cranfield [Edinburgh: T. & T. Clark, 1975–79], 1:20). Watson, on the other hand, doubts the Marcion connection; he thinks inferences from Romans to be a more likely explanation. Yet, another source can hardly be ruled out since nothing in Romans can be said to have "compelled him to such a view" (Watson, *Paul, Judaism and the Gentiles*, 94).

6. Judge and Thomas think that the *katoikountes* of Acts 2:10 refers to Jews from Rome who had taken up residence in Jerusalem, not to Roman travelers at all (E. A. Judge and G. S. R. Thomas, "The Origin of the Church at Rome," 83).

7. Wayne Meeks, "Breaking Away: Three New Testament Pictures of Christianity's Separation from the Jewish Communities," in *To See Ourselves as Others See Us: Christians, Jews, "Others" in Late Antiquity*, ed. Jacob Neusner and Ernest S. Frerichs (Chico, Calif.: Scholars Press, 1985), 96; see also Ramsay MacMullen, *Paganism in the Roman Empire* (New Haven: Yale University Press, 1982), 113–15. The personal greetings in Romans 16, which mention individuals who came to Rome from other locales, suggest that this was in fact the case.

8. John E. Stambaugh, *The Ancient Roman City* (Baltimore: Johns Hopkins University Press, 1988), 90. The figure of a million is derived primarily from the number of adult male citizens included in the grain dole of the late republic and early empire. The numbers range between 150,000 and 320,000. Using this as a basis, allowance is then made for women, children, resident aliens without citizenship, slaves, and soldiers who would not have been included in the dole. The best estimates that result from this approach fall within the range of 750,000–1,000,000 (Julius Beloch, *Die Bevölkerung der griechisch-römischen Welt* [Leipzig: Duncker & Humblot, 1886]; P. A. Brunt, *Italian Manpower, 225 B.C.–A.D. 14* [Oxford: Oxford University Press, 1971], 376–88; Keith Hopkins, *Conquerors and Slaves* [Cambridge: Cambridge University Press, 1978], 96–98;

and W. J. Oates, "The Population of Rome," *Classical Philology* 29 [1934]: 101–16).

9. Sen. *Ad Helviam* 6.

10. It is clear that the growth of Rome cannot be explained solely on the basis of economic and social opportunities in the capital. Rome was no industrial city and its ability to accommodate the economic interests of free foreign immigrants was limited. The population of the capital also increased during the late republic because of the influx of Italian peasants displaced by the formation of large estates (Plutarch *Life of Tiberius Gracchus* 8). Forced immigration resulting from conquest and slave trade continued to swell the population into the imperial period. Delos, the great slave-mart of the Mediterranean, was capable of handling ten thousand slaves per day (Strabo 14.668), many of whom were shipped to Italy. These persons, often manumitted by their owners as freedmen, and the immigrants' descendants made up much of the urban plebeian class (Vell. 2.14.4; Val. Max. 6.2.3). Regardless of the conditions under which an immigrant came to Rome initially, on the streets the immigrants' motives would be impossible to differentiate; hence, the view of Seneca noted above.

11. The 13,900 inscriptions are the ones in CIL, volume 6, parts 2, 3, and 4. See Tenney Frank, "Race Mixture in the Roman Empire," *American Historical Review* 21 (1916): 690.

12. Ibid., 694.

13. He found that 70 percent of the urban inscriptions reflect slaves and freedmen with Greek names (ibid., 700).

14. With a sample of 1347 inscriptions where both the father's and son's names appear Frank observed that in 859 cases where the father had a Greek cognomen the son received a Latin name 399 times (46 percent). However, where the father had a Latin cognomen (488 times), the son received a Greek name only 53 times (11 percent) (ibid., 693). Josephus offers a helpful explanation of name changes in antiquity that no doubt accounts for many such changes in Rome. In his account of the Tower of Babel he says that Hellenization resulted in the adoption of Greek names by local cultures as a matter of accommodation: "Some still preserve the names which were given to them by their founders, some have changed them, while others have adopted a form of name designed to be more intelligible to those who are settled among them" (Jos. *Ant.* 1.121).

15. Ibid., 700.

16. M. Bang, "Die Herkunft der römischen Sklaven," *Mitteilungen des deutschen archaeologischen Instituts* 25 (1910): 223–51. For an expanded list of cases where slaves specified their national extraction, see Marion Edwards Park, *The Plebs in Cicero's Day: A Study of Their Provenance and of Their Employment* (Cambridge, Mass.: Cosmos Press, 1918), 35–36.

17. M. L. Gordon, "The Nationality of Slaves under the Early Roman Empire," *Journal of Roman Studies* 14 (1924): 93ff. She made her case by comparing

the names of the imperial German guard. Her study, however, was challenged by Thylander's analysis of the data (H. Thylander, "Etude sur l'épigraphie latine," *Skrifter utgivna av Svenska Instituet in Rom,* ser. in 8 [Lund: C. W. K. Gleerup, 1952]: 134–52). Susan Treggiari also denies that the Greek cognomen necessarily indicates that its bearers came from the Greek-speaking half of the empire; moreover, she doubts whether East-West categories are ultimately helpful (Treggiari, *Roman Freedmen* [Oxford: Oxford University Press, 1969], 8). She considers the distinction between the civilized and uncivilized and cultured and uncultured to be more relevant to the social situation of freedmen in Rome. Hence, "the Hellenized, or at least Romanized, races...normally provided Rome with her slave craftsmen, teachers, administrators, personal servants" (ibid., 10).

18. Freedmen were more likely to be commemorated in epitaphs because of their pride, or their family's pride, in their achievement. See L. R. Taylor, "Freedmen and Freeborn in the Epitaphs of Imperial Rome," *American Journal of Philology* 82 (1961): 113–32.

19. F. G. Maier, "Römische Bevolkerungsgeschichte und Inschriftenstatik," *Historia* 2 (1954): 318–51, esp. 341–47.

20. Ibid., 321–35, 336–44, 344–47, and 347–50.

21. He points out that there lived in Rome at least 550 slaves or freedmen for each epitaph used by Frank to project his estimates (ibid., 344). With regard to Bang's sample the ratio is 25,000 to 1, while Kuhn bases his predictions concerning the Roman artisans on only 560 epitaphs that are supposed to represent all the artisans who lived and died in the capital over a three-hundred-year period (ibid., 348–50).

22. R. P. Duncan-Jones, review of P. Huttunen's *Social Strata in the Imperial City of Rome, Journal of Roman Studies* 68 (1978): 195.

23. The most compelling case that has been made for this viewpoint is that of Keith Hopkins, *Conquerors and Slaves,* 46–74.

24. Garnsey, however, argues for a greater number of slave-craftsmen in Rome in order to account for the large numbers of freedman-craftsmen. In his words, "The freedman-craftsmen were the most successful members of a distinctly larger group of slave-craftsmen" (Peter Garnsey, "Non-Slave Labour in the Roman World," in *Non-Slave Labour in the Greco-Roman World,* ed. Peter Garnsey [Cambridge: Cambridge Philological Society, 1980], 44).

25. P. Huttunen, *The Social Strata in the Imperial City of Rome,* Acta Universitatis Ouluensis, series B humaniora III, historica I (Oulu, Finland: The University, 1974), 142.

26. Ibid., 193

27. Huttunen, *Social Strata,* 193. See Duncan-Jones, review of Huttunen, 196.

28. That slaves and ex-slaves were in the majority is also the conclusion of P. A. Brunt, *Italian Manpower,* 377, 386.

29. Solin, *Beiträge zur Kenntnis der griechischen Personennamen in Röm* (Helsinki: Societas Scientiarum Fennica, 1971).

30. This may have been especially true of emigrants from southern Italy, where the large animal-farming estates were located (E. Badian, "Tiberius Gracchus and the Roman Revolution," *Aufstieg und Niedergang in der römischen Welt*, I, 1, ed. H. Temporini [New York: Walter de Gruyter, 1974], 672).

31. Few scholars have shown as much creativity in gathering sources for demographic calculations as Keith Hopkins. Yet, with regard to the ratio of slave to free in Rome he refuses to postulate a guess. He simply admits that their numbers must have been substantial, though he doubts that they were a majority (Hopkins, *Conquerors and Slaves*, 115–17).

32. J. P. V. D. Balsdon, *Romans and Aliens* (Chapel Hill: University of North Carolina Press, 1979), 15. See also P. A. Brunt, *Italian Manpower*, 376–79.

33. Ibid., 14. Eastern slaves may have been used to fill artisan positions associated with Oriental luxuries, at least until the Eastern skills were acquired by Romans (Susan Treggiari, "Urban Labour in Rome: Mercennarii and Tabernarii," in *Non-Slave Labour in the Greco-Roman World*, ed. Peter Garnsey [Cambridge: Cambridge Philological Society, 1980]: 56). This might explain why some slaves were sent to *latifundia* while others were directed to Rome. With regard to Juvenal's comment, Courtney points out that Juvenal's xenophobia is not indiscriminate; "he reserves his venom for the Eastern provinces" (E. Courtney, *A Commentary on the Satires of Juvenal* [London: Athlone Press, 1980], 27).

34. Treggiari, *Roman Freedmen*, 8.

35. Courtney, *Commentary on the Satires of Juvenal*, 27. For Juvenal the Western races were being Romanized (*Sat.* 7.147–49, 214; 15.111), while the Easterners "refused to submerge" in Roman culture. In contrast he felt they were trying to absorb the Romans (*Sat.* 3.13–14; 6.542–47; 14.96–106; 6.522–41; 15.1–174). Numismatic evidence supports the same conclusion. By the time of Claudius, Rome had managed to suppress city and other independent coinages in the West. However, it was a different story in the East, where free cities continued to mint coins for centuries (Richard Reece, "Rome in the Mediterranean World: The Evidence of Coins," in *Papers in Italian Archaeology*, vol. 4, The Cambridge Conference, ed. Caroline Malone and Simon Stoddart [1985]: 91 [85–98]). In fact, as late as the third century C.E. there were about 530 separate coinages minted mainly by Greek cities in the East. See bibliography in Meyer Reinhold, *From Republic to Principate: An Historical Commentary of Dio Cassius's Roman History, Books 49–52 (36–29 B.C.)* (Atlanta: Scholars Press, 1988), 203.

36. Geza Alfoldy, *The Social History of Rome*, trans. David Braund and Frank Pollock (London: Croom Helm, 1975), 113.

37. Ibid. See also Meyer Reinhold, *From Republic to Principate*, 141, 188–89 and appendix 11, 227–28.

38. Sen. *De Ira* 2.34.4. Similarly, Tacitus has Claudius addressing the Senate

with these words: "What was the ruin of Sparta and Athens, but this, that mighty as they were in war, they spurned from them as aliens those whom they conquered? Our founder Romulus, on the other hand, was so wise that he fought as enemies and then hailed as fellow-citizens several nations on the same day" (Tac. *Ann.* 11.24).

39. Discussing the resistance to Hellenization along the northwest shore of the Mediterranean, Morel points out, "The most striking symptom of the partial (or superficial or moderate) character of this acculturation resides, perhaps, in the fact that the natives kept their own language" (Jean-Paul Morel, "Greek Colonization in Italy and in the West," in *Crossroads of the Mediterranean*, ed. T. Hackens, Nancy D. Holloway, and R. Ross Holloway, Archaeologia Transatlantica II, papers delivered at the International Conference on Archaeology of Early Italy [May 1981, published 1984], 132).

40. Cic. *De Orat.* 2.265

41. Suet. *Iul.* 39; *Aug.* 24.

42. Juv. *Sat.* 3.62–65

43. M. L. Gordon, "The Nationality of Slaves under the Early Roman Empire," 110.

44. The term *cistiber* seems to designate special police assistants, a shortened form of *quinquevir cis Tiberim.* If so, it is a carry-over from the republican period when such appointments were made to aid the suppression of the Bacchanalian rites (186 B.C.E.). Relevant texts include: Pomponius *Dig.* I, 2.2.31f and also Livy 39.14.10. Deciphering the term has been a matter of considerable debate. Helpful discussions are available in Georg Wissowa, "Cistiber-Deipnokrites," *Hermes* 49 (1914): 626–29; Gunter Wesener, "Quinqueviri (1)," *Paulys Realencyclopädie der classischen atlertumswissenschaft* 24 (1963): 1166–67. For an up-to-date survey of the various arguments that have been put forward concerning the interpretation of the term, see Nicholas Goodhue, *The Lucus Furrinae and the Syrian Sanctuary on the Janiculum* (Amsterdam: Adolf M. Hakkert, 1975), appendix II, 79–89.

45. CIL 6.32316; S. M. Savage, "The Cults of Ancient Trastevere," *Memoirs of the American Academy in Rome* 16 (1940): 37, 45–46; concerning the Syrian sanctuary, see N. Goodhue, *The Lucus Furrinae and the Syrian Sanctuary on the Janiculum.*

46. Ath. *Deipnosophistae* 1.20

47. Appian 2.120

48. Suet. *Jul.* 84.5

49. Balsdon, *Romans and Aliens,* 16.

50. Philo *Embassy* 155–57.

51. Ramsay MacMullen, *Roman Social Relations* (New Haven: Yale University Press, 1974), 83.

52. John E. Stambaugh, *The Ancient Roman City,* 17. The initial development of the Aventine as a place for foreign groups probably goes back to

a fourth-century B.C.E. law aimed at providing new building space for the over-crowded plebeians (Dion. Hal. *Ant. Rom.* 10.31–32).

53. Gellius 13.14.

54. La Piana, "Foreign Groups in Ancient Rome," 214.

55. Suet. *Aug.* 30.

56. S. M. Savage, "The Cults of Ancient Trastevere," 29.

57. For an analysis of the evidence for synagogue groups in Rome, see pp. 33–37 of this study.

58. Archaeological and literary evidence for these has been brought together by G. Lafaye, *Histoire du culte des divinités d'Alexandrie hors de l'Égypte* (Paris, 1884), 200–228.

59. MacMullen, *Roman Social Relations,* 84.

60. Examples of leases of this type are available in Roman legal sources. See Bruce Woodward Frier, "The Rental Market in Early Imperial Rome," *Journal of Roman Studies* 67 (1977): 27–37. La Piana offers an interesting example of an Egyptian who upon coming to Rome looked up a well-known Alexandrian painter and shared his living space until other accommodations became available (La Piana, "Foreign Groups in Ancient Rome," 211).

61. MacMullen, *Roman Social Relations,* 85.

62. Augustus's reorganization of the city into 14 districts and 265 vici served not only administrative aims of urban control but also served to heighten the sense of community feeling that stronger neighborly relations in commerce and cult produced (Karl Christ, *The Romans,* trans. Christopher Holme [Berkeley: University of California Press, 1984], 77). Josephus notes that upon Vespasian's return to Rome the city celebrated in the following groupings: tribes, families, neighborhoods (Jos. *War* 7.473).

63. Juv. *Sat.* 3.62–65.

64. Livy 39. 15. 3.

65. Commenting on the worship of the Phrygian Mother in Rome, Dionysius wrote: "By a law and decree of the senate no native Roman walks in procession through the city arrayed in a parti-coloured robe, begging alms or escorted by flute players, or worships the goddess with the Phrygian ceremonies. So cautious are they about admitting any foreign religious customs and so great is their aversion to all pompous display that is wanting in decorum" (Dion. Hal. *Ant. Rom.* 2.19). It is worth noting that Dionysius was himself in Rome during the reign of Augustus.

66. La Piana, "Foreign Groups in Ancient Rome," 282–320. The grant of official acceptance that Claudius gave to the cult of Attis is just such a case. The choice was to ignore the cult or recognize it in order to regulate it. If recognized, the Romans would press for adaptation according to the cult's Roman context. Judaism obviously fell outside the bounds of such an approach. The Jewish religion could not be assimilated because of its exclusivity, ethnic focus, and cult practices.

67. Jules Toutain, *Les cultes paiëns dans l'empire romain* (Paris: E. Leroux, 1907–20): 1, 2, 34. Note contrast with Franz Cumont, *The Oriental Religions in Roman Paganism* (Chicago: Open Court, 1911, 1929), pp. 81ff.

68. See La Piana, "Foreign Groups in Ancient Rome," 286; Tenney Frank, "Race Mixture in the Roman Empire," 706; L. R. Taylor, "Foreign Groups in Roman Politics of the Late Republic," in *Hommages à Joseph Bidez et à Franz Cumont*, Latomus Collection 2, 323 (fn. 2); and recently Ramsay MacMullen, *Paganism in the Roman Empire* (New Haven: Yale University Press, 1981), 116.

69. The inscription that bears witness to the college of the Paeanistae (146 C.E.) explicitly states that its members were Alexandrians (*CIG* 5898).

70. Jean Waltzing, *Étude historique sur les corporations professionelles chez les Romains* (Louvain: Peeters, 1895–1900), 1:205. These cults no doubt attracted some Romans and made some proselytes; however, the complaints of Roman authors should not be read without awareness of their own prejudices and the limited sample they needed to sound an alarm.

71. This situation is also reflected in the familiar "hyphenated gods" one meets in epigraphic and literary records of the empire. Immigrants who found the worship of their native gods observed in an unfamiliar manner organized their own groups. See Franz Poland, *Geschichte des griechischen Vereinswesens* (Leipzig: Teubner, 1909), 84.

72. Arthur Darby Nock, "The Gild of Zeus Hypsistos," in *Essays on Religion and the Ancient World*, 2 vols. (Cambridge, Mass.: Harvard University Press, 1920), 1:432.

73. Samuel Dill, *Roman Society: From Nero to Marcus Aurelius* (New York: Macmillan, 1905), 261.

74. For a list of funerary collegia, see Waltzing, *Étude historique sur les corporations professionelles chez les Romains*, 4:202–8. The average size of associations based on epigraphic evidence was about 150; however, some were as small as 12. The figure of 150 may be high because of the likelihood that smaller groups would not have been as prone to specify their size (Ramsay MacMullen, *Enemies of the Roman Order* [Cambridge, Mass.: Harvard University Press, 1966], 342).

75. *ILS* 7212 (136 C.E.); a translation of the inscription is available in Naphtali Lewis and Meyer Reinhold, *Roman Civilization*, 3rd ed. (New York: Columbia University Press, 1990), 2:186–88.

76. The inscription (*ILS* 7212) outlines the mechanics of collecting funds and dispersing them at the death of a member. In addition, a calendar of special dinners is included with a detailed procedure by which ample food and drink would be insured for the gatherings. The social focus of the association is highlighted toward the end of the inscription: "It was voted that if any member desires to make any complaint or bring up any business, he is to bring it up at a business meeting, so that we may banquet in peace and good cheer on festive days." The inscription concludes with the responsibilities of officials to provide specific services including the conduct of worship.

77. According to L. R. Taylor, neighborhood guilds of foreign stock, concentrated with persons of common homeland and/or cult, were exploited for political purposes during the late republic. It is in this light that she reads the crackdown on associations during that period (L. R. Taylor, "Foreign Groups in Roman Politics of the Late Republic," 326).

78. The *lex Clodia de collegiis* of 58 B.C.E.

79. Suet. *Jul.* 42.3; Josephus uses the Jewish exemption to show the privileged status the Jews enjoyed under the Roman emperors (Jos. *Ant.* 14.18.8).

80. Suet. *Aug.* 32

81. Ibid.

82. Stambaugh, *The Ancient Roman City*, 212.

83. Treggiari argues that slaves and freedmen "played the main part in the cult of the Lares" (Susan Treggiari, *Roman Freedmen*, 198–200).

84. Ramsay MacMullen, *Enemies of the Roman Order*, 174.

85. "Sans doute, à l'origine comme plus tard, le gouvernement, redoutait les groupes qui se formaient en dehors de la religion, et le culte des collèges paraissait une garantie sérieuse. Il est certain aussi que la religion fut souvent un prétexte mis en avant par des collèges pour cacher un autre dessein; cela prouve seulement, que la religion suffisait pour donner des apparences inoffensives, pourvu qu'il ne s'agit pas d'un culte interdit. Mais rien n'autorise à croire que le culte fut une condition de l'autorisation, ou seulement de la tolérance accordée par le gouvernement" (Waltzing, *Étude historique sur les corporations professionelles chez les Romains*, 1:255). Consequently, it is difficult or impossible to differentiate between religious and secular clubs. All involved the celebration of religious rituals and most met under the patronage of some deity (Dill, *Roman Society*, 262).

86. See Waltzing, *Étude historique sur les corporations professionelles chez les Romains*, 1:136ff.

87. Peter Garnsey, "Religious Toleration in Classical Antiquity," in *Persecution and Toleration*, Papers of the Ecclesiastical History Society, ed. W. J. Sheils (Oxford: Blackwell, 1984), 9.

88. MacMullen, *Roman Social Relations*, 77.

89. For a discussion of the term *cistiber*, see note 44, p. 102 above.

90. Attempts to reconcile Gaionas's titles with membership in one *collegium* have been unsuccessful. It is best to assume that he was a member of two associations, an urban *collegium* (*quinqueviri cis Tiberim*) and a Syrian cult society (Savage, "The Cults of Ancient Trastevere," 37; Goodhue, *The Lucus Furrinae and the Syrian Sanctuary on the Janiculum*, 89).

91. Some have questioned the interpretation of *cistiber* advocated in this study on the grounds that it is unimaginable that one would boast of such a lowly office. Yet, as Ashby has noted, "even the lowest official position at Rome would probably have seemed to an Oriental of considerable importance"

(Thomas Ashby, "Recent Excavations in Rome," *Classical Quarterly* 2 [1908]: 149).

92. CIL 6.36804 = *IGRR* I.1388. The relevant inscriptions along with an interpretation of them is found in Savage, "The Cults of Ancient Trastevere," 37.

93. La Piana, "Foreign Groups in Ancient Rome," 305; Waltzing, *Étude historique sur les corporations professionelles chez les Romains*, 1:205.

94. La Piana, "Foreign Groups in Ancient Rome," 234. Ramsay MacMullen in his book *Roman Social Relations* includes an appendix detailing districts of Rome where specific crafts were concentrated (MacMullen, *Roman Social Relations*, 132–35).

95. La Piana, "Foreign Groups in Ancient Rome," 271.

96. Lanciani wrote of the discovery and excavation in Rome of a single pit that measured 160' x 100' x 30'. He estimated that the grave had been filled with 24,000 corpses, victims of a plague (R. Lanciani, *Ancient Rome in Light of Recent Discoveries* [Boston: Houghton, Mifflin & Co., 1888], 66). Widespread traditions relating to the importance of a proper burial in the Graeco-Roman world only provided further incentive. For the internal workings of a burial society, see the by-laws of the group that met under the patronage of Diana and Antinoüs cited earlier (p. 15).

97. See Keith Hopkins, *Death and Renewal* (Cambridge: Cambridge University Press, 1983), 211–17.

98. La Piana, "Foreign Groups in Ancient Rome," 255.

99. Inscriptions of the Piazzale delle Corporazioni (the heart of Ostia's commercial activity) document the presence of foreign groups from many northern African cities, Spain, Gaul, Asia Minor, Egypt, and several other cities of Italy. Cult structures have been found associated with Cybele, Attis and Bellona, Serapis, Mithras (eleven different Mithraic temples), Jupiter Dolichenus, Sabazius, and a synagogue of the Jews. See R. Meiggs, *Roman Ostia* (Oxford: Clarendon, 1973), 327–33, 354–77.

100. Tyre was well-known in antiquity for its history as a trading and colonizing people (Strab. *Geog.* 756–57). See M. F. Baslez, "Le rôle et la place des Pheniciens dans la vie économique des ports de l'Egee," in *Studia Phoenicia V,* ed. E. Lipinski (Leuven: Peeters, 1987), 267–86. In explaining the persistence of Phoenician culture Millar compares its conscious historical tradition and identity to that of the Jews (Fergus Millar, "The Phoenician Cities: A Case Study of Hellenisation," *Proceedings of the Cambridge Philological Society* 209 [1983]: 59).

101. J. H. D'Arms challenges the view that Puteoli declined in the second century because of Ostia. He maintains that the problem of the *statio* of the Tyrians proves a crisis only for the Tyrians, not Puteoli. He takes the high rent that they pay (the highest for any Italian city on record) to be an indication of continuing prosperity for the city (J. H. D'Arms, "Puteoli in the Second Century

of the Roman Empire: A Social and Economic Study," *Journal of Roman Studies* 64 [1974]: 105).

102. *OGIS* 595 = *CIG* 5853; the letter from Tyre is dated December 8, 174 C.E. For the texts of both letters in translation see La Piana, "Foreign Groups in Ancient Rome," 257–58.

103. Although the Tyrians of Rome attempted to cut off the payments, this does not vitiate my point. It must be borne in mind that the stoppage of funds was a deviation from the previous practice.

104. When the Tyrians of Puteoli describe their lack of ability to meet the rent payments of their *statio,* they point out the financial drain they already experience "for the sacrifices and cult of our national deities who have their temples here" (*CIG* 5853). Another inscription, though fragmentary, mentions the move of "the holy god of Sarepta," to Puteoli from Tyre (*IGRR* I, 420 = *OGIS* 594). See C. C. Torrey, "The Exiled God of Sarepta," *Berytus* 9 (1948–9): 45–49.

105. Delos, another important port for Mediterranean shipping (this one located on an Aegean island), has provided valuable evidence for foreign residents involved in local commercial enterprises. Interestingly, Tyrian merchants also show up on Delos worshiping their ancestral god as Herakles-Melkart (see Philippe Bruneau, *Recherches sur les cultes de Délos* [Paris: Boccard, 1970], 458–93, 622–30).

106. Ath. *Deipnosophistae* 1.20.

Chapter Two
Jewish Socialization in Ancient Rome

1. For a helpful survey with bibliography, see Baruch M. Bokser, "Recent Developments in the Study of Judaism 70–200 C.E.," *Second Century* 3 (1983): 1–68.

2. Philo *Embassy* 281–83. For similar statements see Jos. *War* 7.43; Strabo, as quoted by Jos. *Ant.* 14.115; Philo *Flac.* 45; *Sibyl. Or.* 3.271. There is widespread agreement that the number of Jews living outside of Palestine exceeded those within. Attempts have been made to quantify the population of the Jews during the early empire, but data on which to base predictions are scant and problematic. See Stern's review of the evidence from antiquity and its limitations: S. Safrai and M. Stern, *The Jewish People in the First Century* (Philadelphia: Fortress, 1974), 117–22.

3. Martin Hengel, *Judaism and Hellenism,* trans. John Bowden (Philadelphia: Fortress, 1974), 1:310–14. Even the anti-Hellenistic Hasmonaeans soon "went the way of Hellenization and began to resemble the normal type of Hellenistic monarch" (V. Tcherikover, *Hellenistic Civilization and the Jews* [New York: Atheneum, 1970], 253). See John Collins, who notes that given the extent of Hellenistic influence in Palestine it is not surprising that scholars encounter

difficulty distinguishing between the literature of the Diaspora and that of Judea (i.e., the scholarly debate concerning the provenance of the Testaments of the Twelve Patriarchs). John Collins, *Between Athens and Jerusalem* (New York: Crossroad, 1983), 10.

4. "Palestinian Judaism" is unfortunately the phrase used by E. P. Sanders for "covenantal nomism," allegedly the basic type of religion evidenced by Jews in Palestine from 200 B.C.E. to 200 C.E. (E. P. Sanders, *Paul and Palestinian Judaism* [Philadelphia: Fortress, 1977], 426).

5. With regard to the methodological issues underlying Neusner's work, see Jacob Neusner, "The Use of the Later Rabbinic Evidence for the Study of First-Century Pharisaism," in *Approaches to Ancient Judaism: Theory and Practice*, Brown Judaic Studies 1 (Missoula, Mont.: Scholars Press, 1978), 215–28.

6. See for example, Kraabel's comments regarding Cumont's interpretation of the Valerius Maximus text: A. Thomas Kraabel, "The Roman Diaspora: Six Questionable Assumptions," *Journal of Jewish Studies* 33 (1982): 450.

7. Note for example the comments in Martin Persson Nilsson, *Geschichte der griechischen Religion*, 2 vols. (Munich: Beck, 1941–50), 2:661–67.

8. Magical papyri and gems reflect the most common examples. Sometimes, however, expressions of friendly neighbors have been interpreted as proof of openness to syncretism. The case of Julia Severa is indicative of this problem. The fact that this wealthy woman (from Acmonia in Phrygia) was a high priestess of a pagan cult and a benefactor of a local synagogue certainly indicates that social relations could exist between Jews and pagans. However, it says nothing about the combining of two religions. The inscription is *CIJ* 766 = *MAMA* VI no. 264-B. For a discussion see A. R. R. Sheppard, "Jews, Christians and Heretics in Acmonia and Eumeneia," *Anatolian Studies* 29 (1979): 169–80. Actual examples of syncretistic attitudes in the Diaspora are more common in Egypt. This was no doubt due to the antiquity of the Jewish community in the region coupled with the wealth, status and education of many Alexandrian Jews. Under these circumstances Jews were under greater pressure to reconcile their Judaism and Hellenism and had more freedom to do so. See Emil Schürer, *The History of the Jewish People in the Age of Jesus Christ*, vol. 3.1, revised and edited by Fergus Millar (Edinburgh: T. & T. Clark, 1986 [1885–1924]), 138–39.

9. A. T. Kraabel, "Unity and Diversity among Diaspora Synagogues," in *The Synagogue in Late Antiquity* (Winona Lake, Ind.: Eisenbrauns, 1987), 50.

10. Andrew R. Seager and A. T. Kraabel, "The Synagogue and the Jewish Community," in George M. A. Hanfmann, *Sardis from Prehistoric to Roman Times* (Cambridge, Mass.: Harvard University Press, 1983), 185.

11. A. Thomas Kraabel, "The Diaspora Synagogue: Archaeological and Epigraphic Evidence since Sukenik," in *Aufstieg und Niedergang in der römischen Welt*, II.19.1., ed. Wolfgang Haase (Berlin and New York: Walter de Gruyter, 1979), 483–84.

12. Tcherikover demonstrated in an important essay that "apologetic" is

not a proper label for this literature. It was intended for a Jewish audience, not gentiles. These Jews were grappling with the dissonance they experienced living in the Hellenistic world (V. Tcherikover, "Jewish Apologetic Literature Reconsidered," *Eos* 48 [1956]: 169–93).

13. See the discussion in John Collins, *Between Athens and Jerusalem*, 104–6.

14. Philo *Migration of Abraham* 89. See Alan F. Segal, *Rebecca's Children: Judaism and Christianity in the Roman World* (Cambridge, Mass.: Harvard University Press, 1986), 57.

15. Cultic matters are avoided, even Sabbath and circumcision. See H. C. Kee, "Ethical Dimensions of the Testaments of the XII as a Clue to Provenance," *New Testament Studies* 24 (1978): 259–70.

16. Collins, *Between Athens and Jerusalem*, 12.

17. One has only to compare Philo's Hellenistic portrayal of Judaism with his criticism of Jews who neglected distinctive Jewish cult practices to be reminded of this fact. Were it not for explicit references (e.g., *Migration of Abraham* 89), few would have predicted that Philo would have been so insistent on the literal observance of cultic practices.

18. Terminological disputes abound in modern discussions. Many prefer "anti-Judaism" to "anti-Semitism"; however, other expressions are also suggested. This author favors "anti-Judaism" for the period under consideration because the term "semitic" is too broad and implies that the issues were primarily ethnic rather than religious. For recent discussions, see the introductions to J. N. Sevenster, *Roots of Pagan Anti-Semitism in the Ancient World* (Leiden: E. J. Brill, 1975), and John Gager, *The Origins of Anti-Semitism* (New York: Oxford University Press, 1983).

19. For example, persecution serves to reinforce a sect's "us-versus-them" view of reality.

20. Peter L. Berger, *The Sacred Canopy: Elements of a Sociological Theory of Religion* (Garden City, N.Y.: Doubleday, 1969), 16.

21. Jules Issac, *Jésus et Israël* (New York: Holt, Rinehart and Winston, 1971; translated from revised edition of 1959; originally published 1948); Marcel Simon, *Verus Israël: Etude sur les relations entre chrétiens et juifs dans l'empire romain* (Paris: E. de Boccard, 1964).

22. John C. Meagher, "As the Twig Was Bent: Antisemitism in Greco-Roman and Earliest Christian Times," in Alan T. Davies, ed. *Anti-Semitism and the Foundations of Christianity* (New York: Paulist Press, 1979), 4.

23. Gager, *The Origins of Anti-Semitism*, 9.

24. Meagher, "As the Twig Was Bent," 6.

25. See Tac. *Hist.* 5.4–5; Juv. *Sat.* 14.96–106; Tib. *Carmina* 3.15–18; Hor. *Serm.* 1.9.60–78; Ovid *Rem. Am.* 217–20.

26. A large and powerful Jewish community existed in Alexandria. Jews felt that their status in the city should be comparable to that of the Greeks, given the antiquity of the Jewish community in the city. The Greeks on the

other hand objected to the attempt of the Jews to have it both ways: They wished to "belong" but at the same time wished to remain distinct. Apion's comment, "Why, then, if they are citizens, do they not worship the same gods as the Alexandrians" (Jos. *Ag. Apion* 2.66), reflects at least one aspect of that complaint. When the Romans introduced the poll-tax (*laographia*) following the annexation of Egypt, the tension peaked. By exacting the tax from Egyptians and Jews but not Greeks, the Romans in effect distinguished between citizens and non-citizens in a fashion that effectively lowered the status of the Jews. This set off a bitter struggle that finally prompted Claudius to intervene. In his letter, dated 41 C.E., he refers to the Jews as persons living "in a city not their own," and contrasts their situation with that of the Alexandrians. Although equal status is denied, he does protect the Jews' right to observe their religion without hindrance according to previous Roman practice. For the letter of Claudius, see *CPJ* 153; for a discussion of the papyrus letter, see Tcherikover, *CPJ* 1:39–41, 61–64.

27. Kraabel stresses the implications of the Jewish community having control of such a large building on "main street" in an important city (Kraabel, "The Diaspora Synagogue: Archaeological and Epigraphic Evidence since Sukenik," 488).

28. The inscription has been recently published by J. M. Reynolds and R. Tannenbaum, *Jews and God-fearers at Aphrodisias* (Cambridge: Cambridge Philological Society, 1987), 5–7.

29. Shaye Cohen, *From the Maccabees to the Mishnah* (Philadelphia: Westminster Press, 1987), 37.

30. Robert Goldenberg, "Review of Gager's *Origins of Anti-Semitism,*" *Religious Studies Review* 11 (October 1985): 336.

31. As with other questions regarding antiquity, historians are attempting to describe the world of the common person through the use of sources that were neither written by common persons nor about common persons. For example, the prejudices and conservative tendencies of the Roman *literati* must be taken into account lest the naive reader take their virulent attacks as an accurate indicator of popular opinion; these writers represent *a* viewpoint, not *the* viewpoint. This problem has of course received considerable attention in recent years. See Millar's stark statement of the problem and his approach in "The World of the Golden Ass," *Journal of Roman Studies* 71 (1981): 63–75.

32. A. Thomas Kraabel, "The Diaspora Synagogue: Archaeological and Epigraphic Evidence since Sukenik," 488.

33. Kraabel, "The Roman Diaspora," 457.

34. It should be noted that given the focus of this study the evidence of Sardis is late. It does not appear that the Jews assumed control of the building near the bath-gymnasium complex until the middle of the third century C.E. See A. R. Seager, "The Building History of the Sardis Synagogue," *American Journal of Archaeology* 76 (1972): 425–35. Furthermore, there is evidence that during the earlier period the Jews of Sardis, like their co-religionists in other

locales, had to pursue the protection of their rights against local leaders. During the Augustan period the Romans instructed the city authorities not to hinder the Jews in their collection of sacred funds bound for Jerusalem (Jos. *Ant.* 16.6.6).

35. This is the mistake that John Gager has made. He has in essence replaced the old paradigmatic role of Alexandria with that of Sardis (note the basis of his critique of Sevenster, Gager, *The Origins of Anti-Semitism*, 31).

36. John Gager, *The Origins of Anti-Semitism*, 31.

37. Terms used by the Jews to represent the notion of "community" (*Ioudaioi, politeuma, katoikia, laos, ethnos*) indicate in themselves some level of separateness. Concerning these terms Millar writes: "All the terms . . . reflect the fact that the Jews lived as a foreign people among strangers. The two last-mentioned instances express this directly, while *politeuma* and *katoikia* indicate the fact that they occupied a position in some ways politically independent alongside the rest of the inhabitants" (Schürer, *The History of the Jewish People*, 3.1, 90).

38. Shaye Cohen, *From the Maccabees to the Mishnah*, 35.

39. The term "synagogue" was used of the congregation itself while places of worship were generally known as "proseuchai" in the Diaspora. See Martin Hengel, "Proseuche und Synagoge: Jüdische Gemeinde, Gotteshaus und Gottesdienst in der Diaspora und in Palästina," in *Tradition und Glaube: Das frühe Christentum in seiner Umwelt*, Festgabe für Karl Georg Kuhn, ed. G. Jeremias (Göttingen: Vandenhoeck & Ruprecht, 1971), 157–83.

40. Joseph Gutmann, *The Synagogue: Studies in Origins, Archaeology, and Architecture* (New York: Ktav, 1975); another study edited by Gutmann, *Ancient Synagogues: The State of Research*, Brown Judaic Studies 22 (Chico, Calif.: Scholars Press, 1981); Lee I. Levine, *The Synagogue in Late Antiquity*, JTS Centennial (Winona Lake, Ind.: Eisenbrauns, 1987). See also Michael White, *Building God's House in the Roman World* (Baltimore: Johns Hopkins University Press, 1990).

41. Shaye J. D. Cohen, "Pagan and Christian Evidence on the Ancient Synagogue," in *The Synagogue in Late Antiquity*, 175.

42. This list includes Priene, a site where the identity of the structure as a synagogue has been debated. See Kraabel, "The Diaspora Synagogue," 489–91.

43. Kraabel, "The Diaspora Synagogue," 501–3.

44. In this regard see the recent article by Howard Clark Kee, "The Transformation of the Synagogue after 70 C.E.: Its Import for Early Christianity," *New Testament Studies* 36 (1990): 1–24. Even if third-century patterns were monolithic, it would be ill-advised to use them as sources for the earlier period because of the great changes that took place between the pre-rabbinic and rabbinic periods.

45. Michael White summarizes the current state of affairs as follows:

> The question of origins has come to rest on the Palestinian setting and on the nature of the "synagogue" not as institution in the later Talmudic

sense, but as "assembly." There is no clear archaeological evidence for synagogue buildings from Second Temple Palestine. Only after 70 C.E. and the destruction of the Temple, did it emerge as the central institution of Pharisaic-Rabbinic Judaism. (L. Michael White, "The Delos Synagogue Revisited: Recent Fieldwork in the Graeco-Roman Diaspora," *Harvard Theological Review* 80 [1987]: 133)

46. "Place of gathering," "place of prayer," "sanctuary," "holy place," "Sabbath meeting place," "place of instruction." See Levine, "The Second Temple Synagogue," 13. Cohen states that the "repeated use of the term 'synagogue' results from the erroneous view that there was a single phenomenon that can be designated by this term." He goes on to question whether using the term is helpful (Cohen, "Pagan and Christian Evidence," 175).

47. For a survey of these, see S. Krauss, *Synagogale Altertümer* (Hildesheim: Olms, 1966), 182–98. Some of these include study, prayer, law courts, collection of local charity funds, social and political gatherings, banqueting, etc.

48. Lee Levine, "The Second Temple Synagogue," 23.

49. Kraabel, "The Diaspora Synagogue," 502.

50. White, *Building God's House*, 44.

51. Ibid., 62.

52. White, "The Delos Synagogue Revisited," 135. The Sardis synagogue was an adaptation of a previously existing structure that did not come into Jewish hands until the middle of the third century C.E. See A. R. Seager, "The Building History of the Sardis Synagogue," 425–35.

53. White, "The Delos Synagogue Revisited," 152. With regard to the antiquity of the synagogue at Delos, see the comment of Kraabel, "The Diaspora Synagogue," 493.

54. This is central to the thesis of White's book *Building God's House in the Roman World:* "The establishment of synagogue communities throughout the Diaspora must have generally followed the same steps as those followed at Delos, Priene, and Stobi. Private household gatherings gradually gave rise to formal establishments through a process of architectural adaptation sponsored in large measure by private benefactions" (92). On the basis of the Polycharmos inscription (*CIJ* 694) from the synagogue at Stobi, Hengel argues that the structure had been the private home of Polycharmos. Yet at some point Polycharmos turned the house over to the Jewish community with the condition that he and his heirs would retain the upper rooms, where they probably continued to reside (Hengel, "Die Synagogeninschrift von Stobi," *Zeitschrift für neutestamentlichen Wissenschaft* 57 [1966]: 173–76).

55. White, *Building God's House*, 86. It is indeed interesting, as White notes, that Paul "never once referred to the synagogue, either as institution or edifice, even though he clearly knew Jewish communities or individuals in several localities in Greece and Asia Minor" (ibid., 87).

56. L. Michael White, "The Delos Synagogue Revisited," 154. The Jewish community of Delos is hardly unique in this regard, a conclusion readily drawn from Roman administrative dealings with Jewish groups in light of regulations regarding private associations. This topic will be treated in more detail in subsequent sections of this study.

57. Psalm 137:4. John Collins utilizes this quotation in a provocative manner to introduce his book *Between Athens and Jerusalem*. According to Collins, "The problem of singing the song of the Lord in a foreign land was the problem of maintaining the identity of the people and its survival as a distinct entity" (*Between Athens and Jerusalem*, 1).

58. Kraabel, *The Roman Diaspora*, 455.

59. Val. Max. in *Facta et Dicta Memorabilia* 1.3.3, in Stern, *Greek and Latin Authors*, 147a and 147b.

60. The identification of these Jews as syncretistic worshipers of the Phrygian deity Sabazius has been challenged by the text-critical reconstruction of Eugene Lane, "Sabazius and the Jews in Valerius Maximus: A Re-examination," *Journal of Roman Studies* 69 (1979): 35–38.

61. G. Fuks, "Where Have All the Freedmen Gone? On an Anomaly in the Jewish Grave-Inscriptions from Rome," *Journal of Jewish Studies* 35 (1984): 26.

62. Philo *Embassy* 155.

63. Tac. *Ann.* 2.85.4. It is likely that more Jewish captives were brought to Rome following the siege of Jerusalem by the Roman general Gaius Sosius in 37 B.C.E. His forces assisted Herod in taking control of Jerusalem from Antigonus, the last of the Hasmonaean kings. Following the victory, Sosius received the title "imperator" and was granted a triumphal procession that finally took place in September 34 B.C.E. Though little is known about this event, it is reasonable to assume that Jewish captives marched in the procession according to the usual practice. See G. Fuks, "Where Have All the Freedmen Gone?" 27; Jos. *War* 1.343–53; *Ant.* 14.465–81.

64. Cic. *Flac.* 66.

65. Safrai and Stern, *The Jewish People in the First Century*, 161.

66. Hor. *Serm.* 1.4.139–43; 5.96–104; 9.60–78; Ovid *Ars Am.* I.75–80, 413–16; *Rem. Am.* 217–20.

67. Jos. *Ant.* 17.11.1; *War* 2.6.1.

68. Harry Joshua Leon, *The Jews of Ancient Rome* (Philadelphia: Jewish Publication Society of America, 1960), 15, 135–36. Calculations of forty to fifty thousand are most common. Kettunen estimates thirty to forty thousand (Markku Kettunen, *Der Abfassungszweck des Römerbriefes* [Helsinki: Suomalainen Tiedeakatemia, 1979]). The lowest estimate I have seen is that of Penna, who thinks it could have been as few as twenty thousand (see Romano Penna, "Les Juifs à Rome au temps de l'apôtre Paul," *New Testament Studies* 28 [1982]: 328).

69. Leon, *The Jews of Ancient Rome*, 136. The great synagogue in Rome today is still in Trastevere.

70. Ibid.

71. T. Reinach, *Textes d'auteurs grecs et romains relatifs au judaïsme* (Hildesheim: G. Olms, 1963), 265, fn. 3.

72. Sevenster, *The Roots of Pagan Anti-Semitism*, 102.

73. Jewish epitaphs referring to a synagogue of the *Kampesioi* include: *CIJ* no. 88, 319, 343, 523. See the discussion in *CIJ* I, lxxiv. For the *Sibouresioi*, see *CIJ* no. 18, 22, 37, 67, 140, 380. See also the discussion in *CIJ* I, lxxiii–lxxiv. The fact that this region is located within the *pomerium* presents no real difficulty since restrictions on the performance of foreign cults within the *pomerium* were not enforced from the second century onwards (Schürer, *The History of the Jewish People*, 3.1, 97, fn. 28 and bibliography noted there).

74. Juv. *Sat.* 3.12–16.

75. One almost opposite the Calixtus catacombs and another opposite the Vigna Randanini.

76. Suzanne Collon, "Les Quartiers juifs de la Rome antique," *Mélanges d'Archéologie et d'Histoire* 57 (1940): 74.

77. See Leon's criticism regarding Collon's conjectures: Leon, *The Jews of Ancient Rome*, 140.

78. See Balsdon's comment, for example: Balsdon, *Romans and Aliens* (Chapel Hill: University of North Carolina Press, 1979), 16.

79. Philo *Flac.* 8

80. Solin writes, "Ob es in Rom ganze reine Judenviertel gab, wie es in Alexandrien der Fall war, lässt sich nicht ausmachen" (Heikki Solin, "Juden und Syrer in der römischen Welt," *Aufstieg und Niedergang der römischen Welt*, ed. Wolfgang Haase [Berlin and New York: Walter de Gruyter, 1983], 587–789).

81. Safrai and Stern, *The Jewish People in the First Century*, 166. The four synagogues that most assuredly existed as early as the Julio-Claudian period were located in Trastevere: the synagogue of the Hebrews and those named after Augustus, Agrippa, and Volumnius.

82. Philo *Embassy* 155. See comments concerning the character of the Transtiberine region made earlier in this study on pp. 11–13.

83. Packer's analysis of the evidence in Ostia leads him to conclude that *insula* is a broad term designating any type of multiple dwelling (J. P. Packer, "The Insulae of Imperial Ostia," *Memoirs of the American Academy at Rome* 31 [1971]: 79). Data concerning the ratio of *insulae* to *domus* are from the "Regionary Catalogue" of the fourteen districts of imperial Rome preserved in a fourth-century C.E. document (*Curiosum Urbis Regionum XIV*, or *Notitia Regionum Urbis XIV*). The text is most accessible in H. Jordan, *Topographie der Stadt Rom im Altherthum* (Berlin, 1871), 2:539–74.

84. Stambaugh, *The Ancient Roman City*, 90.

85. Tac. *Ann.* 2.85.

86. For an analysis of the general process, see Arnold M. Duff, *Freedmen in the Early Roman Empire* (Oxford: Oxford University Press, 1928), 12–35.

87. Fuks, "Where Have All the Freedmen Gone?" 30.

88. Although over five hundred inscriptions have been recovered from the Jewish catacombs in Rome, none attests that the deceased person was either a freedman or a slave. This does not mean, however, that these persons were not the descendants of slaves, some of whom may have come to Rome following Pompey's actions in Judaea. The family or friends of a deceased person of servile ancestry would hardly have included such information in an inscription intended to honor them. Prosopographical studies offer some help. Of the twenty typical servile names mentioned by Duff, thirteen are among the catacomb inscriptions and the sample indicates that as many as 10 percent of those buried in the catacombs may have been freedmen. For a fuller discussion of the evidence, see G. Fuks, "Where Have All the Freedmen Gone?" 25–32.

89. Philo *Embassy* 158. On the distribution of grain and money, see M. Rostovtzeff, "Die römischen Bleitesserae," *Klio* 3 (1905): 10–12, and more recently, Z. Yavetz, *Plebs and Princeps* (Oxford: Clarendon Press, 1969), esp. 43–49.

90. Freedmen and their descendants were Roman citizens, though the citizenship of freedmen carried certain restrictions (Ramsay MacMullen, *Roman Social Relations* [New Haven: Yale University Press, 1974], 104f).

91. B. Lazare, *L'Antisémitisme: Son histoire et ses causes* (Paris: L. Chailley, 1894).

92. A. Blaudau, *Juden und Judenverfolgungen im alten Alexandria* (Münster: Aschendorff, 1906), 45.

93. Mart. *Epig.* 12.57.13; Juv. *Saturn.* 3.10–18; 6.542–47

94. Juv. *Sat.* 3:14–18.

95. Ibid., 6.544–48.

96. Mart. *Epig.* 12.57.

97. Sevenster, *The Roots of Pagan Anti-Semitism*, 81.

98. Leon, *The Jews of Ancient Rome*, 235.

99. Ibid.

100. None of the funerary inscriptions recovered from the catacombs in Rome were able to honor a deceased Jew by referring to any public post in the government or bureaucracy.

101. Between 46 B.C.E. and 37 C.E. the number of persons on the grain dole in Rome fluctuated between 150,000 and 320,000 (see Stambaugh, *The Ancient Roman City*, 337, fn. 1). Moreover, these figures represent only the citizen poor.

102. L. R. Taylor, "Foreign Groups in Roman Politics of the Late Republic," in *Hommages à Joseph Bidez et à Franz Cumont*, Latomus Collection 2, 327.

103. Cicero accuses the Jews of being inappropriately influential in political matters because of their exclusivism and lobbying efforts in one another's behalf (Cic. *Flac.* 28.68–69). See also Josephus's account of eight thousand Jews in

Rome joining an embassy from Palestine in protesting the actions of Archelaus in Palestine (Jos. *Ant.* 17.11.1).

104. A piece of Alexandrian Greek propaganda, the *Acts of the Alexandrian Martyrs* (*CPJ* 2), reflects the extreme to which this criticism could be taken. Here Roman leaders are consistently portrayed as biased in favor of the Jews.

105. Shaye Cohen, "Pagan and Christian Evidence," 160.

106. The use of domestic architecture for a synagogue is attested near Rome, at the port city of Ostia (White, *Building God's House*, 69).

107. Ibid., 44–47.

108. Three or four of the eleven synagogues noted by Leon would not be known except for the survival of one or two inscriptions. It is safe to assume, therefore, that more than eleven synagogues existed, though tangible evidence has not survived. The six Jewish catacombs of Rome have yielded the richest concentration of Jewish grave inscriptions of any city of antiquity with the exception of Jerusalem. H. J. Leon's careful analysis of these materials is still the most detailed study of the inscriptions as a whole. He also includes a survey of the catacombs themselves with information regarding the history of their discovery and excavation as well as their unique characteristics. A more recent analysis of catacomb materials is available in a broader study of Jewish funerary inscriptions in Denali Poliakoff, "The Acculturation of Jews in the Roman Empire: Evidence from Burial Places," Ph.D. dissertation, Boston University, 1989.

109. Laurence H. Kant, "Jewish Inscriptions in Greek and Latin," *Aufstieg und Niedergang der römischen Welt*, II.20.2, ed. Wolfgang Haase (Berlin and New York: Walter de Gruyter, 1987), 674.

110. This warning is especially important because the institutional development of the synagogue experienced its greatest evolution during the post-70 period.

111. The uncertainty concerning the Calcaresians stems from whether this group was made up of limekiln workers (Schürer, *The History of the Jewish People*, 3:84; La Piana, "Foreign Groups in Ancient Rome," 352, 370) or was merely named from the street or section where it was located (Leon, *The Jews of Ancient Rome*, 143).

112. The explanation of La Piana for the synagogue of the Hebrews is the most plausible. Rather than referring to a group that spoke Hebrew or conducted services in Hebrew, the name results from the fact that it was the earliest synagogue; hence, there was no need to differentiate it from other Jewish groups (La Piana, "Foreign Groups in Ancient Rome," 356). The synagogue of the Vernaclesians was made up (at least originally) of native-born Romans who wished to differentiate themselves from immigrants. The name comes from the Latin *vernaculus* meaning "indigenous." Common theories that associate this group with Jews of servile origin mistakenly take the name to be a diminutive of *verna* (see the discussion in Leon, *The Jews of Ancient Rome*, 155–56).

113. Ibid., 140–66.

114. This discussion is taken largely from H. J. Leon's analysis of the language of the inscriptions (ibid., 75–92).

115. Leon, *The Jews of Ancient Rome*, 76. His figures are based on comparisons of 536 inscriptions. Jonathan Smith sorted 584 inscriptions and concluded that 70 percent were Greek ("Fences and Neighbors: Some Contours of Early Judaism," in *Approaches to Ancient Judaism*, vol. 2, ed. W. S. Green [Chico, Calif.: Scholar's Press, 1980], 16).

116. Poliakoff, "The Acculturation of Jews in the Roman Empire," 33.

117. Ibid.

118. Leon, *The Jews of Ancient Rome*, 77, 110.

119. The fact that the Monteverde catacomb is the oldest should also be considered. This catacomb may have already been in use during the first century B.C.E. Therefore, time may be as significant a factor as the social context for estimating the relative acculturation of the deceased buried there.

120. White, *Building God's House*, 61.

121. It should be noted that Rome and Alexandria in the Diaspora are the only cities where detailed information about the Jewish population and community structure exists. Therefore it would be a mistake to take either case to be paradigmatic.

122. La Piana, "Foreign Groups in Ancient Rome," 361f; Juster, *Les Juifs dans l'empire romain: Leur condition juridique, économique, et sociale*, 2 vols. (Paris, 1914), 1:418–24; Kant, "Jewish Inscriptions in Greek and Latin," 694. Frey spends considerable time in the introduction to the corpus refuting La Piana on this matter. See Frey, *CIJ* I, cii–cxi.

123. Schürer, *The History of the Jewish People*, 3.1, 91.

124. Because of the dating problem already noted with regard to funerary inscriptions, it is not possible to detail the institutional development of synagogues in Rome. Nonetheless, it is significant that even by the end of the third century C.E., the Jews of Rome were not highly organized when compared to contemporary cities, nor were they involved in the public affairs of the city in a way comparable to Alexandria.

125. *CIJ* I, no. 284, 368, 425. Kant rightly observes that "the frequent linking of an office to the name of a synagogue points toward a decentralized organization" ("Jewish Inscriptions in Greek and Latin," 694).

126. See for example *CIJ* 291, 304, 538.

127. See the discussion in Leon, *The Jews of Ancient Rome*, 173–80. For the title "twice archon," see *CIJ* 397, 316, 391.

128. "Le premier objet de son culte [the synagogue's] et de sa piété" (*CIJ* II, cxlii).

129. Jonathan Z. Smith, "Fences and Neighbors," 17.

130. Ibid. Kant finds it "interesting" that funerary inscriptions stressing "piety and love of law, learning, community, and family" often come from Rome ("Jewish Inscriptions in Greek and Latin," 683).

131. Neusner reflects awareness of this social dynamic when he writes:

My best guess is that when the Jews found themselves in a world in which their small numbers in great cities rendered them distinguished and special, acutely different, then the Judaism of corporate and coherent society had to make provision for a new sort of social experience. That experience was one of intense self-consciousness, one in which the Jews were Jews before they were differentiated persons, and in which the presence and power of the gentile world imposed upon the Jews that acute self-awareness of being "Israel" that, in ancient times, we find in the rabbinical writings only when the writers meditate on enormous historical and national issues. (Jacob Neusner, "The Experience of the City in Late Antique Judaism," in *Approaches to Ancient Judaism*, vol. 5, ed. William Scott Green [Atlanta: Scholars Press, 1985], 52)

132. Kraabel, "Unity and Diversity among Diaspora Synagogues," 55.

133. Kraabel contrasts Rome and Sardis in this regard (Kraabel, "The Roman Diaspora: Six Questionable Assumptions," 457). A number of funerary inscriptions from the Jewish catacombs in Rome indicate that the deceased was an immigrant. Most of these references specify an Eastern provenance, usually Palestine. This could either mean that most immigrants came from the East or that those coming from the East were more likely to have it noted on their grave markers. Specific references include, Aquileia, *CIJ* 147; Laodicea, *CIJ* 296; Lebanon, *CIJ* 501; Caesarea, *CIJ* 65, 370; Sepphoris, *CIJ* 362; Tiberias, *CIJ* 502. Although Palestinian origins predominate, the sample of inscriptions is too small to draw any definitive conclusions from this evidence alone.

134. Jos. *Ant.* 17.11.1; *War* 2.6.1. In fact the Jews of Rome may have served as a sort of lobbying group for Palestine and various Diaspora cities, a practice that drew scorn from Cicero. See Cic. *Flac.* 28.66. See also Safrai and Stern, *The Jewish People in the First Century,* 162.

135. This fact is evidenced in Cicero's defense of Flaccus; see Cic. *Flac.* 28.66–67.

136. Either because they wrote during the period or described the period based on earlier sources.

137. Penna divides the sources into three groups: references to Jews prior to the time of Paul, contemporary with Paul, or from a slightly later time but descriptive of the earlier period. Romano Penna, "Les Juifs a Rome au temps de l'Apôtre Paul," 321–47. See Stern, *Greek and Latin Authors,* for translations of the texts themselves.

138. Tac. *Hist.* 5.4–5.

139. Cic. *Flac.* 28.68–69. These sentiments may not accurately reflect Cicero's own views because allowance must be made for his trial rhetoric. See Bilhah Wardy, "Jewish Religion in Pagan Literature during the Late Republic and Early Empire," *Aufstieg und Niedergang der römischen Welt,* II.19.1, ed. Wolfgang Haase (Berlin and New York: Walter de Gruyter, 1979), 596–613. However, the speech

was prepared with the assumption that these views existed among the jurors and could be exploited to the defendant's advantage.

140. Hor. *Serm.* I.9.60–78; 4.139–43.

141. Ovid *Rem. Am.* 217–20

142. Val. Max. in *Facta et Dicta Memorabilia* I.3.3.

143. Sen. *De Superstit.*, preserved in Aug. *De Civ.* 6.11.

144. Pers. *Sat.* 5.176–84.

145. Petron. *Sat.* 68.4–8.

146. Petron. *Frag.* 37.

147. Quintil. *Inst.* 3.7.21.

148. Mart. *Epig.* 7.82.

149. Ibid., 11.94.

150. Ibid., 12.57.1–14; 4.4.

151. Juv. *Sat.* 14.96–106.

152. Tac. *Hist.* 5.4–5.

153. A more detailed analysis of these texts is included later in this chapter.

154. Suet. *Claud.* 25.4; *Tit.* 7; *Dom.* 12. Dio Cass. 60.6.6; 66.7.2; 67.14.

155. As indicated earlier in this study (p. 24) the separateness of the Jews in a given locale was affected by factors other than their desire to be separate. Separateness may reflect the only option available in the social situation rather than a community's desire to isolate itself from larger society. However, to a critical observer, it all appears the same: They are aloof. The language of the catacomb inscriptions suggests that limited options may have been the chief factor in the isolation of the Jews in Rome rather than their desire to be separate. Over 70 percent of the inscriptions are in Greek, indicating a cohesive community where Greek was the lingua franca. However, they used more Roman names — though sometimes transliterated into Greek — than Greek names (47 percent of the names are Latin while 31 percent are Greek). This preference for Roman names does not suggest a community that rejected Roman culture; however, the preponderance of Greek in the inscriptions suggests that their opportunities in Roman culture were limited. See Poliakoff, "The Acculturation of Jews in the Roman Empire," 38.

156. Alan Wardman, *Religion and Statecraft among the Romans* (London: Granada Publishing, 1982), 108.

157. John Ferguson, *The Religions of the Roman Empire* (Ithaca, N.Y.: Cornell University Press, 1970), 211.

158. See La Piana, "Foreign Groups in Ancient Rome," 282–320.

159. J. A. North, "Conservatism and Change in Roman Religion," *Papers of the British School at Rome* 44 (1976): 5.

160. It is clear that the slightest error in the performance of a ritual invalidated it and risked precipitating the anger of the gods. Note Pliny's witness:

> We also observe that our highest magistrates use certain formulae for praying: not a single word may be omitted or pronounced out of its proper

place; it is somebody's duty to precede the magistrate in reading out the formula from a written text; somebody else's to listen to every word; a third person's to see that the silence is not ominously broken; meanwhile a musician performs on the flute to prevent any other words being heard. There are memorable instances recorded in the annals in which either the sacrifice has been interrupted, and thus marred, by imprecations, or where a mistake has been made in the recitation of the formula. (Pliny *N.H.* 13.10; see also Cic. *Har.* 23)

161. Peter Garnsey and Richard Saller, *The Roman Empire: Economy, Society and Culture* (Berkeley: University of California Press, 1987), 163.

162. Ibid., 170.

163. This seeming paradox has received considerable attention in recent years. See for example J. H. W. G. Liebeschuetz, *Continuity and Change in Roman Religion* (Oxford: Clarendon Press, 1979).

164. Garnsey and Saller, *The Roman Empire*, 170.

165. See pp. 13–15 above for further information regarding foreign persons and their cults in Rome.

166. Garnsey and Saller, *The Roman Empire*, 171.

167. The apprehensions of Cicero regarding participation of women in various cults are noteworthy: "Assuredly we must make most careful provision that the reputation of our women be guarded by the clear light of day, when they are observed by many eyes, and that initiations into the mysteries of Ceres be performed only with those rites which are in use in Rome" (Cic. *Laws* 2.35). In this regard, see David Balch's discussion of Greco-Roman criticism of Eastern religions in his *Let Wives Be Submissive: The Domestic Code in 1 Peter*, SBL Monograph Series 26 (Chico, Calif.: Scholars Press, 1981), 65–80.

168. Claudius, for example, in a letter returning the high-priestly vestments to Jewish control commented: "I cherish religion myself and wish to see every nation maintain the religious practices that are traditional with it" (Jos. *Ant.* 20.1.2).

169. Garnsey and Saller, *The Roman Empire*, 170. Indications of the relation between Hannibal's invasion and importation of the cult occur in Livy's account of the period. See Livy 21.62; 25.1.

170. Dion. Hal. *Ant. Rom.* 2.19. See also Cic. *Balb.* 24.55.

171. Cic. *Laws* 2. 8. 19.

172. See the discussion of this event with a quotation of a portion of the text from Livy on p. 14 of this study. Note also Cicero's reference to the Bacchanal crisis in his warnings regarding the effect of Eastern religions on Roman women (Cic. *Laws* 2.35–37).

173. Livy 39.15.3.

174. Suet. *Aug.* 93.

175. Hugh Last, "The Study of 'Persecutions,'" *Journal of Roman Studies* 27 (1937): 88.

176. A. D. Nock, "Religious Developments from the Close of the Republic to the Death of Nero," in *Cambridge Ancient History,* 10:490.

177. Such property included whatever was consecrated to a god. Thus, it could include temples and cult objects, as well as tombs or burial grounds (Gaius *Inst.* 2.4.5). An example of this usage can be seen in the famous "Nazareth Inscription," which enjoins serious penalties on those who violate graves. A translation and brief description of the inscription is found in Meyer Reinhold, *The Golden Age of Augustus* (Toronto: Samuel Stevens, 1978), 177. On the protection of temples, see a recently discovered inscription recording a general order of Augustus (27 B.C.E.) in Naphtali Lewis and Meyer Reinhold, *Roman Civilization,* 3rd ed. (New York: Columbia University Press, 1990), 1:616–17.

178. T. D. Barnes, "Legislation against the Christians," *Journal of Roman Studies* 58 (1968): 48.

179. See Last, "The Study of 'Persecutions,' " 80–92.

180. Cic. *Att.* 2.17.2; Tert. *Apol.* 6.8; Dio Cass. 40.47.3–4; Val. Max. 1.3.3; Dio Cass. 42.26.1–2. The last of these included the destruction of their temple and the execution of Isiac priests. See the helpful discussion in Sharon Kelly Heyob, *The Cult of Isis among Women in the Graeco-Roman World* (Leiden: E. J. Brill, 1975), 18ff.

181. Ibid., 19.

182. W. H. C. Frend, *Martyrdom and Persecution in the Early Church* (Oxford: Basil Blackwell, 1965), 112.

183. Ibid.

184. Ramsay MacMullen, *Enemies of the Roman Order* (Cambridge, Mass.: Harvard University Press, 1966), 133.

185. Tac. *Ann.* 2.32; 12.52.

186. Livy's account of the suppression of the Bacchic cult illustrates the matter. Once fear of the cult prompted activity on the part of Roman officials, a mechanism for administrating the crisis was created. Rewards were provided for informers, warnings against harboring fugitives were issued, trials were held, and the regulations for the future were proscribed:

> The next task entrusted to the consuls was the destruction of all shrines of Bacchic worship, first at Rome and then throughout Italy, except in places where an ancient altar or statue had been consecrated. For the future it was provided by decree of the Senate that there should be no Bacchanalia in Rome or in Italy. If any person regarded such ceremonies as hallowed by tradition and as essential for him, and believed himself unable to forgo them without being guilty of sin, he was to make a declaration before the city praetor, and the applicant, at a meeting attended by at least a hundred members of the Senate, he would be allowed to perform the rite, provided that no more than five people took part; and there was to be no common fund of money, no president of the ceremonies, and no priest. (Livy 39.18)

187. Tac. *Ann.* 12.52.

188. Pliny *Let.* 10.96, 97.

189. For a discussion of the precise reason why Christians were perse-cuted according to the Pliny-Trajan correspondence, see De Ste. Croix, "Why Were the Early Christians Persecuted?" *Past and Present* 26 (1964): 6–38, and A. N. Sherwin-White, "Why Were the Early Christians Persecuted? An Amendment," *Past and Present* 27 (1963): 23–33.

190. Wardman, *Religion and Statecraft among the Romans,* 126.

191. E. Mary Smallwood, "Jews and Romans in the Early Empire," *History Today* 15 (1965): 233.

192. *CPJ* 153 in Meyer Reinhold, *Diaspora* (Toronto: Samuel Stevens, 1983), 113–14.

193. Dio Cass. 60.6.6.

194. Jos. *Ant.* 20.10–14. The baffling flip-flops reflected in Rome's pol-icy regarding the vestments of the high priest indicate the difficulty Rome encountered administering the affairs of Judaea following the death of Herod.

195. Suet. *Claud.* 25.4. For a detailed discussion of the date of this episode and its interpretation, see below pp. 49–53.

196. A more general look at the array of decisions Claudius handed down also shows the occasional nature of his approach to religions. Sharing the conservative tendencies of Augustus, Claudius sought to restore traditional Roman religion but, like Augustus, tolerated non-Roman cults. However, analysis of his reign indicates that the matter was more complex than this generalization suggests. He expelled the astrologers from Italy and suppressed the Druid religion in Gaul. Yet, at the same time, he attempted to introduce the Eleusinian Mysteries into Rome and recognized the cult of Attis (Arnaldo Momigliano, *Claudius: The Emperor and His Achievement,* trans. W. D. Hogarth [New York: Barnes and Noble, 1934], 28).

197. Jos. *Ant.* 14.10.1–8.

198. Jos. *Ant.* 14.10.8; Suet. *Jul.* 42.3 That the Jews themselves were aware of the beneficence of Caesar's policies toward them is indicated by Suetonius's note that the Jews of Rome mourned his death more than any other national group (Suet. *Jul.* 84.5).

199. Josephus has preserved a considerable number of official documents and other administrative actions that illustrate this fact. See Jos. *Ant.* 14.10; 16.6. For a discussion of the documents and their significance, see Rajak, "Was There a Roman Charter for the Jews?" *Journal of Roman Studies* 74 (1984): 107–33.

200. Stambaugh, *The Ancient Roman City,* 53.

201. Fidélité aux dieux romains; attachement à la Magna Mater; défiance envers les cultes étrangers non soumis au contrôle de l'État (Michel Malaise, *Les conditions de pénétration et de diffusion des cultes égyptiens en Italie* [Leiden: E. J. Brill, 1972], 389).

202. Augustus's removal of the Egyptian cults from the *pomerium* (the sacred area of the Roman gods) and his forbidding of Romans from participating in the ceremonies of Druidism indicate the focus of his policy (Dio Cass. 53.2.4; 54.6.6; for a discussion, see Last, "The Study of the Persecutions," 88).

203. Leon, *The Jews of Ancient Rome*, 140–42.

204. Philo *Embassy* 158.

205. Commenting on Augustus's procedure for dealing with the infiltration of foreign religions, Malaise says that "Toutefois les mesures prises par Auguste se révélèrent peu efficaces." He maintains that if Augustus's approach had been effective, Tiberius — who was a follower of Augustus's policies — would not have resorted to the use of force to stem the tide: "Les persécutions declenchées par Tibére suffiront à démontrer l'échec des tentatives augustéennes" (Malaise, *Les conditions de pénétration et de diffusion des cultes égyptiens en Italie*, 389).

206. Jos. *Ant.* 18.3.5; Tac. *Ann.* 2.85; Suet. *Tib.* 36.

207. Tac. *Ann.* 2.85. Suetonius's account is very similar and probably dependent on the same source; however, he does mention that proselytes were among those expelled (Suet. *Tib.* 36).

208. Jos. *Ant.* 18.65.

209. H. J. Leon argues that the chief motivation for the event was religious and that it was prompted by Jewish proselytism (Leon, *The Jews of Ancient Rome*, 16–20). See also E. Mary Smallwood, "Some Notes on the Jews under Tiberius," *Latomus* 15 (1956): 314–29. David Balch utilizes the crackdowns on the Jewish and Isis cults in 19 C.E. — along with many others — to make his case that Roman censorship of Oriental religions was prompted by fear that their Roman women were corrupted by such cults (David Balch, *Let Wives Be Submissive*, 65–80).

The severity and breadth of the expulsion is indicated by the methods used to remove the Jews from Rome. Because *peregrini* had no technical right of residence they could be summarily expelled. Jews with Roman citizenship, on the other hand, could be legally evicted only after a trial and conviction. Conscription was a convenient way of removing this sector of the Jewish community. See Elmer Truesdell Merrill, "The Expulsion of the Jews from Rome under Tiberius," *Classical Philology* 14 (1919): 365–72, esp. 368. Tacitus's figure of four thousand *libertini generis* probably includes freedmen and their descendants, although this is not strict legal terminology. Otherwise, the figures are out of proportion to what is reasonable, given the time period that had elapsed since the Roman war in Judaea at the time of the installation of the provincial administrative system (Stern, *Greek and Latin Authors*, 1:72).

210. Dio Cass. 57.18.5a, preserved by John of Antioch = Stern, 2:419.

211. Tac. *Ann.* 2.85.

212. Sen. *Epist.* 108.22

213. Smallwood, *The Jews under Roman Rule* (Leiden: E. J. Brill, 1976), 205.

214. Barbara Levick, _Tiberius the Politician_ (London: Thames and Hudson, 1976), 136–38. Philo mentions no expulsion but rather an "upheaval" (Philo _Embassy_ 159).

215. Stern dates the upheaval Philo refers to in 31 C.E. (Stern, _Greek and Latin Authors_, 2:71). Sejanus was an influential force by this time but not as early as 19 C.E. (Smallwood, _The Jews under Roman Rule_, 209). Philo's comment that Tiberius abandoned the anti-Jewish measures following the death of Sejanus makes no sense if connected to an event that took place twelve years earlier. Philo must have been referring to a incident subsequent to the expulsion in 19 C.E.

216. Philo _Embassy_ 159.

217. Dio Cass. 60.6.6

218. For a brief review of reasons why the account of Philo is to be preferred, see Smallwood, _The Jews under Roman Rule_, 174. A fuller discussion is available in Emil Schürer, _The History of the Jewish People_, 1:394–97. For the purposes at hand, a solution to this question is not required.

219. Philo explains that the action of Gaius was in retaliation for the Jews' destruction of an imperial image that had been set up in Jamnia by the gentile population. Philo believes that those who set up the image were more interested in annoying the Jewish inhabitants of the city than rendering homage to Gaius (Philo _Embassy_ 200–206).

220. Ibid., 218–19.

221. Barnett, "Under Tiberius All Was Quiet," _New Testament Studies_ 21 (1975): 569.

222. Nock, "Religious Developments," _Cambridge Ancient History_, 10:496.

223. Jos. _Ant._ 19.1.5; for more on Gaius and the Egyptian cults see J. Colin, "Les consuls de César-Pharaon Caligula et l'héritage de Germanicus," _Latomus_ 13 (1954): 398–416.

224. For an extensive and recent discussion of the issues, see Gerd Luede-mann, _Paul: Apostle to the Gentiles_, trans. F. Stanley Jones (Philadelphia: Fortress, 1984), 164–71.

225. Dio Cass. 60.6.6

226. Suet. _Claud._ 25.4

227. Leon, _The Jews of Ancient Rome_, 23–27.

228. Gerd Luedemann, for example, corroborates his claim that Dio Cassius corrects Suetonius's claim of an expulsion by noting the conflict between Rome and Alexandria that would result if, at roughly the same time, Claudius was protecting the rights of Jews in Alexandria and expelling them from Rome (Luedemann, _Paul, Apostle to the Gentiles_, 164ff).

229. See the discussion of the Alexandrian episode earlier in this study, p. 44.

230. Nock, "Religious Developments," _Cambridge Ancient History_, 10:498.

231. Vincent M. Scramuzza, _The Emperor Claudius_ (Cambridge, Mass.: Harvard University Press, 1940), 184.

232. Tac. *Ann.* 11.15.

233. Ibid., 11.25.3

234. Ibid., 23.3 This was an augury for ascertaining whether prayers for the safety of the state might be offered.

235. Ibid., 12.23.4. This would have necessitated the removal of any non-Roman cults that may have been worshiped at precincts in the area newly incorporated.

236. Tac. *Ann.* 12.22.1–2; 12.52.1; 12.59.1–2. Tacitus suggests that the calamity of Lollia Paulina was the result of the jealousy of Agrippina, who saw her as a rival for the hand of Claudius and produced an accuser. Even so, it seems that Agrippina was aware of Claudius's aversion to foreign rites and found in the same a predictable opportunity to achieve her end. For the expulsion of astrologers, see Tac. *Ann.* 12.52.3.

237. Scramuzza, *The Emperor Claudius,* 145.

238. One other source, the *Scholia* to Juvenal (*Scholia in Iuvenalem vetustiora,* ed. Wessner, 64) mentions Jews expelled from Rome who had settled in Aricia. Some scholars, including Schürer and Juster, think this refers to an expulsion during the reign of Claudius (Schürer, *The History of the Jewish People in the Age of Jesus Christ,* 3:63; Juster, *Les Juifs dans l'empire romain,* 1:180, n. 9).

239. Salvaging 41 C.E. as the date by asserting that the couple may have "spent several years elsewhere in the interim" surely begs the question (Leon, *The Jews of Ancient Rome,* 25). See also Safrai and Stern, *Jewish Diaspora,* 182. Furthermore, an action against the Jewish community toward the end of the decade fits the general crackdown on foreign superstitions already noted during that period.

240. E. Mary Smallwood, *The Jews under Roman Rule,* 215. Other scholars who opt for two events include: H. Smilda, *C. Suetonii Vita Divi Claudii* (1896), 123–25; E. Meyer, *Ursprung und Anfänge des Christentums III* (1923), 37–38; E. Bammel, *Zeitschrift für Theologie und Kirche* (1959), 294–97; F. F. Bruce, *Bulletin of the John Rylands Library* (1961–62): 313–18; W. H. C. Frend, *Martyrdom and Persecution in the Early Church* (1965), 160; A. D. Nock, "Religious Developments," *Cambridge Ancient History,* 10:500; Momigliano, *Claudius, the Emperor and His Achievement* (1934), 31–32, 98–99.

241. Although absolute clarity is desired, neither the date of the action(s), nor the relationship between the two sources significantly affect the reconstruction proposed in this study. For example Luedemann's conclusion that there was only one episode (41 C.E.) and that Dio Cassius suppressed the reference to Christianity would not greatly alter the picture (Luedemann, *Paul, Apostle to the Gentiles,* 164ff).

242. Tert. *Apol.* 3.5

243. Lactant. *Inst.* 4.7.5

244. Watson, *Paul, Judaism and the Gentiles,* 91.

245. Smallwood, *The Jews under Roman Rule,* 211. The case for this view is cogently made by H. Janne, *Mélanges Bidez* (1934), 531–53. For the opposing view that "Chrestus" was a Jewish political agitator in Rome with no Christian connection, see Stephen Benko, "The Edict of Claudius of A.D. 49 and the Instigator Chrestus," *Theologische Zeitschrift* 25 (1969): 406–18.

246. This explains in part why in the letter of Claudius to Alexandria he threatened to accuse the Jews of fomenting a worldwide plague if they did not cease their riots and submit to his directives (*CPJ,* no. 153, lines 73–104, in Reinhold, *Diaspora,* 113–14).

247. Scramuzza, *The Emperor Claudius,* 152.

248. Jos. *Ant.* 20.8.11. Josephus calls Poppaea "God-fearing"; yet, such terminology need not demand that she was a proselyte.

249. After all, if Nero had not been more open to Orientals these court connections would not have existed.

250. See the evidence for his philhellenism collected in Miriam T. Griffin, *Nero: The End of a Dynasty* (New Haven: Yale University Press, 1984), 208ff.

251. Note the comment of Malaise:

> Néron, le successeur de Claude, le petit-fils de Germanicus et d'Agrippine, paraît avoir été attiré par l'Égypte comme son oncle Caligula. Le nouvel empereur avait d'ailleurs reçu comme précepteur le stoïcien Chérémon de Naucratis, directeur de la Bibliothèque d'Alexandrie et auteur de plusieurs ouvrages sur l'Égypte, dont une étude théologique sur Isis et Osiris. Son attirance pour la Vallée du Nil fut cependant surtout importante dans la deuxième partie de son règne caractérisée par la rupture avec le Principat et le retour au despotisme de type oriental. (Malaise, *Les conditions de pénétration et de diffusion des cultes égyptiens en Italie,* 403)

252. Tac. *Ann.* 15.40ff. See Griffin, *Nero: The End of a Dynasty,* 132ff.

Chapter Three
Christians and Jews in Rome Between 49 and 64 C.E.

1. Marcel Simon, *Verus Israel: A Study of the Relations between Christians and Jews in the Roman Empire, 135–425,* trans. H. McKeating (Oxford: Oxford University Press, 1986), 98.

2. Gamble, *The Textual History of the Letter to the Romans* (Grand Rapids, Mich.: Eerdmans, 1977), 136.

3. Willi Marxsen was the first to suggest that Paul's letter to the Romans should be read in light of the edict of Claudius: Willi Marxsen, *Introduction to the New Testament,* trans. G. Buswell (Philadelphia: Fortress, 1968), 100.

4. See Karris's criticism of Donfried's analysis of the situation based on the Claudian edict: Robert Karris, "The Occasion of Romans: A Response to

Professor Donfried," in *The Romans Debate,* ed. Karl Donfried (Minneapolis: Augsburg Press, 1977), 151.

  5. Wiefel is among those who believe the edict expelled the entire Jewish community (Wolfgang Wiefel, "The Jewish Community in Ancient Rome and the Origins of Roman Christianity," in *The Romans Debate,* ed. Karl Donfried [Minneapolis: Augsburg Press, 1977], 110–13).

  6. Ibid., 110.

  7. Ibid., 110–13.

  8. Luke consistently uses "Jew" to specify a member of the Jewish *ethnos.* See Peter Lampe, *Die Stadtrömischen Christen in den ersten beiden Jahrhunderten* (Tübingen: J. C. B. Mohr, 1987), 5.

  9. L. A. Thompson, "Domitian and the Jewish Tax," *Historia* 31 (1982): 329–42.

  10. Tac. *Ann.* 15.28.

  11. Dio Cass. 37.17.1.

  12. Petron. *Sat.* 102.13–15; Mart. 7.55.7–8; for further information regarding Roman perceptions of Jews and Judaism, see pp. 37–40 and 45–53 of this study.

  13. Epict. *Diss.* 2.9.19–20. Whether Epictetus refers to proselyte baptism or Christian baptism does not affect the point at issue here.

  14. See Jos. *Ant.* 14.10.13–19.

  15. Suet. *Dom.* 12.2.

  16. It is unlikely that citizens would have been expelled out of hand without due process. However, as has already been noted with regard to the action of Tiberius in 19 C.E., even citizens could be removed from the city by conscription into the military if the government was too impatient to handle offenders on a case-by-case basis.

  17. Marxsen, *Introduction to the New Testament,* 100. Dio Cassius's comment (57.18.5) that during the reign of Claudius the Jews were back in Rome in great numbers indicates that the eviction order under Tiberius had either lapsed or ceased to be enforced following Tiberius's death.

  18. Alan Segal, "The Costs of Proselytism and Conversion," *Seminar Papers,* Society of Biblical Literature, no. 27 (Atlanta: Scholars Press, 1988), 336–69, esp. 363.

  19. A similar version of the Noahide Commandments is found in a pre-Christian source, *Jubilees* 7:20–21.

  20. Segal, "The Costs of Proselytism and Conversion," 365.

  21. Ibid.

  22. Philip Francis Esler, *Community and Gospel in Luke-Acts* (Cambridge: Cambridge University Press, 1987), 22. The boundary-keeping role that unique Jewish practices played is poignantly reflected in Philo's interpretation of Numbers 23:9: Israel cannot be harmed by foreign influence as long as it is a "people dwelling alone." Philo states the reason for his conclusion in the clearest of

terms: "because in virtue of the distinction of their peculiar customs they do not mix with others to depart from the ways of their fathers" (Philo *Mos.* 1.278). Wayne Meeks drew proper attention to the significance of Paul's threat to the boundaries between Jews and gentiles when he wrote:

> By abandoning these rules, the Pauline Christians gave up one of the most effective ways by which the Jewish community had maintained its separate identity in pagan society. That was the practical issue at dispute between Paul and his opponents in Galatia, although the complexity of Paul's theological and midrashic arguments has often led later interpreters to forget this simple question. (Wayne Meeks, *The First Urban Christians* [New Haven: Yale University Press, 1983], 97)

23. R. O. Hoerber, "The Decree of Claudius in Acts 18:2," *Concordia Theological Monthly* 31 (1960): 690. Regarding the notion that beliefs in the Messiahship of Jesus would not have caused disturbances of themselves, see David Aune's observation: "Jewish scholars are virtually unanimous in the opinion that uniformity of observance (orthopraxy) is a more fundamental constituent of historical Judaism than is theological orthodoxy" (David Aune, "Orthodoxy in First Century Judaism?" *Journal for the Study of Judaism* 7 [1976]: 1–10, 2).

24. Paul's statement that some Christian missionaries preached circumcision to escape persecution is a clear example (Gal. 6:12).

25. R. A. Markus calls this the "fundamental uncertainty." See R. A. Markus, *Christianity in the Roman World* (New York: Charles Scribner's, 1974), 22.

26. Peter Lampe, who takes the Dio Cassius and Suetonius accounts to refer to the same episode, notes that the assembly restrictions placed on the Jewish synagogues would have contributed to the separation of the communities as well. However, he also notes that the same conclusion would have been drawn from the Suetonius text without the Dio Cassius version (Peter Lampe, *Die Stadtrömischen Christen*, 8).

27. Tac. *Ann.* 15.44; Suet. *Nero* 16. The study of this event has produced a massive literature. For a fairly extensive bibliography, see Paul Keresztes, "The Imperial Roman Government and the Christian Church," in *Aufstieg und Niedergang der römischen Welt*, II.23.1, ed. Wolfgang Haase (Berlin and New York: Walter de Gruyter, 1979), 248. Considerable attention has been focused on the question of whether Christians were persecuted as scapegoats for the burning of Rome or simply as Christians. For discussions of this matter, see Keresztes, ibid., 247–57; Michael Grant, *Nero* (London: Weidenfeld and Nicolson, 1970), 155ff; A. Momigliano, *Cambridge Ancient History* 10 (1934), 887. Ronald Syme, *Tacitus* (Oxford: Clarendon, 1958), 2:533. The Tacitus passage (*Ann.* 15.44) is the first extant reference in a pagan author to the origin of Christianity. Michael White thinks that "Tacitus' histories may have projected onto the actions of

Nero a cognizance of group identity not possible in the earlier period" (White, *Building God's House,* 102). It may well be true that Nero and his contemporaries might not have been able to explain the identity of Christianity by recounting its origin with Tacitus's accuracy. However, the literary record from antiquity is clear (both from Christian and pagan writers) that Nero persecuted Christians in Rome and not Jews. Some level of recognition of Christian identity vis-à-vis the Jews is required to account for Nero's action. Fergus Millar has correctly noted that the ancient materials are silent regarding how Christians were identified and prosecuted; nonetheless, they were identified, and that is the crucial point here! (Fergus Millar, *The Emperor in the Roman World* [Ithaca, N.Y.: Cornell University Press, 1977], 554).

28. Peter Richardson, *Israel in the Apostolic Church* (Cambridge: Cambridge University Press, 1969), 41. Those reluctant to accept Rome's ability to distinguish Jews from Christians as early as 64 C.E. should ask why Roman administrators in 64 C.E. would not be able to learn through interrogations fundamentally the same information Pliny learned in 112 C.E.

29. Gerhard Krodel, "Persecution and Toleration of Christianity until Hadrian" in *The Catacombs and the Colosseum,* ed. Stephen Benko and John J. O'Rourke (Valley Forge, Pa.: Judson Press, 1971), 259.

30. John J. O'Rourke, "Roman Law and the Early Church" in *The Catacombs and the Colosseum,* ed. Stephen Benko and John J. O'Rourke (Valley Forge, Pa.: Judson Press, 1971), 179.

31. Richardson points out that only the Jews (as opposed to the Christians) were in a position to make the distinction clear to the Romans because they had some imperial court contacts. Furthermore, the indignation that the Jews would have felt over the expulsion and related disruptions served as sufficient motivation (Richardson, *Israel in the Apostolic Church,* 42).

32. Esler's sociological description of how the "church-sect" model relates to tension between the Jewish and Christian communities is consonant with this conclusion. He points out that the "church" — the Jewish community in this case — is likely to use the "state" to get at the "sect" — the Christian community in this case. The state is more likely to support the church because it is more conservative and stable (Esler, *Community and Gospel in Luke-Acts,* 22–23).

33. Tacitus stands alone among ancient historians in linking the execution of the Christians with the great fire (Tac. *Ann.* 15.44). Suetonius presented Nero's measures as merely the suppression of a "pernicious superstition" (Suet. *Nero* 16.2). Early Christian writers do not depend on the fire to explain the outburst. Clement of Rome, writing within a generation of the event, says that "malice" and "jealousy" toward the Christians was the cause (1 Clem. 5–6). Smallwood and others have noted that the only people who would have felt malice and jealousy toward the Christians during this period would have been the Jews (E. Mary Smallwood, *The Jews under Roman Rule* [Leiden: E. J. Brill, 1976], 218).

34. T. D. Barnes, "Legislation against the Christians," 49. W. H. C. Frend

in his volume *Martyrdom and Persecution in the Early Church* (Oxford: Basil Blackwell, 1965) writes of this period:

> The persecution represented a triumph for the orthodox Jews, who were able, through influence at Court, to shift the odium of the outbreak on the hated schismatics, the Christian synagogue. This they hoped to destroy at a single tremendous blow. In the persons of Poppaea Sabina and the actor Tigellinus they had the ear of the Emperor, and they succeeded in so far as a great number of Christians were killed, including the leaders, Peter and Paul. (164)

Although evidence is lacking to support Frend's hypothesis that the Jews were directly responsible for the persecution of the Christians under Nero, it is possible that the outbreak was in fact related to the Jewish-Christian conflict, albeit indirectly. Marcel Simon nuances "the Jewish factor" carefully in his explanation of the anti-Christian measures taken by the Romans:

> Even if we cannot unreservedly follow the early Christian apologists when they blame the Jews for initiating the persecutions, we must still ask to what extent the Jews were involved and what part they did play. The question of their responsibility, even if it was only indirect, must still be raised and it seems to me it is capable of being answered. (Simon, *Verus Israel,* 98)

35. Wayne Meeks, "Breaking Away: Three New Testament Pictures of Christianity's Separation from the Jewish Communities," in *To See Ourselves as Others See Us: Christians, Jews, "Others" in Late Antiquity,* ed. Jacob Neusner and Ernest S. Frerichs (Chico, Calif.: Scholars Press, 1985), 106.

36. This may explain why Paul gets so personal in Romans 9; his experience is paradigmatic for them. The pain of Jewish Christians in Rome was not unlike that which Paul experienced in his own radical resocialization — from sharing table with Pharisees to sharing table with gentiles.

37. Alan F. Segal, *Rebecca's Children: Judaism and Christianity in the Roman World* (Cambridge, Mass.: Harvard University Press, 1986), 114.

38. Although it may have been safe to return sooner, the edict would have become a dead letter with the death of Claudius in 54 C.E. (James D. G. Dunn, *Romans,* 2 vols. Word Biblical Commentary [Dallas: Word Books, 1988], 1:liii).

39 The existence of house-churches independent of the Jewish synagogues by the time of the Roman letter attests this transition. Note the absence of a singular salutation ("to the church at Rome") in the letter. Furthermore, the admonition to greet the church in the house of Aquila and Priscilla assumes the existence of other house-churches (16:3–5). See Paul Minear, *Obedience of Faith,* Studies in Biblical Theology 19 (London: SCM Press, 1971), 24.

40. Most of these converts would have come from foreign immigrants who lived and worked among the Christians across the Tiber.

41. See 1 Thessalonians 2:14ff, as well as the gospel accounts of the crucifixion.

42. The turmoil they experienced would have been similar to that reflected in the Fourth Gospel, where coping with exclusion from the synagogue community was clearly problematic. Of the Johannine situation Meeks writes: "Traumatically divorced from the synagogues, Johannine Christians made a new life for themselves within private houses, starting anew just as Jewish or Samaritan immigrants in Diaspora cities had often done when they first arrived" (Meeks, "Breaking Away," 102).

43. The expulsion of the Jewish couple Aquila and Priscilla is tangible evidence of a leadership change that was prompted by the edict (Acts 18:2; Rom. 16:3–5).

44. Wolfgang Wiefel, "The Jewish Community in Ancient Rome and the Origins of Roman Christianity," 113.

45. Victor Furnish, *The Moral Teaching of Paul* (Nashville: Abingdon, 1979), 116–17.

46. A representative of the first group would be J. C. O'Neill, *Paul's Letter to the Romans* (Baltimore: Penguin, 1975), 209–10. Characteristic of the second group would be Ernst Bammel, "Romans 13," in *Jesus and the Politics of His Day*, ed. Ernst Bammel and C. F. D. Moule (Cambridge: University Press, 1984), 381. The latter group would include Furnish, *The Moral Teaching of Paul*, 135.

47. The notion of governing authorities operating under authority granted by God did not originate with Paul. Similar statements are found in Israel's literature, particularly in the wisdom tradition (see Prov. 24:21 and Wisd. 6:4–11). The possibility of Paul expressing himself in this way may also reflect Stoic influence. Not only does the strong notion of creative order closely parallel Stoic views, but Paul's appeal to "conscience" as the reason why Christians should be subject reverberates with Stoic overtones. In this regard, see Howard Clark Kee, "Pauline Eschatology: Relationships with Apocalyptic and Stoic Thought," in *Glaube und Eschatologie*, Festschrift für Werner Georg Kümmel zum 80. Geburtstag, ed. E. Grasser and O. Mark (Tübingen: J. C. B. Mohr, 1985), 149. Furthermore, the notion is not without at least a rough parallel in the New Testament canon (see 1 Pet. 2:17) and may reflect widespread Christian paraenesis.

48. Some scholars, like Barrett, have maintained in a general way that "there may have been good reasons, unknown to us, why this example [obedience to magistrates] should have been chosen" in a discussion of practical Christian virtues. Though he is no doubt correct that there were good reasons why this text was included, his claim that the reasons are wholly unknown unreasonably ignores considerable evidence. See C. K. Barrett, *The Epistle to the Romans,* Black's New Testament Commentaries (London: Adam and Charles Black, 1957), 244. Even Käsemann agrees that "it must be oriented concretely to the situation

in Rome" (*Commentary on Romans*, trans. G. Bromiley [Philadelphia: Fortress, 1980], 364).

49. Not surprisingly, J. Christiaan Beker, a scholar committed to the apocalyptic structure of Paul's gospel, argues that the pericope must be interpreted in light of a *Sitz im Leben* that occasioned it and helps to explain its difficult contents.

50. Scholars have often been intrigued by the rather pointed command in Romans 13:6, 7 to pay one's taxes. Three German scholars, Friedrich, Pohlmann, and Stuhlmacher, have recently argued that the command has a correspondingly pointed explanation (Johannes Friedrich, Wolfgang Pohlmann, and Peter Stuhlmacher, "Zur historischen Situation und Intention von Rom 13, 1–7," *Zeitschrift für Theologie und Kirche* 73 [1976]: 131–66). They have drawn attention to the fact that historical records of tax riots under Nero correspond to the time frame of the Roman letter. Tacitus says that the popular sentiment against the excessive greed of the revenue collectors was so great that Nero considered repealing all "indirect taxes." However, he was discouraged by senators who after initial praises warned that after these were abolished there would be demands for the abolition of the "direct taxes" as well. The extent of the uprising is indicated not only by the initial response of Nero but also by the extensive overhaul of the system that was subsequently ordered (Tac. *Ann.* 13.50f).

The epistle to the Romans was written approximately two years prior to the enactment of these changes. Hence, it comes during the very period when the protests were occurring that finally precipitated changes in the system.

Although the timing of this crisis alone raises intriguing possibilities for correlation, it is the vocabulary of 13:6, 7 that has convinced scholars of the connection. Friedrich, Pohlmann, and Stuhlmacher have pointed out that the terms Paul used for the taxes in the passage are the Greek equivalents of the Latin terms for "direct" and "indirect" taxes. The direct taxes (Latin: *tributum;* Greek: *phoros;* RSV: "taxes") were collected by government officials. The indirect taxes (Latin: *portoria* [and *vectigalia*]; Greek: *telos;* RSV: "revenue") were primarily harbor fees and *ad valorem* duties on exports and imports. It is these taxes, collected (and exploited) by companies of Roman knights, that were chiefly responsible for the crisis mentioned by Tacitus.

Chapter Four
Ethnic Issues in Romans

1. A. J. M. Wedderburn, *Reasons for Romans* (Edinburgh: T. & T. Clark, 1988), 64.

2. Unlike most scholars, E. P. Sanders makes no attempt to harmonize the chapter with Pauline thought or the content of the Roman letter. He emphasizes (exaggerates?) how uncharacteristic of Paul the content of chapter 2 actually is:

In Romans 2 we are dealing with a point of view which at no point reflects specifically Christian thinking.

... It stands out because it deals directly with salvation and makes salvation dependent on obedience to the law. What is said about the law in Romans 2 cannot be fitted into a category otherwise known from Paul's letters, and for that reason it has been dealt with in an appendix. (E. P. Sanders, *Paul, the Law and the Jewish People* [Philadelphia: Fortress, 1983], 132)

A similar approach is adopted by Heikki Räisänen. See his *Paul and the Law* (Philadelphia: Fortress, 1983), 97–109.

For recent attempts at explaining the tension, see Snodgrass, "Justification by Grace — To the Doers: An Analysis of the Place of Romans 2 in the Theology of Paul," *New Testament Studies* 32 (1986): 72–93; and Karl Donfried, "Justification and Last Judgment in Paul," *Zeitschrift für die neutestamentliche Wissenschaft* 67 (1976): 90–110; Douglas J. Moo, " 'Law,' 'Works of the Law,' and Legalism in Paul," *Westminster Theological Journal* 45 (1983): 73–100.

3. Krister Stendahl, *Paul among Jews and Gentiles* (Philadelphia: Fortress, 1976), 3.

4. Nils Alstrup Dahl, *Studies in Paul: Theology for the Early Christian Mission* (Minneapolis: Augsburg Press, 1977), 80.

5. Jouette M. Bassler, "Divine Impartiality: Paul and a Theological Axiom," Society of Biblical Literature Dissertation Series 59 (Chico, Calif.: Scholars Press, 1982), 121. See also her "Divine Impartiality in Paul's Letter to the Romans," *Novum Testamentum* 26 (1984): 43–58.

6. J. A. Fischer, "Pauline Literary Forms and Thought Patterns," *Catholic Biblical Quarterly* 39 (1977): 209–23.

7. Bassler, "Divine Impartiality," 135.

8. See for example, Ernst Käsemann, *Commentary on Romans*, trans. G. Bromiley (Philadelphia: Fortress, 1980), 52. For a lengthy bibliography, see Bassler, "Divine Impartiality," 249, n. 1.

9. "The sudden turning in 2:1 is a well known problem to commentators, but is completely in tune with this style of address" (Stanley Stowers, *The Diatribe and Paul's Letter to the Romans*, Society of Biblical Literature Dissertation Series 57 [Chico, Calif.: Scholars Press, 1981], 93ff).

10. Ibid., 110.

11. Lietzmann argues that *dio* can be a colorless particle (*An die Römer,* Handbuch zum Neuen Testament [Tübingen: Mohr, 1906], 37–39). That the problem results from a gloss is the suggestion of Bultmann ("Glossen im Römerbrief," *Theologische Literaturzeitung* 72 [1947]: 197–202). A. Fridrichsen thinks it is a mistake; *dis* is not supposed to be there ("Quatre conjectures sur le texte du Nouveau Testament," *Revue d'historie et de philosophie religieuses* 3 [1923]: 439ff). Käsemann smooths out the problem by suggesting 2:1 is an interpolation (*Commentary on Romans,* 54).

12. Wayne Meeks, "Judgment and the Brother: Romans 14:1–15:13," in *Tradition and Interpretation in the New Testament,* essays in honor of E. Earle Ellis, ed. Gerald F. Hawthorne with Otto Betz (Grand Rapids, Mich.: Eerdmans, 1987), 296.

13. Bassler, "Divine Impartiality," 128.

14. The typical nature of the polemic has been long compared to that of Wisdom of Solomon 11–15 (see Dunn, *Romans,* 1:53ff.). Allusions to Israel's idolatry are Psalm 106:20 and Jeremiah 2:11 (see C. E. B. Cranfield, *Commentary on Romans,* International Critical Commentary [Edinburgh: T. & T. Clark, 1975], 1:119f).

15. Meeks, "Judgment and the Brother," 296. The repetition of the formula "to the Jew first and also the Greek" (1:16) at 2:9, 10 also indicates that 2:1–10 belongs to the argument of 1:16–32. In fact, a deliberate *Ringkomposition* has been postulated by Pohlenz in a detailed study that highlights both the return to "the Jew first and also the Greek" as well as the revelation of divine wrath (1:18) that is picked back up at 2:5. Another obvious link between the chapters is *anapologetos* (2:1) which parallels the *anapologetous* of 1:20 (Max Pohlenz, "Paulus und die Stoa," *Zeitschrift für de neutestamentliche Wissenschaft* 42 [1949]: 69–104, esp. 73f).

16. Cranfield, *Commentary on Romans,* 1:105.

17. Bassler, "Divine Impartiality," 135.

18. Ibid., 128.

19. E. Klostermann, "Die Adäquate Vergeltung in Rom 1:22–31," *Zeitschrift für die neutestamentliche Wissenschaft* 32 (1933): 1–6.

20. Klostermann outlines the argument into three periods, which begin in verses 22, 25, and 28. This breakdown results from his contention that Paul consistently follows the reference to the sin by its corresponding retribution.

21. Bassler, "Divine Impartiality," 128.

22. Ibid., 135.

23. Ibid., 121.

24. Meeks, "Judgment and the Brother," 296.

25. Note especially the vocabulary connections: *erga, kauchesis, pistis, dikaioo.* For a discussion of the continuity of the argument between 3:27 and 4:25 based on the dialogical exchanges of 3:27–4:2, see Stowers, *The Diatribe,* 155–74.

26. See Dunn's analysis of chapter 4 as a midrash on Genesis 15:6 (James D. G. Dunn, *Romans,* 2 vols. Word Biblical Commentary [Dallas: Word Books, 1988], 1:196ff).

27. W. S. Campbell, "The Freedom and Faithfulness of God in Relation to Israel," *Journal for the Study of the New Testament* 13 (1981): 27–45, esp. 39.

28. Bassler, "Divine Impartiality," 160.

29. It also reappears in chapters 9–11, but its function there will be examined later in this study.

30. Bassler's comment that they (Jews and gentiles) will be judged "in different, but equivalent ways," allows more "difference" than Paul does (see Bassler, "Divine Impartiality," 140).

31. On the contrary, it can place one at the head of the line for tribulation and distress (2:9).

32. Stowers, *The Diatribe*, 96ff. Note the parallels in Epictetus, "Why then, do you call yourself a Stoic?" (Epict. *Diss.* 2.19.19; 3.7.17; 3.24.41).

33. The description of the Jew, particularly as one who possesses the law and functions as teacher of the nations reflects the situation of Diaspora synagogues (Käsemann, *Commentary on Romans*, 70f).

34. The veracity of this claim is shown by Paul's own usage of circumcision/ uncircumcision as equivalent to Jew/gentile (Rom. 2:26; 3:30; Gal. 2:7). That circumcision was the basic identity marker for Jews in the city of Rome is illustrated by references in Roman authors (Petron. *Sat.* 102.14; Tac. *Hist.* 5.5.2; Juv. *Sat.* 14.99). For more information regarding Roman views of Jews and Judaism in the capital, see pp. 37–40 and 45–53 of this study.

35. Bassler, "Divine Impartiality," 151.

36. The radical redefinitions Paul offers inevitably raise the question, Then what advantage has the Jew? (3:1). Paul assures the reader at this point that the advantages of the Jews are not erased. However, his defense of this apparently contradictory assertion is postponed until chapter 9.

37. Even the Jews would have accepted the theologumenon in principle since Jewish literature commonly defended the justice of God's judgment by affirming God's impartiality (Deut. 1:16–17; 16:18–19; Lev. 19:15; Ps. 82:1–2; Pss. Sol. 2:17–19; 1 Enoch 63:8–9; Jub. 5:12–16, et al.).

38. The assumption that they are Christians runs counter to the logic of the passage but is often assumed because of the theological tension caused by Paul's affirmations in chapter 2 that seem to run counter to the theme of justification by faith. For a discussion of views that are put forward to explain the tension, see Sanders, *Paul, the Law and the Jewish People*, 125–27. See also Snodgrass, "Justification by Grace — To the Doers," 73–74.

39. Dunn, *Romans*, 1:106. For a discussion of the various "ways of evading the text," see Snodgrass, "Justification by Grace — to the Doers," 73–74, and the bibliography cited there.

40. See the excellent discussion by Kuhr, "Römer 2:14f. und die Verheissung bei Jeremia 31:31ff.," *Zeitschrift für die neutestamentliche Wissenschaft* 55 (1964): 243–61.

41. Dunn, *Romans*, 1:107.

42. E.g., Sen. *Epist.* 28.10; Philo assumes as much, see Philo *Abr.* 275–76. See Grundmann, *"agathos"* in *Theological Dictionary of the New Testament*, 1:11f; and Maurer, *"suneidesis"* in *Theological Dictionary of the New Testament*, 7:902ff; Margaret Thrall, "The Pauline Use of *Suneidesis*," *New Testament Studies* 14 (1967–68): 897–918. Connections with Stoic thought abound in the passage.

The Stoic understanding of nature and conscience are useful for Paul's argument for common ground because they assume the universality of knowledge and moral insight. For a discussion of the connections between Paul and Stoic ideas, see Howard Clark Kee, "Pauline Eschatology: Relationships with Apocalyptic and Stoic Thought," in *Glaube und Eschatologie,* Festschrift für Werner Georg Kümmel zum 80. Geburtstag, ed. E. Grasser and O. Mark (Tübingen: J. C. B. Mohr, 1985), 135–58.

43. Ernst Käsemann rejects the gentile Christian interpretation of 2:6–16 but interprets the "true Jew" of 2:28–29 as a gentile Christian (Käsemann, *Commentary on Romans,* 73–75). However, the nature of Paul's argument also vitiates the insertion of "Christian" in 2:28–29. Christians are neither mentioned nor alluded to from 1:18–3:20! For the arguments in favor of identifying the gentiles as Christian gentiles, see Cranfield, *The Epistle to the Romans,* 1:152ff; Felix Flückiger, "Die Werke des Gesetzes bei den Heiden (nach Röm 2,14ff)," *Theologische Zeitschrift* 8 (1952): 17–42.

44. Bassler, "Divine Impartiality," 142.

45. The contrast here between Galatians and Romans is striking. See Beker, *Paul the Apostle* (Philadelphia: Fortress, 1980), 99, and Sampley, "Romans and Galatians: Comparison and Contrast," in *Understanding the Word,* essays in honor of Bernard Anderson, ed. J. Butler, E. Conrad, B. Ollenburger (Sheffield: JSOT, 1985): 315–39.

46. Ibid., 322–23. Sampley points out that in Romans Paul speaks of

> God's righteousness (1:17), God's wrath (1:18), God's judgment (2:2), God's kindness (2:4; 11:21), God's love (8:39), God's severity (11:21), God's gifts and call (11:29)....In the same way, the questions that focus Paul's reflection are questions that center upon God: "Is God unjust to inflict wrath on us?" (3:5); "Has the word of God failed?" (9:6); "Is there injustice on God's part?" (9:19); "Has the potter no right over the clay?" (9:21); and "Has God rejected Israel?" (11:1). By contrast to all these questions concerning God and God's purposes, there is only one question about Christ in all of Romans (8:34).

47. I.e., "All Israel will be saved" (11:26). Note especially 11:25–32. See the discussion of the argument in Romans 11 later in this study, pp. 77–84.

48. Meeks, "Judgment and the Brother," 295f.

49. It is interesting that Käsemann has argued that 2:1 is an interpolation because accepting it would place the accent of the verse on judging. "But Paul's concern is not with judging others," he writes. However, that is precisely Paul's concern if the opening argument is properly understood in relation to the situation in Rome!

50. Stowers, *The Diatribe,* 115. Although Stowers is convinced that the rhetorical approach Paul utilizes so often in Romans (the diatribe) is responsible for the development of the argument at times, he does admit that the diatribe's function in the teacher-student relationship can reflect the actual situation of

the student. Hence, mirror reading every interlocutor's objection is unacceptable. However, that does not at all mean that the general views of the "student" cannot be recognized by looking at patterns in the exchanges. Unmasking pretentiousness and arrogance, for example, seem to be standard functions of the diatribe. On diatribe in general and its influence of Christian polemic literature, see *Oxford Classical Dictionary,* 2nd ed., 338, and bibliography cited there.

51. But see 2 Tim. 2:8. Scott Gambrill Sinclair, *Jesus Christ according to Paul* (Berkeley, Calif.: Bibal Press, 1988), 34. For Jesus' Davidic descent in early Christian usage, see Raymond Brown, *The Birth of the Messiah* (New York: Doubleday, 1977), 505–12.

52. The fact that "the exposition of that theme ('The gospel is a power of God for salvation') continues through Rom. 9–11 ('Jew first and Greek') and right up to the conclusion of the paraenesis in 15:7–13" leads Dahl to insist that 1:16 is not only the theme of chapters 1–8 but of the "whole body" (1:16–15:13) (Dahl, "Missionary Theology in Romans," in *Studies in Paul,* 82).

53. The phrase has received a variety of interpretations though three are most common, as Sampley has noted ("Romans and Galatians," 329):

1. A rhetorically inclusive way of saying "everybody."

2. A reflection of the growth of early Christianity, beginning as a sectarian movement within Judaism and among Jews, and then becoming predominantly non-Jewish ("the Jew first, and then the Greek").

3. A claim of some significant priority of the Jews over gentiles.

The third option is the only viable alternative in view of the actual content and argument of the Roman letter, particularly chapters 9–11. This will be apparent in the following analysis of this section.

54. See Philippians 3:5, where a similar list is set aside by Paul as indicative of self-confident boasting.

55. It was F. C. Baur who first attempted to free these chapters from dogmatic treatments concerned primarily with the theology of election by asserting a *Sitz im Leben* that would explain their contents. Regarding chapters 9–11 Baur wrote:

> Everything which the apostle develops in the first eight chapters is the necessary presupposition for cutting off at its roots the Jewish particularism, which opposes the apostle's universalism not in Judaism as a whole, but in the Christian church itself. (Ferdinand Christian Baur, *The Church History of the First Three Centuries* [London, 1875], 1:174)

Baur's premise of a dominant Jewish Christianity in Rome caused him to read almost everything in the letter as an attack on Jewish particularism. Consequently, he failed to recognize that Paul was attempting to defend the priority of Israel, not destroy it. Francis Watson's approach offers a modern version of Baur's thesis (Watson, *Paul, Judaism and the Gentiles*).

56. R. David Kaylor, *Paul's Covenant Community: Jew and Gentile in Romans* (Atlanta: John Knox Press, 1988), 159.

57. Nils Dahl has argued that Romans 9–11 reflects an epistolary style that suggests that in these chapters Paul "addresses the epistolary situation more directly than in most parts of Romans 1–8" (Dahl, "The Future of Israel," in *Studies in Paul,* 141). Although Dahl grants that the situation may have been related to the edict of Claudius (49 C.E.), he prefers to read chapters 9–11 in terms of the delivery of the contribution to Jerusalem (*Studies in Paul,* 141–42).

58. See for example Cranfield, *Romans* 2:568. Williams also sees the exhortation in terms of gentile Christians disposed to write off the Jews' special relationship to God as over and done with; this stands out in view of his inclination to read Romans in light of Paul's defense in Jerusalem (S. K. Williams, "The 'Righteousness of God' in Romans," *Journal of Biblical Literature* 99 [1980]: 252).

59. Getty is correct when she acknowledges:

> The two parts of 11:28 juxtapose apparently contradictory ideas in a way characteristic of the development throughout Romans 9–11. The Jews are said to be enemies of God as regards the gospel, but beloved of God as regards their election. The two poles of Paul's tension are the gospel and the abiding faithfulness of God to Israel. These are two fundamentals Paul is unable to surrender. (Mary Ann Getty, "Paul and the Salvation of Israel: A Perspective on Romans 9–11," *Catholic Biblical Quarterly* 50 [July 1988]: 462)

60. See the comments of Campbell regarding the relationship between the beginning of chapter 3 and chapters 9–11: W. S. Campbell, "Romans 3 as a Key to the Structure and Thought of the Letter," *Novum Testamentum* 23 (1981): 33.

61. J. Christiaan Beker, "The Faithfulness of God and the Priority of Israel in Paul's Letter to the Romans," in *Christians among Jews and Gentiles,* essays in honor of Krister Stendahl, ed. George Nickelsburg and George MacRae (Philadelphia: Fortress, 1986), 14.

62. Stowers, *The Diatribe,* 114.

63. This is the same way Paul used the cross in 1 Corinthians 1 and the resurrection of Christ in 1 Corinthians 15.

64. Although Paul does not allude to the faithfulness of God until verse 6, the reader already has it in sight because of the conclusion of chapter 8. Paul commonly begins the transition to the next section in the conclusion of the preceding one in the Roman letter. This can cause considerable problems for outliners on occasion (e.g., the problems determining whether to put chapter 5 with what precedes it or what follows it). See Cranfield, *Romans,* 1:252ff. Paul's paradoxical division of Israel at 9:6 ("For not all who are descended from Israel belong to Israel") does not differentiate between the *ethnos* of Israel and believing Israel ("the church"). The argument of chapter 11 clearly confirms this

(H. Hübner, *Gottes Ich und Israel: Zum Schriftgebrauch des Paulus in Römer 9–11* [Göttingen: Vandenhoeck & Ruprecht, 1984], 17).

65. Dahl, "Future of Israel," 143. The inability of Räisänen and Watson to avoid the conclusion that decisive contradictions exist between chapters 9 and 11 results from their failure to recognize that 9:6ff is concerned with the nature of election, how it works. Paul is not attempting to defend the faithfulness of God by denying Israel was ever elected (contra Watson, *Paul, Judaism and the Gentiles*, 227, n. 9) but to prove the priority of Israel on the basis of God's faithfulness. The view of H. Räisänen is similar to that of Watson; see "Römer 9–11: Analyse eines geistigen Ringens," *Aufstieg und Niedergang der römischen Welt*, 2.25.4, ed. Wolfgang Haase (Berlin and New York: Walter de Gruyter, 1987), 2891–2939.

66. Sampley, "Romans and Galatians: Comparison and Contrast," 331.

67. Without this clarification at the outset of Paul's affirmation of Israel's priority, chapters 9–11 would open the door for ethnic pretension and arrogance on the part of the Jewish Christians. Furthermore, by challenging Israel's special status on the basis of ethnicity and works Paul draws gentile readers sympathetically into his argument.

68. Paul deals briefly with the interlocutor's misgivings about God's apparent arbitrary choices but finally accuses those who would get stuck on this point of standing in judgment of God (9:20).

69. The significance of this matter is highlighted by the astute comment of Beker: "The total sweep of the argument of Romans is held together by the theme of the peculiar interaction between Israel's particularity and the universality of the gospel for the Gentiles" ("The Faithfulness of God and the Priority of Israel in Paul's Letter to the Romans," 14).

70. His own ministry had afforded him ample opportunity to experience Jewish rejection of the gospel.

71. "What if some were unfaithful? Does their faithlessness nullify the faithfulness of God? By no means! Let God be true though every man be false" (3:3f).

72. Dunn is correct when he points out that in 9:30–10:21 "Paul has now exposed the fact and character of Israel's unbelief in increasingly explicit terms" (Dunn, *Romans*, 2:632). However, he does not sufficiently account for the function of the passage. Wedderburn's suggestion that Paul has to carry the argument on two fronts reflects the complexity of the situation Paul addresses (Wedderburn, *Reasons for Romans*, 136). However, chapters 9–11 are primarily addressing gentile pretension and arrogance. George Kennedy is correct when he writes, "Verses 9:1–11:36 are addressed to gentiles to provide an understanding of the situation of Jews" (George Kennedy, *New Testament Interpretation through Rhetorical Criticism* [Chapel Hill: University of North Carolina Press, 1984], 154).

73. This is similar to the approach Paul uses in 2 Corinthians 10–13. Paul

readily grants the contention of his opponents that he is weak because his apostolic credentials were not based on his own strength.

74. Dahl, *Studies in Paul,* 149. Or as Boers puts it, "Paul finds assurance in the incident with Elijah that God has not rejected his people" (Hendrikus Boers, "The Problem of Jews and Gentiles in the Macro-Structure of Romans," *Exegetisk Arsbok* 13 [1982]: 192).

75. Getty, "Paul and the Salvation of Israel," 461.

76. Dahl believes that "all Israel" refers to the remnant and the "others" of 11:7 ("Future of Israel," 153). Given Paul's view of judgment it is possible that "all Israel" means Israel as a whole, individual exceptions notwithstanding (Dunn, *Romans,* 2:681; see the bibliography cited in Dunn concerning this question). With regard to the lively debate concerning whether Israel's salvation depends on acceptance of the messiahship of Jesus, see the discussion of Kaylor, who sets out the issues and considers the recent positions represented by Gager and Gaston (Kaylor, *Paul's Covenant Community,* 183–90).

77. "If God in his impartiality could not permit the first situation to prevail (chapters 1–3), no more can he endure the second" (Bassler, *Divine Impartiality,* 162).

78. Meeks, "Judgment and the Brother," 297.

79. Stowers, *The Diatribe,* 115.

80. Getty, "Paul and the Salvation of Israel," 469.

81. Robinson claims that "the aim of Romans is to show the Gentiles how their hope rests on Israel's Messiah" (D. W. B. Robinson, "The Priesthood of Paul in the Gospel of Hope," in *Reconciliation and Hope: New Testament Essays on Atonement and Eschatology,* essays in honor of Leon Morris, ed. R. J. Banks [Exeter: Paternoster, 1974]: 232). Similarly, Sinclair has shown that in three significant christological passages in Romans (1:1–5; 9:1–5; and 15:8–12) Paul attempts to show that the Jews "somehow have a privileged relationship to Jesus — that he is somehow especially their savior" (Sinclair, *Jesus Christ according to Paul,* 30).

82. Although Paul identifies both dietary matters and special days as boundary markers in the pericope, his discussion centers upon dietary concerns. Matters relating to special days do not come up again after 14:6 while those relating to diet arise again in 14:14, 15, 20, 21, 23. The emphasis is probably due to the greater effect of dietary restrictions on community interaction.

83. Romans 14:14 also reflects this consideration: "I know and am persuaded in the Lord Jesus that nothing is unclean in itself; but it is unclean for any one who thinks it unclean."

84. Meeks, "Judgment and the Brother," 291.

85. See Cranfield's discussion of the six most common theses in Cranfield, *The Epistle to the Romans,* 2:690–98; see also Käsemann's survey of the various approaches along with his critical comments (Käsemann, *Commentary on Romans,* 367–68).

86. Robert Karris, "Romans 14:1–15:13 and the Occasion of Romans," in *The Romans Debate*, ed. Karl Donfried (Minneapolis: Augsburg Press, 1977), 81. Jewett has a similar criticism (Robert Jewett, *Paul's Anthropological Terms* [Leiden: E. J. Brill, 1971], 45–46), and Käsemann's critique of several approaches comes down ultimately to the same criticism (see Käsemann, *Commentary on Romans*, 367–68).

87. Dunn, *Romans*, 2:799–800. Käsemann grants the problem is Jewish but opts for a syncretistic group comparable to persons reflected in Galatians 4:9f and Colossians 2:16ff. However, correlation with the larger document remains problematic given this view. Käsemann's awareness of this weakness is apparent in his introduction to 14:1–15:13; he can find firm connections between 1 Corinthians 8 and other parts of 1 Corinthians, but cannot find evidence of his syncretistic group elsewhere in Romans (*Commentary on Romans*, 364).

88. The mention of abstention from wine in 14:21 receives less attention because in the text it is not directly mentioned as a practice of the "weak" and because the context favors its inclusion for rhetorical purposes. Drinking is naturally paired with eating. Moreover, the phrase "or drink wine" is the second in a series of three, the last of which is "nor do anything." See Cranfield, *Romans*, 2:725 and Meeks, "Judgment and the Brother," 292. Rauer has observed that if the "weak" actually abstained from wine they would not have been able to participate in the Lord's Supper (M. Rauer, *Die "Schwachen" in Korinth und Rom nach den Paulusbriefen* [Freiburg im Breisgau: Herder, 1923], 97).

89. This is the view advocated by Peter Lampe, *Die Stadtrömischen Christen in den ersten beiden Jahrhunderten* (Tübingen: J. C. B. Mohr, 1987), 57.

90. Jos. *Life*, 14.

91. Barrett is still correct here, *pace* Dunn. See Barrett, *Romans*, 256; Dunn, *Romans*, 2:801.

92. Against Watson, *Paul, Judaism and the Gentiles*, 95f. See the interpretation of the edict and its effect on the Jewish and Christian communities of Rome presented earlier, pp. 57–64.

93. W. Sanday and A. C. Headlam, *Romans*, International Critical Commentary (Edinburgh: T. & T. Clark, 1895; 1902), 385. This is in fact the view of Karris ("Romans 14:1–15:13 and the Occasion of Romans," 90). Note also the comment of Jewett:

> It is clear from the wording of these verses (14:1–3) that Paul selected the extreme positions on opposite ends of the liberal-conservative spectrum in Rome, with the absolute vegetarian on one end and the complete libertarian on the other, in order to make the principle of tolerance inclusive of all the positions inside this range. (Robert Jewett, *Christian Tolerance* [Philadelphia: Westminster, 1982], 30)

94. Harry Gamble, *The Textual History of the Letter to the Romans* (Grand Rapids, Mich.: Eerdmans, 1977), 136. Gamble makes this comment in the same paragraph where he already stated, "If this section (14:1–15:6) were found in another letter it would not be regarded as merely 'theoretical' or paradigmatic; it would be understood in a highly specific way."

95. Meeks, "Judgment and the Brother," 292f.

96. This rhetorical strategy is not limited to the pericope at hand. In the opening argument of the letter Paul indicts gentiles and Jews for their sins in correspondingly oblique terms (see esp. 1:18–2:11). The apostle's use of the terms *pas* and *anthropos* in the indictment betray Paul's strategy. For a fuller discussion, see the discussion of God's impartiality earlier in this chapter (pp. 68–77).

97. Jewett also stresses the rhetorical function of Paul's "vagueness." He finds the approach consistent with Paul's "ambassadorial purpose" in Romans (Jewett, *Christian Tolerance*, 26).

98. See the discussion of Israel's priority earlier in this chapter (pp. 77–84).

99. Because it was the distinctive character of Judaism that attracted many of these gentiles initially and because they had been willing to make significant sacrifices to "live the life of a Jew," it is doubtful that upon conversion to Christianity they would have quickly dropped Jewish observances.

100. Peter Lampe, *Die Stadtrömischen Christen*, 57; U. Wilckens, *Der Brief an die Römer* (Zurich: Neukirchener Verlag, 1979–82), 3:112f; Dunn, *Romans*, 2:800; note the following examples of the distinctive usage of *koinon:* 1 Maccabees 1.47.62; Jos. *Ant*, 3.1811; 11.346; 12.320; 13.4.

101. Wedderburn, *Reasons for Romans*, 32. Contra Karris who claims that "love" is the link between 15:1–6 and 15:7–13, not Jews and gentiles (Karris, "Romans 14:1–15:13 and the Occasion of Romans," 93f). Karris argues this in spite of the fact that the word "love" appears nowhere in the two paragraphs (see Donfried's criticisms of Karris's effort in "False Presuppositions in the Study of Romans," in *The Romans Debate*, ed. Karl Donfried [Minneapolis: Augsburg Press, 1977], 130–31).

102. Meeks, "Judgment and the Brother," 292. Similarly Dunn, "Above all Paul's whole point is that Christ became servant of the circumcised not with a view to their salvation alone, but to confirm both phases of God's saving purpose: to Jew first but also to Gentile" (*Romans*, 2:848). For a detailed discussion concerning the problematic relationship between verses 8 and 9, see A. E. S. Nababan, "Bekenntnis und Mission in Römer 14 und 15," Ph.D. dissertation (Heidelberg, 1963), 115–18.

103. Victor Furnish, *The Love Command in the New Testament* (Nashville: Abingdon, 1972), 115.

104. Karris, "Romans 14:1–15:13 and the Occasion of Romans," 86f.

105. The common material is readily explicable in terms of the prior writing of the Corinthian letter and Paul's own conviction regarding proper behav-

ior in circumstances wherein the behavior of some endangered the faith of others.

106. Ibid., 88.

107. Ibid.

108. Käsemann calls mutual acceptance the "catchword in this whole portion of the epistle" (Käsemann, *Commentary on Romans*, 365).

109. Pressure of this kind is reflected in the list of minimal requirements to be observed by gentiles in Acts 15:19–21. Gentiles are to submit to these restrictions because "from early generations Moses has had in every city those who preach him, for he is read every sabbath in the synagogues" (15:21).

110. Although he treats the effects of the Claudian edict too simplistically, the comments of Wiefel are perceptive: Wolfgang Wiefel, "The Jewish Community in Ancient Rome and the Origins of Roman Christianity," in *The Romans Debate*, ed. Karl Donfried (Minneapolis: Augsburg Press, 1977), 110–13.

111. Dunn, *Romans*, 2:800; see Daniel 1:3–16; 10:3; Tobit 1:10–12; Judith 12:2,19; Add. Esth. 14:17; Jos. As. 7.11; 8.5. See also the lengthy discussion of Philip Francis Esler, *Community and Gospel in Luke-Acts* (Cambridge: Cambridge University Press, 1987), 73–109.

112. Dunn, *Romans*, 2:797.

113. Ibid., 2:811.

114. Meeks, "Judgment and the Brother," 290.

115. Michel finds an important link between 14:1–15:13 and the earlier portions of the letter in the tendency of Paul to utilize the quotation of scripture at decisive points to undergird the argument (O. Michel, *Der Brief an der Römer* [Göttingen: Vandenhoeck & Ruprecht, 1966], 335). Wedderburn has argued that the "renewed mind" ties together the entire section 12:1–15:13: "In this way 12:2 may be said to introduce the main thrust of Paul's exhortations in Romans 12:1–15:13, a thrust that is highly relevant to, and directed towards, a specific situation in the Roman church" (Wedderburn, *Reasons for Romans*, 87).

116. Meeks, "Judgment and the Brother," 296.

117. Ibid.

118. In view of the diversity of early Christianity and especially in light of the situation in Rome the assumption that the various house-churches in Rome were distinguished only by geography hardly seems likely.

119. It is clear from the argument of Romans as well as others of Paul's letters that the acceptance of separate Jew-gentile versions of Christianity is unthinkable for the apostle. Romans 1:16 comes to mind as do Galatians 3:28 and 1 Corinthians 12:13. In fact the whole collection enterprise is based on this conviction (Rom. 15:25–27).

Epilogue
The Purpose of Romans
in Light of the Ethnic Issues It Treats

1. See the bibliography cited by James D. G. Dunn, *Romans,* 2 vols. Word Biblical Commentary (Dallas: Word Books, 1988), 1:liv–lv.

2. What "support" entails depends on the interpretation of Romans 15:24: "I hope to see you in passing as I go to Spain, and to be sped on my journey there by you, once I have enjoyed your company for a little." It likely includes provisions and/or monetary help, contacts for hospitality, and possibly even assistants (see Käsemann, *Commentary on Romans,* trans. Geoffrey W. Bromiley [Philadelphia: Fortress, 1980], 398; Dunn, *Romans,* 2:872–73).

3. See also 2 Corinthians 10:13–16. Paul's apostolic mission also includes Roman gentiles. This is evident in Romans 1:14–16. In 15:15–16 it is noteworthy that Paul associates his authority to write the Roman Christians so boldly with the grace given him by God "to be a minister of Christ Jesus to the gentiles."

4. Minear's suspicions were correct here (Paul Minear, *Obedience of Faith,* Studies in Biblical Theology 19 [London: SCM Press, 1971], 2–3).

5. Beker's synopsis of the contents and development of Romans is on target: "The total sweep of the argument of Romans is held together by the theme of the peculiar interaction between Israel's particularity and the universality of the gospel for the Gentiles" (J. Christiaan Beker, "The Faithfulness of God and the Priority of Israel in Paul's Letter to the Romans," in *Christians among Jews and Gentiles,* essays in honor of Krister Stendahl, ed. George Nickelsburg and George MacRae [Philadelphia: Fortress, 1986], 14).

Paul's desire to create common ground is also apparent in chapters 5–8 of Romans. Although ethnic vocabulary is ubiquitous in chapters 1–4 and 9–11, ethnic terms — "Jew," "Jewish," "Israel," "Israelite," or "gentile" — never occur in chapters 5–8. This lengthy passage, though lacking the ethnic terms that indicate Paul's aim in other parts of the letter, functions to highlight common ground as well. In this portion of the letter Paul presents Roman Christians with a "life-world" wherein those in Christ already participate in the triumph of God while awaiting final redemption. Within this framework the alternatives are "Adam" and "Christ," ethnic issues become irrelevant. I believe Beker's synopsis is correct: "Jew and Gentile are now subsumed under the one figure of Adam, who by his transgression sealed 'all men' (*pantas anthropous,* 5:18) under sin and death. The subject is no longer Jew or gentile but 'the many' (*hoi polloi,* 5:19)" (Beker, *Paul the Apostle* [Philadelphia: Fortress, 1980], 85).

6. Jervell, "The Letter to Jerusalem," 68. However, Romans is more than an extended prayer request concerned only with the delivery of the collection, contra Jervell (ibid., 64).

7. Hence Wedderburn's title, *Reasons for Romans.* See also Beker, *Paul the Apostle,* 71–74.

Bibliography

Alfoldy, Geza. *The Social History of Rome.* Translated by David Braund and Frank Pollock. London: Croom Helm, 1975.

Appian. *Civil Wars.* Translated by Horace White. Loeb Classical Library. Cambridge, Mass.: Harvard University Press, 1913.

Ashby, Thomas. "Recent Excavations in Rome." *Classical Quarterly* 2 (1908): 142–50.

Athenaeus. *The Deipnosophists.* Translated by Charles Burton Gulick. Loeb Classical Library. Cambridge, Mass.: Harvard University Press, 1951.

Aune, David. "Orthodoxy in First Century Judaism?" *Journal for the Study of Judaism* 7 (1976): 1–10.

Badian, E. "Tiberius Gracchus and the Roman Revolution." *Aufstieg und Neidergang der römischen Welt* I.1. Edited by Hildegard Temporini. Berlin and New York: Walter de Gruyter, 1974, 668–731.

Balch, David. *Let Wives Be Submissive: The Domestic Code in 1 Peter,* SBL Monograph Series, no. 26. Chico, Calif.: Scholars Press, 1981.

Balsdon, J. P. V. D. *Romans and Aliens.* Chapel Hill: University of North Carolina Press, 1979.

Bammel, Ernst. "Judenverfolgung und Naherwartung: zur Eschatologie des ersten Thessalonicherbriefs." *Zeitschrift für Theologie und Kirche* 56 (1959): 294–315.

———. "Romans 13." In *Jesus and the Politics of His Day.* Edited by Ernst Bammel and C. F. D. Moule. Cambridge: University Press, 1984.

Bang, M. "Die Herkunft der römischen Sklaven." *Mitteilungen des deutschen archaeologischen Instituts* 25 (1910): 223–51.

Barnes, T. D. "Legislation against the Christians." *Journal of Roman Studies* 58 (1968): 32–50.

Barnett, Paul W. "Under Tiberius All Was Quiet." *New Testament Studies* 21 (1975): 564–71.

Barrett, C. K. *The Epistle to the Romans.* Black's New Testament Commentaries. London: Adam and Charles Black, 1957.

Baslez, M. F. "Le rôle et la place des Pheniciens dans la vie économique des ports de l'Egee." In *Studia Phoenicia V.* Edited by E. Lipinski. Leuven: Peeters, 1987.

Bassler, Jouette M. *Divine Impartiality: Paul and a Theological Axiom.* Society of Biblical Literature Dissertation Series 59. Chico, Calif.: Scholars Press, 1982.

————. "Divine Impartiality in Paul's Letter to the Romans." *Novum Testamentum* 26 (1984): 43–58.

Baur, Ferdinand Christian. *Paul the Apostle of Jesus Christ.* Vol. 1, London, 1873.

————. *The Church History of the First Three Centuries.* Vol. 1, London, 1875.

Beker, J. Christiaan. *Paul the Apostle.* Philadelphia: Fortress, 1980.

————. "The Faithfulness of God and the Priority of Israel in Paul's Letter to the Romans." In *Christians among Jews and Gentiles.* Essays in honor of Krister Stendahl. Edited by George Nickelsburg and George MacRae. Philadelphia: Fortress, 1986, 10–16.

Beloch, Juluis. *Die Bevölkerung der griechisch-römischen Welt* Leipzig: Duncker & Humblot, 1886.

Benko, Stephen. "The Edict of Claudius of A.D. 49 and the Instigator Chrestus." *Theologische Zeitschrift* 25 (1969): 406–18.

Berger, Peter L. *The Sacred Canopy: Elements of a Sociological Theory of Religion.* Garden City, N.Y.: Doubleday, 1969.

Berger, Peter L., and T. Luckmann. *The Social Construction of Reality.* Garden City, N.Y.: Doubleday, 1967.

Best, Thomas. "The Sociological Study of the New Testament: Promise and Peril of a New Discipline." *Scottish Journal of Theology* 36 (1983): 245–61.

Blaudau, A. *Juden und Judenverfolgungen im alten Alexandria.* Münster: Aschendorff, 1906.

Boers, Hendrikus. "The Problem of Jews and Gentiles in the Macro-Structure of Romans." *Exegetisk Arsbok* 13 (1982): 184–96.

Bokser, Baruch M. "Recent Developments in the Study of Judaism 70–200 C.E." *Second Century* 3 (1983): 1–68.

Bornkamm, Gunther. "The Letter to the Romans as Paul's Last Will and Testament." In *The Romans Debate.* Edited by Karl Donfried. Minneapolis: Augsburg Press, 1977, 17–31.

Brown, Raymond. *The Birth of the Messiah.* New York: Doubleday, 1977.

Bruce, F. F. "The Romans Debate — Continued." *Bulletin of the John Rylands Library* 64 (1961–62): 334–59.

Bruneau, Philippe. *Recherches sur les cultes de Délos.* Paris: Boccard, 1970.

Brunt, P. A. *Italian Manpower 225 B.C.–A.D. 14.* Oxford: Oxford University Press, 1971.

Bultmann, Rudolf. "Glossen im Römerbrief." *Theologische Literaturzeitung* 72 (1947): 197–202.

Campbell, W. S. "The Freedom and Faithfulness of God in Relation to Israel." *Journal for the Study of the New Testament* 13 (1981): 27–45.

————. "Romans 3 as a Key to the Structure and Thought of the Letter." *Novum Testamentum* 23 (1981): 22–40.

Christ, Karl. *The Romans.* Translated by Christopher Holme. Berkeley: University of California Press, 1984.

Cicero. *De Legibus.* Translated by Clinton W. Keyes. Loeb Classical Library. Cambridge, Mass.: Harvard University Press, 1928.

————. *Letters to Atticus.* Translated by E. O. Winstedt. Loeb Classical Library. Cambridge, Mass.: Harvard University Press, 1912.

————. *Orations.* Vol. 10. Translated by C. Macdonald. Loeb Classical Library. Cambridge, Mass.: Harvard University Press, 1976.

————. *Orations.* Vol. 11. Translated by N. H. Watts. Loeb Classical Library. Cambridge, Mass.: Harvard University Press, 1923.

————. *Orations.* Vol. 13. Translated by R. Gardner. Loeb Classical Library. Cambridge, Mass.: Harvard University Press, 1958.

Cohen, Shaye. *From the Maccabees to the Mishnah.* Philadelphia: Westminster Press, 1987.

————. "Pagan and Christian Evidence on the Ancient Synagogue." In *The Synagogue in Late Antiquity.* Edited by Lee I. Levine. JTS Centennial. Winona Lake, Ind.: Eisenbrauns, 1987.

Colin, J. "Les consuls de César-Pharaon Caligula et l'héritage de Germanicus." *Latomus* 13 (1954): 398–416.

Collins, John. *Between Athens and Jerusalem.* New York: Crossroad, 1983.

Collon, Suzanne. "Les Quartiers juifs de la Rome antique." *Mélanges d'Archéologie et d'Histoire* 57 (1940): 74.

Courtney, E. *A Commentary on the Satires of Juvenal.* London: Athlone Press, 1980.

Cranfield, C. E. B. *The Epistle to the Romans.* 2 vols. International Critical Commentary. Edited by J. A. Emerton and C. E. B. Cranfield. Edinburgh: T. & T. Clark, 1975–79.

Cumont, Franz. "Les Mystères de Sabazius et le Judaïsme." *Comptes Rendus de l'Academie des Inscriptions et Belles Lettres* (1906): 63–67.

D'Arms, J. H. "Puteoli in the Second Century of the Roman Empire: A Social and Economic Study." *Journal of Roman Studies* 64 (1974): 104–24.

Dahl, Nils Alstrup. *Studies in Paul: Theology for the Early Christian Mission.* Minneapolis: Augsburg Press, 1977.

Dill, Samuel. *Roman Society: From Nero to Marcus Aurelius.* New York: Macmillan, 1905.

Dio Cassius. *Roman History.* Translated by Earnest Cary. Loeb Classical Library. Cambridge, Mass.: Harvard University Press, 1924.

Dionysius of Halicarnassus. *Roman Antiquities.* Translated by Earnest Cary. Loeb Classical Library. Cambridge, Mass.: Harvard University Press, 1937.

Donfried, Karl Paul. "Justification and Last Judgment in Paul." *Zeitschrift für die neutestamentliche Wissenschaft* 67 (1976): 90–110.

————. "False Presuppositions in the Study of Romans." In *The Romans Debate.* Edited by Karl Donfried. Minneapolis: Augsburg Press, 1977, 120–48.

————. "Introduction: The Nature and Scope of the Romans Debate." In *The Romans Debate.* Edited by Karl Donfried. Minneapolis: Augsburg Press, 1977, ix–xvii.

————, ed. *The Romans Debate.* Minneapolis: Augsburg Press, 1977.

Dittenberger, W. *Orientis Graeci Inscriptiones Selectae.* 2 vols. Leipzig, 1903–5.

Duff, Arnold M. *Freedmen in the Early Roman Empire.* Oxford: Oxford University Press, 1928.

Duncan-Jones, R. P. Review of *Social Strata in the Imperial City of Rome,* by P. Huttunen. In *Journal of Roman Studies* 68 (1978): 195.

Dunn, James D. G. *Romans.* 2 vols. Word Biblical Commentary. Dallas: Word Books, 1988.

Epictetus. *Discourses.* Translated by W. A. Oldfather. Loeb Classical Library. Cambridge, Mass.: Harvard University Press, 1925.

Esler, Philip Francis. *Community and Gospel in Luke-Acts.* Cambridge: Cambridge University Press, 1987.

Fahy, T. "St. Paul's Romans Were Jewish Converts." *Irish Theological Quarterly* 26 (1959): 182–91.

Ferguson, John. *The Religions of the Roman Empire.* Ithaca, N.Y.: Cornell University Press, 1970.

Fischer, J. A. "Pauline Literary Forms and Thought Patterns." *Catholic Biblical Quarterly* 39 (1977): 209–23.

Flückiger, Felix. "Die Werke des Gesetzes bei den Heiden nach Röm 2, 14ff." *Theologische Zeitschrift* 8 (1952): 17–42.

Frank, Tenney. "Race Mixture in the Roman Empire." *American Historical Review* 21 (1916): 689–708.

Frend, W. H. C. *Martyrdom and Persecution in the Early Church.* Oxford: Basil Blackwell, 1965.

Frey, P. Jean Baptiste. *Corpus Inscriptionum Iudaicarum.* Rome: Pontificio Instituto di Archeologia Christiana, 1936–52.

Friedrich, Johannes, Wolfgang Pohlmann, and Peter Stuhlmacher. "Zur historischen Situation und Intention von Röm 13, 1–7." *Zeitschrift für Theologie und Kirche* 73 (1976): 131–66.

Frier, Bruce Woodward. "The Rental Market in Early Imperial Rome." *Journal of Roman Studies* 67 (1977): 27–37.

Fuks, G. "Where Have All the Freedmen Gone? On an Anomaly in the Jewish Grave Inscriptions from Rome." *Journal of Jewish Studies* 35 (1984): 25–32.

Furnish, Victor. *The Love Command in the New Testament.* Nashville: Abingdon, 1972.

————. *The Moral Teaching of Paul.* Nashville: Abingdon, 1979.

Gager, John. *Kingdom and Community: The Social World of Early Christianity.* Englewood Cliffs, N.J.: Prentice-Hall, 1975.

————. "Shall We Marry Our Enemies? Sociology and the New Testament." *Interpretation* 36 (1982): 256–65.

————. *The Origins of Anti-Semitism.* New York: Oxford University Press, 1983.

Gaius. *Institutes.* Translated by W. M. Gordon and O. F. Robinson. London: Duckworth, 1987.

Gamble, Harry. *The Textual History of the Letter to the Romans.* Grand Rapids, Mich.: Eerdmans, 1977.

Garnsey, Peter. "Non-Slave Labour in the Roman World." In *Non-Slave Labour in the Greco-Roman World.* Edited by Peter Garnsey. Cambridge: Cambridge Philological Society, 1980.

————. "Religious Toleration in Classical Antiquity." In *Persecution and Toleration: Studies in Church History* 21 (1984): 1–28.

————, and Richard Saller. *The Roman Empire: Economy, Society and Culture.* Berkeley: University of California Press, 1987.

Gellius. *Attic Nights.* Translated by John C. Rolfe. Loeb Classical Library. Cambridge, Mass.: Harvard University Press, 1927.

Getty, Mary Ann. "Paul and the Salvation of Israel: A Perspective on Romans 9–11." *Catholic Biblical Quarterly* 50 (July 1988): 456–69.

Goldenberg, Robert. Review of *Origins of Anti-Semitism* by John Gager. In *Religious Studies Review* 11 (October 1985): 336.

Goodenough, E. *Jewish Symbols in the Greco-Roman Period.* 13 vols. New York: Pantheon, 1953–68.

Goodhue, Nicholas. *The Lucus Furrinae and the Syrian Sanctuary on the Janiculum.* Amsterdam: Adolf M. Hakkert, 1975.

Gordon, M. L. "The Nationality of Slaves under the Early Roman Empire." *Journal of Roman Studies* 14 (1924): 93–111.

Grant, Michael. *Nero.* London: Weidenfeld and Nicolson, 1970.

Griffin, Miriam T. *Nero: The End of a Dynasty.* New Haven: Yale University Press, 1984.

Gutmann, Joseph. *The Synagogue: Studies in Origins, Archeology, and Architecture.* New York: Ktav, 1975.

————. *Ancient Synagogues: The State of the Research.* Chico, Calif.: Scholars Press, 1981.

Haenchen, Ernst. *The Acts of the Apostles.* Translated by R. McL. Wilson, et al. Philadelphia: Fortress, 1971.

Harrington, Daniel J. "Sociological Concepts and the Early Church." *Theological Studies* (1980): 181–90.

————. "Second Testament Exegesis and the Social Sciences: A Bibliography." *Biblical Theology Bulletin* 18 (1988): 77–85.

Headlam, A. C., and W. Sanday. *Romans.* International Critical Commentary. Edinburgh: T. & T. Clark, 1902.

Hengel, Martin. "Die Synagogeninschrift von Stobi." *Zeitschrift für neutestamentlichen Wissenschaft* 57 (1966): 167–82.

————. "Proseuche und Synagoge: Jüdische Gemeinde, Gotteshaus und Gottesdienst in der Diaspora und in Palästina." In *Tradition und Glaube: Das frühe Christentum in seiner Umwelt.* Festgabe für Karl Georg Kuhn. Edited by G. Jeremias. Göttingen: Vandenhoeck & Ruprecht, 1971, 157–83.

————. *Judaism and Hellenism.* Translated by John Bowden. Philadelphia: Fortress, 1974.

————. *Jews, Greeks and Barbarians.* Translated by John Bowden. Philadelphia: Fortress, 1980.

Heyob, Sharon Kelly. *The Cult of Isis among Women in the Graeco-Roman World.* Leiden: E. J. Brill, 1975.

Hirsch, E. D. *Validity in Interpretation.* New Haven: Yale University Press, 1967.

Hoerber, R. O. "The Decree of Claudius in Acts 18:2." *Concordia Theological Monthly* 31 (1960): 690–94.

Hopkins, Keith. *Conquerors and Slaves.* Cambridge: Cambridge University Press, 1978.

————. *Death and Renewal.* Cambridge: Cambridge University Press, 1983.

Horace. *Odes and Epodes.* Translated by C. E. Bennett. Loeb Classical Library. Cambridge, Mass.: Harvard University Press, 1914.

————. *Satires, Epistles, Ars Poetica.* Translated by H. R. Fairclough. Loeb Classical Library. Cambridge, Mass.: Harvard University Press, 1926.

Hübner, H. *Gottes Ich und Israel: Zum Schriftgebrauch des Paulus in Römer 9–11.* Göttingen: Vandenhoeck & Ruprecht, 1984.

Huttunen, P. *The Social Strata in the Imperial City of Rome,* Acta Universitatis Ouluensis, series B humaniora III, historica I. Oulu, Finland: The University, 1974.

Issac, Jules. *Jésus et Israël.* New York: Holt, Rinehart and Winston, 1948.

Inscriptiones Graecae. Berlin: Preussische Akademie der Wissenschaften, 1873– .

Jalabert, L., and R. Mouterde, *Inscriptions Grecques et Latines de la Syrie.* 5 vols. Paris, 1929– .

Janne, H. "Impulsore Chresto." In *Mélanges J. Bidez* (1934): 531–53.

Jervell, Jacob. "The Letter to Jerusalem." *The Romans Debate.* Edited by Karl Donfried. Minneapolis: Augsburg Press, 1977, 61–74.

Jewett, Robert. *Paul's Anthropological Terms.* Leiden: E. J. Brill, 1971.

————. *Dating Paul's Life.* London: SCM, 1979.

————. "Romans as an Ambassadorial Letter." *Interpretation* 34 (1980): 17–31.

————. *Christian Tolerance.* Philadelphia: Westminster, 1982.

Johnson, Sherman E. "The Present State of Sabazios Research." *Aufstieg und Niedergang der römischen Welt.* II.17.3. Edited by Wolfgang Haase. Berlin and New York: Walter de Gruyter, 1984, 1583–1613.

Jordon, H. *Topographie der Stadt Röm im Altherthum.* Berlin, 1871.

Josephus. *Against Apion.* Translated by J. Thackeray. Loeb Classical Library. Cambridge, Mass.: Harvard University Press, 1926.

————. *Antiquities.* Translated by R. Marcus. Loeb Classical Library. Cambridge, Mass.: Harvard University Press, 1943.

————. *Jewish War.* Translated by J. Thackeray. Loeb Classical Library. Cambridge, Mass.: Harvard University Press, 1928.

————. *The Life.* Translated by J. Thackeray. Loeb Classical Library. Cambridge, Mass.: Harvard University Press, 1926.

Judge, E. A., and G. S. R. Thomas. "The Origin of the Church at Rome." *Reformed Theological Review* 25 (1966): 81–93.

Juster, J. *Les Juifs dans l'empire romain: Leur Condition juridique, économique, et sociale.* 2 vols. Paris, 1914.

Juvenal and Persius. Translated by G. G. Ramsay. Loeb Classical Library. Cambridge, Mass.: Harvard University Press, 1918.

Kant, Laurence H. "Jewish Inscriptions in Greek and Latin." *Aufstieg und Niedergang der römischen Welt.* II.20.2. Edited by Wolfgang Haase. Berlin and New York: Walter de Gruyter, 1987, 671–713.

Karris, Robert. "The Occasion of Romans: A Response to Professor Donfried." In *The Romans Debate.* Edited by Karl Donfried. Minneapolis: Augsburg Press, 1977, 149–51.

———. "Romans 14:1–15:13 and the Occasion of Romans." In *The Romans Debate.* Edited by Karl Donfried. Minneapolis: Augsburg Press, 1977, 75–99.

Käsemann, Ernst. *Commentary on Romans.* Translated by Geoffrey W. Bromiley. Philadelphia: Fortress, 1980.

Kaylor, R. David. *Paul's Covenant Community: Jew and Gentile in Romans.* Atlanta: John Knox Press, 1988.

Kee, Howard Clark. "Ethical Dimensions of the Testaments of the XII as a Clue to Provenance." *New Testament Studies* 24 (1978): 259–70.

———. "Pauline Eschatology: Relationships with Apocalyptic and Stoic Thought." In *Glaube und Eschatologie.* Festschrift für Werner Georg Kümmel zum 80. Geburtstag. Edited by Erich Grasser and Otto Mark. Tübingen: J. C. B. Mohr, 1985, 135–58.

———. *Knowing the Truth: A Sociological Approach to New Testament Interpretation.* Minneapolis: Fortress, 1989.

———. "The Transformation of the Synagogue after 70 C.E.: Its Import for Early Christianity." *New Testament Studies* 36 (1990): 1–24.

Kennedy, George. *New Testament Interpretation through Rhetorical Criticism.* Chapel Hill: University of North Carolina Press, 1984.

Keresztes, Paul. "The Imperial Roman Government and the Christian Church." In *Aufstieg und Niedergang der römischen Welt.* II.23.1. Edited by Wolfgang Haase. Berlin and New York: Walter de Gruyter, 1979, 247–315.

Kettunen, Markku. *Der Abfassungszweck des Römerbriefes.* Helsinki: Suomalainen Tiedeakatemia, 1979.

Klein, Gunter. "Paul's Purpose in Writing the Epistle to the Romans." In *The Romans Debate.* Edited by Karl Donfried. Minneapolis: Augsburg Press, 1977, 32–49.

Klostermann, E. "Die Adäquate Vergeltung in Röm 1:22–31." *Zeitschrift für die neutestamentliche Wissenschaft* 32 (1933): 1–6.

Kraabel, A. Thomas. "The Diaspora Synagogue: Archaeological and Epigraphic Evidence since Sukenik." In *Aufstieg und Niedergang der römischen Welt.* II.19.1. Edited by Wolfgang Haase. Berlin and New York: Walter de Gruyter, 1979, 477–510.

———. "The Roman Diaspora: Six Questionable Assumptions." *Journal of Jewish Studies* 33 (1982): 445–77.

————. "Unity and Diversity among Diaspora Synagogues." In *The Synagogue in Late Antiquity*. JTS Centennial. Winona Lake, Ind.: Eisenbrauns, 1987, 49–60.

————, and Andrew R. Seager. "The Synagogue and the Jewish Community." In *Sardis from Prehistoric to Roman Times*. Edited by George M. A. Hanfmann. Cambridge, Mass.: Harvard University Press, 1983, 168–90.

Krauss, S. *Synagogale Altertümer*. Hildesheim: Olms, 1966.

Krodel, Gerhard. "Persecution and Toleration of Christianity until Hadrian." In *The Catacombs and the Colosseum*. Edited by Stephen Benko and John J. O'Rourke. Valley Forge, Pa.: Judson Press, 1971.

Kuhn, Helmut. "The Phenomenological Concept of Horizon." In *Philosophical Essays in Memory of Edmund Husserl*. Edited by M. Farber. Cambridge, Mass.: Harvard University Press, 1940, 106–23.

Kuhr, F. "Römer 2:14f. und die Verheissung bei Jeremia 31:31ff." *Zeitschrift für die neutestamentliche Wissenschaft* 55 (1964): 243–61.

La Piana, George. "Foreign Groups in Ancient Rome." *Harvard Theological Review* 20 (1927): 183–403.

Lafaye, G. *Histoire du culte des divinités d'Alexandrie hors de l'Égypte*. Paris, 1884.

Lampe, Peter. *Die Stadtrömischen Christen in den ersten beiden Jahrhunderten*. Tübingen: J. C. B. Mohr, 1987.

Lanciani, R. *Ancient Rome in Light of Recent Discoveries*. Boston: Houghton, Mifflin & Co., 1888.

Lane, Eugene. "Sabazius and the Jews in Valerius Maximus: A Re-examination." *Journal of Roman Studies* 69 (1979): 35–38.

Last, Hugh. "The Study of 'Persecutions.'" *Journal of Roman Studies* 27 (1937): 80–92.

Lazare, B. *L'Antisémitisme: Son histoire et ses causes*. Paris: L. Chailley, 1894.

Leon, Harry Joshua. *The Jews of Ancient Rome*. Philadelphia: Jewish Publication Society of America, 1960.

Levick, Barbara. *Tiberius the Politician*. London: Thames and Hudson, 1976.

Levine, Lee I. "The Second Temple Synagogue: The Formative Years." In *The Synagogue in Late Antiquity*. JTS Centennial; Winona Lake, Ind,: Eisenbrauns, 1987, 7–32.

————. *The Synagogue in Late Antiquity*. JTS Centennial; Winona Lake, Ind.: Eisenbrauns, 1987.

Liebeschuetz, J. H. W. G. *Continuity and Change in Roman Religion*. Oxford: Clarendon Press, 1979.

Lietzmann, H. *An die Römer*. Handbuch zum Neuen Testament. Tübingen: Mohr, 1906.

Livy. Vol. 11. Translated by Evan T. Sage. Loeb Classical Library. Cambridge, Mass.: Harvard University Press, 1936.

Luckmann, T., and A. Schutz. *The Structures of the Life-World*. Translated by R. Zaner and H. Engelhardt. Evanston: Northwestern, 1973.

Luedemann, Gerd. *Paul: Apostle to the Gentiles*. Translated by F. Stanley Jones. Philadelphia: Fortress, 1984.

MacMullen, Ramsay. *Enemies of the Roman Order.* Cambridge, Mass.: Harvard University Press, 1966.

————. *Roman Social Relations.* New Haven: Yale University Press, 1974.

————. *Paganism in the Roman Empire.* New Haven: Yale University Press, 1981.

Maier, F. G. "Römische Bevolkerungsgeschichte und Inschriftenstatik." *Historia* 2 (1954): 318–51.

Malaise, Michel. *Les conditions de pénétration et de diffusion des cultes égyptiens en Italie.* Leiden: E. J. Brill, 1972.

Malherbe, Abraham. *Social Aspects of Early Christianity.* Baton Rouge: Louisiana State University Press, 1977.

Manson, T. W. "St. Paul's Letter to the Romans — and Others." In *The Romans Debate.* Edited by Karl Paul Donfried. Minneapolis: Augsburg Press, 1977, 1–16.

Markus, R. A. *Christianity in the Roman World.* New York: Charles Scribner's, 1974.

Martial. *Epigrams.* Translated by W. C. A. Ker. Loeb Classical Library. Cambridge, Mass.: Harvard University Press, 1919.

Marxsen, Willi. *Introduction to the New Testament.* Translated by G. Buswell. Philadelphia: Fortress, 1968.

Meagher, John C. "As the Twig Was Bent: Antisemitism in Greco-Roman and Earliest Christian Times." In *Anti-Semitism and the Foundations of Christianity.* Edited by Alan T. Davies. New York: Paulist Press, 1979, 1–26.

Meeks, Wayne. *The First Urban Christians.* New Haven: Yale University Press, 1983.

————. "Breaking Away: Three New Testament Pictures of Christianity's Separation from the Jewish Communities." In *To See Ourselves as Others See Us: Christians, Jews, "Others" in Late Antiquity.* Edited by Jacob Neusner and Ernest S. Frerichs. Chico, Calif.: Scholars Press, 1985, 93–116.

————. *The Moral World of the First Christians.* Philadelphia: Westminster, 1986.

————. "Judgment and the Brother: Romans 14:1–15:13." In *Tradition and Interpretation in the New Testament.* Essays in honor of E. Earle Ellis. Edited by Gerald F. Hawthorne with Otto Betz. Grand Rapids, Mich.: Eerdmans, 1987, 290–300.

Meiggs, R. *Roman Ostia.* Oxford: Clarendon, 1973.

Merrill, Elmer Truesdell. "The Expulsion of the Jews from Rome under Tiberius." *Classical Philology* 14 (1919): 365–72.

Michel, O. *Der Brief an der Römer.* Göttingen: Vandenhoeck & Ruprecht, 1966.

Millar, Fergus. *The Emperor in the Roman World.* Ithaca, N.Y.: Cornell University Press, 1977.

————. "The World of the Golden Ass." *Journal of Roman Studies* 71 (1981): 63–75.

————. "The Phoenician Cities: A Case Study of Hellenisation." *Proceedings of the Cambridge Philological Society* 209 (1983): 55–71.

Minear, Paul. *Obedience of Faith.* Studies in Biblical Theology 19. London: SCM Press, 1971.

Momigliano, Arnaldo. *Claudius: The Emperor and His Achievement.* Translated by W. D. Hogarth. New York: Barnes and Noble, 1934.

Moo, Douglas J. "'Law,' 'Works of the Law,' and Legalism in Paul." *Westminster Theological Journal* 45 (1983): 73–100.

Morel, Jean-Paul. "Greek Colonization in Italy and in the West." In *Crossroads of the Mediterranean.* Edited by T. Hackens, Nancy D. Holloway and R. Ross Holloway. Archaeologia Transatlantica II. Papers delivered at the International Conference on Archaeology of Early Italy, May 1981, 123–62.

Nababan, A. E. S. "Bekenntnis und Mission in Römer 14 und 15." Ph.D. dissertation. Heidelberg, 1963.

Neusner, Jacob. "The Use of the Later Rabbinic Evidence for the Study of First-Century Pharisaism." In *Approaches to Ancient Judaism: Theory and Practice.* Brown Judaic Studies 1. Missoula, Mont.: Scholars Press, 1978, 215–28.

————. "The Experience of the City in Late Antique Judaism." In *Approaches to Ancient Judaism,* vol. 5, edited by William Scott Green. Brown Judaic Studies 32. Atlanta: Scholars Press, 1985, 37–52.

Nilsson, Martin Persson. *Geschichte der griechischen Religion.* 2 vols. Munich: Beck, 1941–50.

Nock, Arthur Darby. "The Gild of Zeus Hypsistos." *Harvard Theological Review* 29 (1936): 39–88.

————. "Religious Developments from the Close of the Republic to the Death of Nero." In *The Cambridge Ancient History.* Edited by S. A. Cook, F. E. Adcock, M. P. Charlesworth, J. B. Bury. Cambridge: University Press, 1963, 10:465–511.

Nolland, J. "Uncircumcised Proselytes?" *Journal for the Study of Judaism* (1981): 173–94.

North, J. A. "Conservatism and Change in Roman Religion." *Papers of the British School at Rome* 44 (1976): 5.

Nygren, Anders. *Commentary on Romans.* Philadelphia: Fortress, 1949.

O'Neill, J. C. *Paul's Letter to the Romans.* Baltimore: Penguin, 1975.

O'Rourke, John J. "Roman Law and the Early Church." In *The Catacombs and the Colosseum.* Edited by Stephen Benko and John J. O'Rourke. Valley Forge, Pa.: Judson Press, 1971, 165–86.

Oates, W. J. "The Population of Rome." *Classical Philology* 29 (1934): 101–16.

Ovid. *Ars Amatoria.* Translated by J. H. Mozley. Loeb Classical Library. Cambridge, Mass.: Harvard University Press, 1929.

————. *Remedia Amoris.* Translated by J. H. Mozley. Loeb Classical Library. Cambridge, Mass.: Harvard University Press, 1929.

Packer, J. P. *The Insulae of Imperial Ostia: Memoirs of the American Academy at Rome,* no. 31, 1971.

Park, Marion Edwards. *The Plebs in Cicero's Day: A Study of Their Provenance and of Their Employment.* Cambridge, Mass.: Cosmos Press, 1918.

Penna, Romano. "Les Juifs à Rome au temps de l'apôtre Paul." *New Testament Studies* 28 (1982): 321–47.

Petronius. Translated by M. Heseltine. Loeb Classical Library. Cambridge, Mass.: Harvard University Press, 1913.

Philo. *Abraham.* Translated by F. H. Colson. Loeb Classical Library. Cambridge, Mass.: Harvard University Press, 1935.

———. *Against Flaccus.* Translated by F. H. Colson. Loeb Classical Library. Cambridge, Mass.: Harvard University Press, 1962.

———. *On the Embassy to Gaius.* Translated by F. H. Colson. Loeb Classical Library. Cambridge, Mass.: Harvard University Press, 1962.

———. *Moses.* Translated by F. H. Colson. Loeb Classical Library. Cambridge, Mass.: Harvard University Press, 1935.

———. *On Providence.* Translated by F. H. Colson. Loeb Classical Library. Cambridge, Mass.: Harvard University Press, 1941.

Pliny. *Letters.* Translated by Betty Radice. Loeb Classical Library. Cambridge, Mass.: Harvard University Press, 1969.

———. *Natural History.* Translated by H. Rackham. Loeb Classical Library. Cambridge, Mass.: Harvard University Press, 1945.

Plutarch. *Life of Tiberius Gracchus.* Translated by B. Perrin. Loeb Classical Library. Cambridge, Mass.: Harvard University Press, 1921.

Pohlenz, Max. "Paulus und die Stoa." *Zeitschrift für de neutestamentliche Wissenschaft* 42 (1949): 69–104.

Poland, Franz. *Geschichte des griechischen Vereinswesens.* Leipzig: Teubner, 1909.

Poliakoff, Denali Marie. "The Acculturation of Jews in the Roman Empire: Evidence from Burial Places." Ph.D. dissertation. Boston University, 1989.

Porton, Gary G. "Diversity in Postbiblical Judaism." In *Early Judaism and Its Modern Interpreters.* Edited by Robert Kraft and George Nickelsburg. Philadelphia: Fortress, 1986, 57–80.

Quintilian. *Institutio Oratoria.* Translated by H. E. Butler. Loeb Classical Library. Cambridge, Mass.: Harvard University Press, 1920.

Räisänen, Heikki. *Paul and the Law.* Philadelphia: Fortress, 1983.

———. "Römer 9–11: Analyse eines geistigen Ringens." *Aufstieg und Niedergang der römischen Welt.* II.25.4. Edited by W. Haase. Berlin and New York: Walter de Gruyter, 1987, 2891–2939.

Rajak, Tessa. "Was There a Roman Charter for the Jews?" *Journal of Roman Studies* 74 (1984): 107–33.

Rauer, M. *Die "Schwachen" in Korinth und Röm nach den Paulusbriefen.* Freiburg im Breisgau: Herder, 1923.

Reece, Richard. "Rome in the Mediterranean World: The Evidence of Coins." In *Papers in Italian Archaeology.* Vol. 4, The Cambridge Conference. Edited by Caroline Malone and Simon Stoddart, 1985, 85–98.

Reinach, T. *Textes d'auteurs grecs et romains relatifs au judaïsme.* Hildesheim: G. Olms, 1963.

Reinhold, Meyer. *The Golden Age of Augustus.* Toronto: Samuel Stevens, 1978.

———. *From Republic to Principate: An Historical Commentary on Dio Cassius's Roman History Books 49–52.* American Philological Association Monograph Series, no. 34, Atlanta: Scholars Press, 1988.

Reinhold, Meyer, and Naphtali Lewis. *Roman Civilization.* 3rd ed. New York: Columbia University Press, 1990.

Reynolds, Joyce, and Robert Tannenbaum. *Jews and Godfearers at Aphrodisias.* Cambridge: Cambridge Philological Society, 1987.

Richardson, Peter. *Israel in the Apostolic Church.* Cambridge: Cambridge University Press, 1969.

Robinson, D. W. B. "The Priesthood of Paul in the Gospel of Hope." In *Reconciliation and Hope: New Testament Essays on Atonement and Eschatology.* Essays in honor of Leon Morris. Edited by R. J. Banks. Exeter: Paternoster, 1974, 231–45.

Rodd, Cyril S. "On Applying a Sociological Theory to Biblical Studies." *Journal for the Study of the Old Testament* 19 (1981): 95–106.

Rostovtzeff, M. "Die römischen Bleitesserae." *Klio,* Beiheft No. 3, 1905.

Safrai, S., and M. Stern. *The Jewish People in the First Century.* Philadelphia: Fortress, 1974.

de Ste. Croix, G. E. M. "Why Were the Early Christians Persecuted." *Past and Present* 26 (1964): 6–38

Sampley, J. Paul. "Romans and Galatians: Comparison and Contrast." In *Understanding the Word.* Essays in honor of Bernhard Anderson. Edited by J. Butler, E. Conrad, and B. Ollenburger. Sheffield: JSOT, 1985, 315–39.

Sanders, E. P. "The Covenant as a Soteriological Category and the Nature of Salvation in Palestinian and Hellenistic Judaism." In *Jews, Greeks and Christians: Religious Cultures in Late Antiquity.* Essays in honor of William David Davies. Edited by Robert Hamerton-Kelly and Robin Scroggs. Leiden: E. J. Brill, 1976, 11–44.

———. *Paul and Palestinian Judaism.* Philadelphia: Fortress, 1977.

———. *Paul, the Law and the Jewish People.* Philadelphia: Fortress, 1983.

Savage, S. M. "The Cults of Ancient Trastevere." *Memoirs of the American Academy in Rome* 17 (1940): 26–46.

Schmithals, Walter. *Der Römerbrief als historisches Problem.* Gutersloh: Gerd Mohn, 1975.

Schürer, Emil. *The History of the Jewish People in the Age of Jesus Christ.* Vol. 3.1. Revised and edited by Fergus Millar. Edinburgh: T. & T. Clark, 1986.

Scramuzza, Vincent M. *The Emperor Claudius.* Cambridge, Mass.: Harvard University Press, 1940.

Scroggs, Robin. "The Sociological Interpretation of the New Testament: The Present State of Research." *New Testament Studies* 26 (1980): 164–79.

Seager, A. R. "The Building History of the Sardis Synagogue." *American Journal of Archeology* 76 (1972): 425–35.

Segal, Alan F. *Rebecca's Children: Judaism and Christianity in the Roman World.* Cambridge, Mass.: Harvard University Press, 1986.

———. "The Costs of Proselytism and Conversion." *Seminar Papers.* Society of Biblical Literature 27. Atlanta: Scholars Press, 1988, 336–69.

Seneca. *Epistulae Morales.* Translated by R. M. Gummere. Loeb Classical Library. Cambridge, Mass.: Harvard University Press, 1917–25.

———. *Ad Helviam.* Translated by John W. Basore. Loeb Classical Library. Cambridge, Mass.: Harvard University Press, 1932.

———. *De Ira.* Translated by John W. Basore. Loeb Classical Library. Cambridge, Mass.: Harvard University Press, 1928.

Sevenster, J. N. *Roots of Pagan Anti-Semitism in the Ancient World.* Leiden: E. J. Brill, 1975.

Sheppard, A. R. R. "Jews, Christians and Heretics in Acmonia and Eumeneia." *Anatolian Studies* 29 (1979): 169–80.

Sherwin-White, A. N. "Why Were the Early Christians Persecuted? An Amendment." *Past and Present* 27 (1963): 23–33.

Sibylline Oracles. Translated by Milton S. Terry. New York: Eaton & Mains, 1899.

Simon, Marcel. *Verus Israel: A Study of the Relations between Christians and Jews in the Roman Empire, 135–425.* Translated by H. McKeating. Oxford: Oxford University Press, 1986.

Sinclair, Scott Gambrill. *Jesus Christ according to Paul.* Berkeley, Calif.: Bibal Press, 1988.

Smallwood, E. Mary. "Some Notes on the Jews under Tiberius." *Latomus* 15 (1956): 314–29.

———. "Jews and Romans in the Early Empire." *History Today* 15 (1965): 232–39.

———. *The Jews under Roman Rule.* Leiden: E. J. Brill, 1976.

Smith, Jonathan Z. "The Social Description of Early Christianity." *Religious Studies Review* 1 (1975): 19–25.

———. "Fences and Neighbors: Some Contours of Early Judaism." In *Approaches to Ancient Judaism.* Vol. 2. Edited by W. S. Green. Chico, Calif.: Scholars Press, 1980, 1–25.

Snodgrass, K. R. "Justification by Grace — To the Doers: An Analysis of the Place of Romans 2 in the Theology of Paul." *New Testament Studies* 32 (1986): 72–93.

Solin, Heikki. *Beiträge zur Kenntnis der griechischen Personennamen in Röm.* Helsinki: Societas Scientiarum Fennica, 1971.

———. "Juden und Syrer in der römischen Welt." *Aufstieg und Niedergang der römischen Welt.* Edited by Wolfgang Haase. Berlin and New York: Walter de Gruyter, 1983, 587–789.

Stambaugh, John E. *The Ancient Roman City.* Baltimore: Johns Hopkins University Press, 1988.

Stendahl, Krister. "The Apostle Paul and the Introspective Conscience of the West." *Harvard Theological Review* 56 (1963): 199–215.

———. *Paul among Jews and Gentiles.* Philadelphia: Fortress, 1976.

Stern, Menahem. _Greek and Latin Authors on Jews and Judaism._ 3 vols. Jerusalem: Israel Academy of the Sciences and Humanities, 1974.

Stowers, Stanley Kent. "The Social Sciences and the Study of Early Christianity." In _Approaches to Ancient Judaism,_ vol. 5. Edited by William Scott Green. Brown Judaic Studies 32. Atlanta: Scholars Press, 1985, 149–81.

————. _The Diatribe and Paul's Letter to the Romans._ Society of Biblical Literature Dissertation Series 57. Chico, Calif.: Scholars Press, 1981.

————. "Paul's Dialogue with a Fellow Jew in Romans 3:1–9." _Catholic Biblical Quarterly_ 46 (1984).

Strabo. _Geography._ Translated by Horace L. Jones. Loeb Classical Library. Cambridge, Mass.: Harvard University Press, 1929.

Stuhlmacher, Peter. "Der Abfassungszweck des Römerbriefes." _Zeitschrift für die neutestamentliche Wissenschaft_ 77 (1986): 180–93.

Suetonius. _The Lives of the Caesars._ Translated by J. C. Rolfe. Loeb Classical Library. Cambridge, Mass.: Harvard University Press, 1914.

Syme, Ronald. _Tacitus._ Oxford: Clarendon, 1958.

Tacitus. _Annals._ Translated by John Jackson. Loeb Classical Library. Cambridge, Mass.: Harvard University Press, 1925–37.

————. _Histories._ Translated by Clifford Moore. Loeb Classical Library. Cambridge, Mass.: Harvard University Press, 1925–31.

Taylor, L. R. "Foreign Groups in Roman Politics of the Late Republic." In _Hommages à Joseph Bidez et à Franz Cumont,_ Collection Latomus 2 (1949), 323–30.

————. "Freedmen and Freeborn in the Epitaphs of Imperial Rome." _American Journal of Philology_ 82 (1961): 113–32.

Tcherikover, V. "Jewish Apologetic Literature Reconsidered." _Eos_ 48 (1956): 169–93.

————. _Corpus Papyrorum Judaicarum._ Cambridge, Mass.: Harvard University Press, 1964.

————. _Hellenistic Civilization and the Jews._ New York: Atheneum, 1970.

Tertullian. _Apology._ Translated by T. R. Glover. Loeb Classical Library. Cambridge, Mass.: Harvard University Press, 1931.

Theissen, Gerd. _The Social Setting of Pauline Christianity._ Translated by John Shutz. Philadelphia: Fortress, 1982.

Thompson, L. A. "Domitian and the Jewish Tax." _Historia_ 31 (1982): 329–42.

Thrall, Margaret. "The Pauline Use of _Suneidesis._" _New Testament Studies_ 14 (1967–68): 897–918.

Thylander, H. "Étude sur l'épigraphie latine." _Skrifter utgivna av Svenska Instituet in Rom,_ ser. in 8, Lund: C. W. K. Gleerup, 1952, 134–52.

Tibullus. _Carmina._ Translated by J. P. Postgate. Loeb Classical Library. Cambridge, Mass.: Harvard University Press, 1913.

Torrey, C. C. "The Exiled God of Sarepta." _Berytus_ 9 (1948–49): 45–49.

Toutain, Jules. _Les cultes païens dans l'empire romain._ Paris: E. Leroux, 1907–20.

Treggiari, Susan. _Roman Freedmen._ Oxford: Oxford University Press, 1969.

————. "Urban Labour in Rome: Mercennarii and Tabernarii." In *Non-Slave Labour in the Greco-Roman World.* Edited by Peter Garnsey. Cambridge: Cambridge Philological Society, 1980.

Velleius Paterculus. Translated by F. W. Shipley. Loeb Classical Library. Cambridge, Mass.: Harvard University Press, 1924.

Walbank, Frank. "Nationality as a Factor in Roman History." In *Selected Papers: Studies in Greek and Roman History and Historiography.* Cambridge: Cambridge University Press, 1985, 57–76.

Waltzing, Jean. *Étude historique sur les corporations professionelles chez les Romains.* 4 vols. Louvain: Peeters, 1895–1900.

Wardman, Alan. *Religion and Statecraft among the Romans.* London: Granada Publishing, 1982.

Wardy, Bilhah. "Jewish Religion in Pagan Literature during the Late Republic and Early Empire." *Aufstieg und Niedergang der römischen Welt.* II.19.1. Edited by W. Haase. Berlin and New York: Walter de Gruyter, 1979, 596–613.

Watson, F. *Paul, Judaism and the Gentiles: A Sociological Approach.* Society for New Testament Studies Monograph Series 56. Cambridge: Cambridge University Press, 1986.

Wedderburn, A. J. M. "The Purpose and Occasion of Romans Again." *Expository Times* 90 (1979): 137–41.

————. *The Reasons for Romans.* Edinburgh: T. & T. Clark, 1988.

White, L. Michael. "The Delos Synagogue Revisited: Recent Fieldwork in the Graeco-Roman Diaspora." *Harvard Theological Review* 80 (1987): 133–60.

————. *Building God's House in the Roman World.* Baltimore: Johns Hopkins University Press, 1990.

Wiefel, Wolfgang. "The Jewish Community in Ancient Rome and the Origins of Roman Christianity." In *The Romans Debate.* Edited by Karl Donfried. Minneapolis: Augsburg Press, 1977, 100–19.

Wilckens, U. *Der Brief an die Römer,* 3 vols. Zurich: Neukirchener Verlag, 1979–82.

Williams, S. K. "The 'Righteousness of God' in Romans." *Journal of Biblical Literature* 99 (1980): 241–90.

Wissowa, Georg. "Cistiber-Deipnokrites." *Hermes* 49 (1914): 626–29.

Yavetz, Zvi. *Plebs and Princeps.* Oxford: Clarendon Press, 1969.

Index of Authors

Ambrosiaster, 97 n. 5
Appian, 11
Apuleius, 23
Ashby, Thomas, 105 n. 91
Athenaeus, 10, 18
Augustine, ix
Aune, David, 128 n. 23
Aurelius, Marcus, 23

Badian, E., 101 n. 30
Balch, David, 120 n. 167, 123 n. 209
Balsdon, David, 9, 11, 12
Bammel, Ernst, 131 n. 46
Bang, M., 8
Barnett, Paul W., 49
Barrett, C. K., 131 n. 48, 141 n. 91
Barth, Karl, ix
Bassler, Jouette M., 69, 70, 71, 140 n. 77
Baur, F. C., 137 n. 55
Beker, J. Christiaan, 80, 95 n. 1, 132 n. 49, 136 n. 45, 139 n. 69, 144 n. 5
Beloch, Juluis, 98 n. 8
Benko, Stephen, 126 n. 245
Berger, Peter L., 22, 95 n. 5
Blaudau, A., 32
Boers, Hendrikus, 140 n. 74
Brown, Raymond, 137 n. 51
Brunt, P. A., 98 n. 8
Bultmann, Rudolf, 133 n. 11

Campbell, W. S., 138 n. 60
Christ, Karl, 103 n. 62
Cicero, 10, 23, 29, 37, 42, 115 n. 103, 120 n. 167, 120 n. 172
Clement of Rome, 129 n. 33
Cohen, Shaye, 24, 25, 33, 112 n. 46
Colin, J., 124 n. 223

Collins, John, 107 n. 3, 113 n. 57
Collon, Suzanne, 30
Courtney, E., 101 n. 33
Cranfield, C. E. B., 70, 98 n. 5, 136 n. 43, 138 n. 64, 140 n. 85
Cumont, Franz, 14

Dahl, Nils, 69, 137 n. 52, 138 n. 57, 140 n. 76
D'Arms, J. H., 106 n. 101
Dill, Samuel, 105 n. 85
Dio Cassius, 23, 37, 39, 47, 48, 49, 51, 52, 58, 127 n. 17
Dionysius of Halicarnassus, 14
Donfried, Karl, 126 n. 4, 133 n. 2, 142 n. 101
Duncan-Jones, R. P., 8
Dunn, James D. G., 74, 90, 134 n. 26, 139 n. 72, 140 n. 76, 142 n. 102

Epictetus, 59
Esler, Philip Francis, 127 n. 22, 129 n. 32, 143 n. 111

Fischer, J. A., 69
Flückiger, Felix, 136 n. 43
Frank, Tenney, 7, 8, 9, 99 n. 14
Frend, W. H. C., 129 n. 34
Frey, P. J-B., 36, 117 n. 122
Fridrichsen, A., 133 n. 11
Friedrich, Johannes, 132 n. 50
Frier, Bruce Woodward, 103 n. 60
Fuks, G., 113 n. 63, 115 n. 88
Furnish, Victor, 64, 89, 131 n. 46

Gager, John, 22, 23, 24, 96 n. 8, 109 n. 18
Gaius, 121 n. 177

DATE DUE

DEC 2 0 1994			
MAY 2 5 1998			
DEC 8 2000			
DEC 2 9 2001			
MAR 0 2 2005			
			Printed in USA